COMMERCIAL SPEECH AS FREE EXPRESSION

For many years, commercial speech was summarily excluded from First Amendment protection, without reason or logic. Starting in the mid-1970s, the Supreme Court began to extend protection but it remained strictly limited. In recent years, that protection has expanded, but both Court and scholars have refused to consider treating commercial speech as the First Amendment equivalent of traditionally protected expressive categories such as political speech or literature. *Commercial Speech as Free Expression* stands as the boldest statement yet for extending full First Amendment protection to commercial speech by proposing a new, four-part synthesis of different perspectives on the manner in which free expression fosters and protects expressive values. This book explains the complexities and subtleties of how the equivalency principle would function in real-life situations. The key is to recognize that as a matter of First Amendment value, commercial speech deserves treatment equivalent to that received by traditionally protected speech.

Martin H. Redish is the Louis and Harriet Ancel Professor of Law and Public Policy at Northwestern University Pritzker School of Law. He is the author of 17 books and over 100 scholarly articles. His books include *Judicial Independence and the American Constitution: A Democratic* Paradox (2017) and *The Adversary First Amendment* (2013). He has been consistently ranked among the 25 most cited legal scholars of all time by Hein Online. He has been quoted or cited in 22 Supreme Court opinions and have been included among the list of most cited researchers worldwide by the Institute for Scientific Information.

CAMBRIDGE STUDIES ON CIVIL RIGHTS AND CIVIL LIBERTIES

This series is a platform for original scholarship on US civil rights and civil liberties. It produces books on the normative, historical, judicial, political, and sociological contexts for understanding contemporary legislative, jurisprudential, and presidential dilemmas. The aim is to provide experts, teachers, policymakers, students, social activists, and educated citizens with in-depth analyses of theories, existing and past conditions, and constructive ideas for legal advancements.

General Editor: Alexander Tsesis, *Loyola University, Chicago*

Commercial Speech as Free Expression

THE CASE FOR FIRST AMENDMENT PROTECTION

MARTIN H. REDISH
Northwestern University

CAMBRIDGE
UNIVERSITY PRESS

University Printing House, Cambridge CB2 8BS, United Kingdom

One Liberty Plaza, 20th Floor, New York, NY 10006, USA

477 Williamstown Road, Port Melbourne, VIC 3207, Australia

314-321, 3rd Floor, Plot 3, Splendor Forum, Jasola District Centre, New Delhi - 110025, India

103 Penang Road, #05-06/07, Visioncrest Commercial, Singapore 238467

Cambridge University Press is part of the University of Cambridge.

It furthers the University's mission by disseminating knowledge in the pursuit of education, learning and research at the highest international levels of excellence.

www.cambridge.org
Information on this title: www.cambridge.org/9781108405003
DOI: 10.1017/9781108277563

© Martin H. Redish 2021

This publication is in copyright. Subject to statutory exception and to the provisions of relevant collective licensing agreements, no reproduction of any part may take place without the written permission of Cambridge University Press.

First published 2021
First paperback edition 2021

A catalogue record for this publication is available from the British Library

Library of Congress Cataloging in Publication data
NAMES: Redish, Martin H., author.
TITLE: Commercial speech as free expression : the case for first amendment protection / Martin H. Redish, Northwestern University.
DESCRIPTION: Cambridge, United Kingdom ; New York, NY : Cambridge University Press, 2020. | Series: Cambridge studies on civil rights and civil liberties | Includes index.
IDENTIFIERS: LCCN 2020051781 | ISBN 9781108417402 (hardback) | ISBN 9781108405003 (paperback) | ISBN 9781108277563 (ebook)
SUBJECTS: LCSH: Corporate speech – United States. | Freedom of speech – United States.
CLASSIFICATION: LCC KF4772 .R43 2020 | DDC 342.7308/53–dc23
LC record available at https://lccn.loc.gov/2020051781

ISBN 978-1-108-41740-2 Hardback
ISBN 978-1-108-40500-3 Paperback

Cambridge University Press has no responsibility for the persistence or accuracy of URLs for external or third-party internet websites referred to in this publication, and does not guarantee that any content on such websites is, or will remain, accurate or appropriate.

For Caren

Contents

Preface		*page* ix
Acknowledgments		xi
1	Commercial Speech and the Values of Free Expression	1
2	False Commercial Speech and the First Amendment	21
3	The Right of Publicity, Commercial Speech, and the Equivalency Principle	60
4	Compelled Commercial Speech and the First Amendment	103
5	Scientific Expression and Commercial Speech: The Problem of Product Health Claims	133
	Conclusion: Making the Case for First Amendment Protection	170
Index		175

Preface

This book represents my latest contribution to the modern debate over the level of First Amendment protection to be extended to commercial speech. A number of respected scholars today vigorously resist the extension of significant constitutional protection to commercial speech, finding it unworthy of the protection extended to traditional noncommercial expressive categories. This is so despite the fact that over the last twenty-five years or so the Supreme Court has adopted a doctrinal framework that continues to expand the scope of First Amendment protection given to commercial speech.

Throughout this book I argue, for reasons explained throughout these pages, that both constitutional logic and policy dictate that the level of First Amendment protection extended to commercial speech be equivalent to that extended to all traditionally protected categories of expression. As I explain in the book, I am arguing not that commercial speech should be protected in all instances, but rather that it be afforded a type of "most favored nation" status – that is, it should be judged by the exact same constitutional standard as traditional expression is judged in comparable circumstances.

To be sure, this will not necessarily mean that commercial speech will receive protection in every instance in which comparable noncommercial speech will be protected. But if so (and the instances are likely to be rare), it will be because, in light of the nature and degree of the harm caused, commercial speech gives rise to significant harm while comparable noncommercial speech does not. In all cases, however, both are to be judged by the same compelling interest standard. After making this broad argument grounded in the theory of free expression, the book examines four areas of commercial speech regulation in which the courts have either openly refused to extend commercial speech protection or have left the issue unresolved.

I certainly do not expect everyone to agree with my reasoning or conclusions. I do hope, however, that this contribution to the scholarly debate will, at the very least, force those who disagree to understand and respond to my arguments. If this book accomplishes that much, I will deem it a success.

The book draws on a number of my previously published scholarly articles, though in all instances those articles have been modified, updated, or reshaped in a variety of important ways. The works are as follows:

1. Martin H. Redish, *Product Health Claims and the Twilight Zone of Commercial Speech*, 43 Vand. L. Rev. 1433 (1990)
2. Martin H. Redish & Kelsey B. Shust, *The Right of Publicity and the First Amendment in the Modern Age of Commercial Speech*, 56 Wm. & Mary L. Rev. 1443 (2015)
3. Martin H. Redish & Kyle Voils, *False Commercial Speech and the First Amendment: Understanding the Implications of the Equivalency Principle*, 25 Wm. & Mary Bill Rts. J. 765 (2015)
4. Martin H. Redish, *Compelled Commercial Speech and the First Amendment*, 94 Notre Dame L. Rev. 1749 (2019)
5. Coleen Klasmeier & Martin H. Redish, *Off-Label Prescription Advertising, the FDA and the First Amendment: A Study in the Values of Commercial Speech Protection*, 37 Am. J. L. & Med. 315 (2011)

All are reproduced with the written permission of the journals in which they were published.

Acknowledgments

This book would not have been possible without the moral and physical support of many individuals, most of whom are or were connected in some way with Northwestern University Pritzker School of Law, where I have taught for the last forty-eight years. In particular, very special thanks go to my former students and coauthors, Kyle Voils and Kelsey Shust. Both contributed significantly to the articles that bear their names, and I owe them a tremendous debt of gratitude. To the extent the final product here differs from the original articles, they bear no responsibility for those alterations or additions. Also, I owe thanks to Austin Piatt and Elizabeth Jeffers, both of the class of 2022 at Northwestern Pritzker School of Law, for their valuable research assistance.

I also owe a great debt to the two deans of Northwestern Pritzker School of Law, Daniel Rodriguez and Kimberly Yuracko, who served during the years in which this book was written. Both gave significant moral and financial support, helping make this book possible. In particular, special thanks go out to Dean Rodriguez, both for suggesting and then funding a scholarly conference, held in 2016 at Northwestern Law, honoring the 45th anniversary of my very first article, *The First Amendment in the Marketplace: Commercial Speech and the Values of Free Expression*, published in the *George Washington Law Review* in 1971 (written as a third year law student), which some have suggested influenced the creation and development of the modern commercial speech doctrine. Dean Yuracko deserves additional thanks, for authorizing and funding my 2018 debate about corporate and commercial speech with legal author and entrepreneur, Steve Brill. The debate was held in front of a large audience in Northwestern's famed Lincoln Hall. In addition, I owe thanks to Andy Koppelman, my Northwestern colleague and well-known First Amendment scholar, whose regular disagreements with me over commercial speech have forced me to sharpen my arguments.

The two individuals who have served as my faculty assistants during the years that this book was written, Juana Haskin and Sarah Shoemaker, deserve a medal for their loyal and efficient service in making this book a reality.

Finally, nothing I do would have the slightest significance without the love and support of the three people who make my life meaningful: my wife, Caren, and my daughters, Jessica and Elisa.

1

Commercial Speech and the Values of Free Expression

Over the last forty years, the Supreme Court has extended an ever-increasing level of First Amendment protection to commercial speech. Indeed, it is difficult to find a Supreme Court decision upholding governmental suppression of truthful commercial speech in the last twenty-five years.[1] Yet the Court has continued to provide less protection for commercial speech than is given to traditionally protected categories such as political or artistic expression. Moreover, the scholarly community has, with only rare exception, been either grudging or downright hostile to extending constitutional protection to commercial advertising. Many scholars believe that protecting commercial speech trivializes what the First Amendment is truly about,[2] reintroduces the threat to the smooth functioning of the regulatory system first presented by the specious and harmful pre-New Deal doctrine of economic substantive due process,[3] and risks diluting the strong protection traditionally given to more valuable areas of expression.[4] The goal of this book is to establish not only that these critiques of commercial speech protection are fallacious or misguided but also that the Supreme Court's failure to provide to commercial speech a level of First Amendment protection equivalent to that afforded other categories of fully protected expression is irrational and indefensible. Acceptance of this First Amendment "equivalency principle," however, will not dictate equivalent protection in all cases. Rather, it will only mean that the criteria employed

---

[1] See, e.g., *Lorillard Tobacco Co. v. Reilly*, 533 U.S. 525 (2001); *Greater New Orleans Broadcasting Ass'n, Inc. v. United States*, 527 U.S. 173 (1999); *44 Liquormart v. Rhode Island*, 517 U.S. 484 (1996).

[2] See Vincent Blasi, *The Pathological Perspective and the First Amendment*, 85 Colum. L. Rev. 449 (1985).

[3] Thomas H. Jackson & John Calvin Jeffries, *Commercial Speech: Economic Due Process and the First Amendment*, 65 Va. L. Rev. 1 (1979). Cf. R. George Wright, *Selling Words: Free Speech and Commercial Culture* (New York: New York University Press, 1997).

[4] Ibid.; see discussion on p. 15.

to determine constitutional protection for commercial and noncommercial speech will be identical. It is conceivable that, due to factual differences, applications of those same criteria will give rise to different conclusions in the two situations.

Commercial speech has become one of the most litigated and controversial areas of First Amendment protection. The controversy arises from fundamental misunderstandings of the ways in which commercial speech furthers the values of the First Amendment's guarantee of free expression. To understand the nature of the debate, it is necessary to understand how the Supreme Court has chosen to define the concept of commercial speech. The phrase does not include all expressions concerning the relative merits of commercial products or services. Rather, the Court has confined the concept to speech that does no more than propose a commercial transaction.[5] Thus, speech either opposing a commercial purchase or neutrally describing the qualities of a commercial product or service receives full First Amendment protection,[6] while speech that directly promotes a purchase receives a reduced level of protection.[7]

Reducing or excluding First Amendment protection for commercial advertising contravenes core constitutional values of free expression. I intend to establish this conclusion by means of what I believe to be a fresh conceptual approach to understanding those values – what I call the "perspective" framework. By this I mean that I view the purposes served by free expression from four different focuses – the speaker-centric model, the listener-centric model, the regulatory-centric model, and the rationalist-centric model. Each of these models provides both a formal and an intuitive normative basis for the constitutional guarantee of free expression. The conclusion I reach on the basis of the application of these four sufficient, but not necessary, perspectives is that commercial speech protection serves foundational goals and premises of our democratic system. Correspondingly, rejection of or reduction in the constitutional protection of commercial speech seriously threatens achievement of those goals.

THE EVOLUTION OF COMMERCIAL SPEECH PROTECTION

Prior to its watershed 1976 decision in *Virginia State Board of Pharmacy v. Virginia Citizens Consumer Council, Inc.*, the Supreme Court had given

---

[5] See *Virginia St. Bd. of Pharmacy v. Virginia Citizens Consumer Council, Inc.*, 425 U.S. 748, 762 (1976); *Bolger v. Youngs Drug Products Corp.*, 447 U.S. 557, 561 (1980).
[6] *Bose Corp. v. Consumers Union of U.S.*, 466 U.S. 485 (1984).
[7] *44 Liquormart, Inc. v. Rhode Island*, 517 U.S. 484 (1996).

short shrift to commercial speech.[8] In only one decision, *Valentine v. Chrestensen*, had the Court devoted anything approaching serious attention to the issue of First Amendment protection for commercial speech, and even there the analysis was, at best, cursory.[9] Just as small political and religious organizations had discovered handbills to be a vital ally, commercial advertisers had also found them extremely useful.[10] Long before the Supreme Court decisions in protecting the distribution of religious and political handbills, several state courts had overruled local ordinances that restricted handbill distribution as applied to commercial handbills on the grounds that the ordinances were unreasonable, arbitrary, and unwarranted. They were therefore beyond the constitutionally authorized police power vested in the local legislative units;[11] but mention of the First Amendment had rarely been made.

Valentine[12] involved the question of the constitutionality of a provision of New York City's sanitary code, forbidding distribution of commercial and business advertising matter in the streets. Chrestensen, a citizen of Florida, owned a former US Navy submarine, which he exhibited for profit. Arriving in New York, he printed a handbill advertising the boat and soliciting visitors for a stated fee. New York City's police commissioner advised him that the distribution of these leaflets would violate the previously mentioned ordinance, although Chrestensen was told that he might freely distribute handbills solely devoted to information or to a public protest. He proceeded to prepare a second handbill with the original advertisement on one side, altered only by removing the statement as to an admission fee, and adding, on the other side, a protest, without advertising, against the action of the City Dock Department for refusing him wharf facilities at a city pier to exhibit his submarine. The police department advised him that, although a handbill containing only the protest would be permissible, the fact that the proposed leaflet also contained advertising material rendered it legally undistributable. Chrestensen nevertheless proceeded to distribute the handbill, and after being restrained by the police, brought suit to enjoin the commissioner's action. The district court granted an interlocutory injunction[13] and after trial granted a permanent injunction. A divided Court of Appeals for the Second Circuit affirmed.[14]

[8] 425 U.S. 748 (1976).
[9] 316 U.S. 52 (1942).
[10] James K. Lindsay, *Council and Court: The Handbill Ordinances, 1889–1939*, 39 Mich. L. Rev. 561, 562 (1941).
[11] E.g., *City of Chicago v. Schultz*, 341 Ill. 208, 173 N.E. 276 (1930); *People v. Armstrong*, 73 Mich. 288, 41 N.W. 275 (1889).
[12] 316 U.S. 52 (1942).
[13] *Chrestensen v. Valentine*, 34 F. Supp. 596 (S.D.N.Y. 1941).
[14] *Chrestensen v. Valentine*, 122 F.2d 511 (2d Cir. 1941).

In an earlier decision, the Supreme Court had specifically noted that it was not holding "that commercial soliciting and canvassing may not be subjected to such regulation as the ordinance requires."[15] On the other hand, Judge Clark, speaking for the majority in the Second Circuit's decision in *Chrestensen*, felt that "interpretation of the conclusion of the *Schneider* case is not doubtful. Absolute prohibition of expression 'in the market place' is illegal, not to be saved by any commercial taint attached to the expression."[16] Thus, despite the Court's specific disclaimer regarding commercial advertising in *Schneider v. State*, many had considered the issue unsettled.

The Supreme Court had little trouble disposing of the lower court decisions. Justice Owen Roberts, who had written the opinion in *Schneider*, stated for a unanimous Court:

> This court has unequivocally held that the streets are proper places for the exercise of the freedom of communicating information and disseminating opinion and that, though the states and municipalities may appropriately regulate the privilege in the public interest, they may not unduly burden or proscribe its employment in these public thoroughfares. We are equally clear that the Constitution imposes no such restraint on government as respects purely commercial advertising.[17]

The Court reasoned that commercial advertising was merely ancillary to the proper performance of a business and could therefore be legislatively regulated in the public interest, much like all other business activities. *Valentine* was decided in 1942 – the height of the New Deal period. The New Deal Supreme Court viewed one of its most important goals to be the dismantling of the conservative Court's economic substantive due process regime associated primarily with *Lochner v. New York*.[18] It is therefore perhaps not surprising that the New Deal Court would tend to associate any constitutional protection of commercial activities with what it deemed to be the pathological and misguided framework derived from *Lochner*. In doing so, however, the Court appeared oblivious to the significant difference between *Lochner*-like property rights protection on the one hand and protection of commercial speech on the other hand. While *Lochner* and its progeny protected the commercial *conduct* of selling products and paying workers, *Valentine* involved *speech* by a commercial enterprise, informing its readers

---

[15] *Schneider v. State*, 308 U.S. at 165.
[16] 122 F.2d at 515. For a similar reading of *Schneider*, see note, 8 Geo. Wash. L. Rev. 866, 868 (1940).
[17] 316 U.S. at 54.
[18] 198 U.S. 45 (1905).

and listeners of truthful, and arguably valuable, information in much the same way that political expression seeks to inform and influence its recipients.

The situation remained this way, with only minor change, until the Court's 1976 decision in *Virginia Board*. There the Court invalidated the state's prohibition on prescription drug advertising as a First Amendment violation. "Advertising, however tasteless and excessive it sometimes may seem," the Court wrote, "is nonetheless dissemination of information as to who is producing and selling what product, for what reason, and at what price."[19] But while the decision was in many ways a constitutional breakthrough, subsequent decisions quickly made it clear that the Court was providing "commercial speech a limited measure of protection, commensurate with its subordinate position in the scale of First Amendment values."[20]

In its 1980 *Central Hudson* decision, the Court established a four-pronged test to determine whether commercial speech regulation violates the First Amendment – a test that for approximately the next twelve years shielded commercial speech far less than other protected expression.[21] There can be no doubt that the *Central Hudson* test as applied today provides dramatically greater protection than it did in its early years.[22] Yet the protection given to commercial speech remains below the "compelling interest" standard that protects such categories as political and artistic expression, and equally noteworthy, leading free speech scholars doubt or deny the case for protecting commercial speech.[23] Such skepticism is both unfortunate and unjustified. Commercial speech fosters important First Amendment values that are improperly ignored or dismissed by those who wish to give commercial speech second-class First Amendment protection. A detailed exploration of the Supreme Court's definition of commercial speech shows such skepticism is wholly unwarranted.

DEFINING COMMERCIAL SPEECH

One needs to understand the Court's definition of commercial speech to understand the concept's differences from fully protected expression. While

---

[19] 425 U.S. at 764.
[20] *Ohralik v. Ohio St. Bar Ass'n*, 436 U.S. 447, 456 (1978).
[21] *Central Hudson Gas & Elec. Corp. v. Pub. Service Commission*, 447 U.S. 557 (1980).
[22] For a detailed discussion of that doctrinal evolution, see Martin H. Redish, *Money Talks: Speech, Economic Power, and the Values of Democracy* (New York: New York University Press, 2000), pp. 14–62.
[23] Included on this list are, among others, such leading First Amendment scholars as Robert Post, Fred Schauer, Steven Shiffrin, and the late Ed Baker.

the Supreme Court has on different occasions employed varying, sometimes inconsistent definitions, for the most part it has defined commercial speech as speech that does "no more than propose a commercial transaction."[24] This definition has a significant drawback. The distinction between promotional and nonpromotional commercial speech suggests both the Court and the scholarly community are discriminating against profit-motivated expression. Yet in no other area of free speech jurisprudence has it ever been held that the First Amendment discriminates against speech that is motivated by self-interest, either financial or otherwise. Individuals who advocate for a reduction in their taxes will often be acting out of financial self-interest, yet no one would seriously challenge full First Amendment protection for their advocacy. Indeed, the speech of every candidate for political office could easily be seen as inherently self-promotional.

More ominous is the dangerous viewpoint discrimination that inheres in the prevailing definition. A speaker *opposing* a commercial transaction presumably possesses a full First Amendment right to speak. For example, Ralph Nader has full constitutional protection for his criticism of the safety of the Chevrolet Corvair; however, if General Motors sought to defend the safety of its product, it receives only the reduced protection given to commercial speech.[25] When the press criticizes Nike for using sweatshop labor in its foreign plants, its expression receives full First Amendment protection. Yet when Nike seeks to defend its practices, its arguments merit only the lesser protection-afforded commercial speech because the ultimate purpose and effect of the speech is to promote product sale. It is hard to view such a distinction as anything more than a categorical attack on capitalistic expression – hardly an acceptable basis for stratifying First Amendment protection. Such a dichotomy in constitutional protection is inherently pathological. As I have previously written, "[v]iewpoint based regulations are, by definition, grounded not in a principled effort to interpret and apply the structural values underlying the free speech protection but rather in a subjective assessment of moral and/or sociopolitical considerations that are external to the First Amendment. Those considerations necessarily grow out of normative concerns that exist wholly external to the First Amendment."[26] As Justice Scalia reasoned, in a world of viewpoint regulation, one side of the debate is forced to

---

[24] *Virginia St. Bd. of Pharmacy* v. *Virginia Citizens Consumer Council*, 425 U.S. 748, 762 (1976), quoting *Pittsburgh Press Co.* v. *Human Rights Comm'n*, 413 U.S. 378, 385 (1973).
[25] See Ralph Nader, *Unsafe at Any Speed* (New York: Grossman Publishers, 1965).
[26] Martin H. Redish, *The Adversary First Amendment: Free Expression and the Foundations of American Democracy* (Stanford: Stanford Law Books, 2013), p. 106.

fight according to Marquess of Queensbury Rules, while the other side may hit below the belt.[27]

It is likely for this reason that in *Sorrell v. IMS Health, Inc.*,[28] the Supreme Court subjected discrimination against commercial speech to strict scrutiny.[29] The state statute in question discriminated among speakers, favoring nonmanufacturer expression concerning prescription drugs over speech by manufacturers. But the Court overlooked an important implication of its analysis: if discriminatory *regulation* of expression is constitutionally suspect, then discriminatory *protection* must logically be deemed equally questionable. Yet that is exactly what the Court's own approach to First Amendment protection to commercial speech achieves. For while the level of constitutional protection extended to commercial speech has grown dramatically in recent years, it would be inaccurate to suggest that it has reached the level of full protection.

COMMERCIAL SPEECH AND THE THEORY OF FREE EXPRESSION

It is appropriate to begin making the case for protecting commercial speech by setting out a theoretical baseline – a foundation of normative precepts without which the protection of expression would be rendered either trivial or meaningless. These precepts postulate that a commitment to free expression both reflects and implements a belief in the ability of adult individuals to judge for themselves the wisdom or persuasiveness of competing viewpoints. A commitment to free expression presupposes an equally strong commitment to a principle of democratic self-rule, for neither free expression nor democracy would be of significant meaning or value absent the other. Both precepts are grounded in a normative commitment to the dignity of the individual citizens who, acting within the bounds of democratic government, contribute to the shaping and achievement of the goals they have set for themselves and for democratic society more generally.

Linking free expression and democratic government might seem a strange way to justify full First Amendment protection for commercial speech. One could argue that the matter of speech by "a seller hawking his wares" lies far from the heart of the democratic process.[30] It is thus not surprising that years before *Virginia Board*, a leading First Amendment scholar summarily

---

[27] *R.A.V. v. City of St. Paul*, 504 U.S. 377, 392 (1992) (plurality opinion).
[28] 564 U.S. 552 (2013).
[29] id.
[30] Jackson & Jeffries, *supra* note 3.

concluded that "[c]ommunications in connection with commercial transactions generally relate to a separate sector of social activity involving the system of property rights rather than free expression."[31] The opposite is true. Commercial speech substantially engages citizens on matters of public concern and debate (e.g., issues surrounding governmental regulation of such high-risk industries as drug manufacturing), and correspondingly, governmental suppression of commercial speech undermines such progress in much the same way that suppressing traditionally protected categories of expression does. Why? Commercial speech, much like speech directly concerning collective self-government, reflects a belief in individuals' ability to govern their lives and their right to seek to influence others, who, in turn, have the ability and right to make choices for their own lives.

My conclusions are best understood and defended by fashioning and explaining what I call the "perspective framework" approach to the theory of free expression. This framework significantly departs from traditional approaches to First Amendment theory. Generally, First Amendment scholars use a functionalist categorization methodology. For example, some scholars may draw sharp lines between speech tied directly to the political process and to other subjects of expression.[32] Other scholars focus instead on expression that furthers individual liberty or self-realization.[33] Still others see free expression as fostering a variety of pragmatic goals.[34]

To be sure, my framework subsumes at least some of the factors included in the more traditional functionalist categorization approach. The functionalist categorization approach begs a central question: to posit the special position of political speech assumes away the very issue subject to debate – namely, whether political speech is, in fact, special. My perspective framework does not assume the answer to that disputed question. Rather, it posits four significant perspectives to inform the issue of whether commercial speech merits as much protection as noncommercial expression. This perspective framework compels the conclusion that commercial speech merits full First Amendment protection.

---

[31] Thomas Emerson, *Toward a General Theory of the First Amendment* (New York: Random House, 1966), p.105 n.46.
[32] Alexander Meiklejohn, *Political Freedom* (New York: Harper, 1960); and Robert H. Bork, *Neutral Principles and Some First Amendment Problems*, 47 Ind. L. J. 1 (1971).
[33] Martin H. Redish, *The Value of Free Speech*, 130 U. Pa. L. Rev. 591 (1982).
[34] Steven H. Shiffrin, *The First Amendment and Economic Regulation: Away from a General Theory of the First Amendment*, 78 Nw. U. L. Rev. 1212 (1984).

THE PERSPECTIVE FRAMEWORK

My perspective framework includes four subcategories: the speaker-centric perspective, the listener-centric perspective, the regulatory-centric perspective, and the rationalist-centric perspective. The speaker-centric perspective focuses on how freedom of expression fosters the democratic needs and interests of the speaker. In contrast, the listener-centric perspective considers the liberal democratic values fostered for the recipient of the expression. The two are by no means necessarily the same. Expression that has no value to a recipient could still have value to a speaker – for example, writing in a private diary. In contrast, speech without value to a speaker might benefit a recipient in ways that further recognize values of free expression. For example, when a corporation disseminates communication, the developmental benefits traditionally associated with free speech are arguably remote at best. But the recipient of that corporate expression can benefit substantially from the educational, informative, or thought-provoking impact of that corporate communication. However, when viewed as an organic whole, the two perspectives reflect the First Amendment's commitment to individual development, growth, and self-government. These benefits can derive equally from individuals' participation in collective self-government and the individuals' control of their personal affairs – what I have long referred to as "private self-government."[35] In a pragmatic manner, speech simultaneously enables speakers to achieve their goals by persuading others and listeners to reach collective or personal choices by absorbing information and opinion.

The regulatory-centric and rationalist-centric perspectives add an entirely different analytical framework. The speaker-centric and listener-centric perspectives focus on the direct impact on the specific participants. The regulatory-centric and rationalist-centric perspectives consider broader, more systemically pervasive values and concerns. The regulatory-centric perspective posits that government may not do some things and still remain a liberal democracy. Some regulations of expression may undermine the democratic system by manipulatively skewing public debate. Others will do so by imposing a paternalism that contravenes the liberal democratic social contract between government and citizen. Both sorts of regulations must be invalidated to preserve liberal democracy.

The regulatory-centric perspective reflects what I have referred to as optimistic skepticism – a somewhat paradoxical belief in both the possibilities of

---

[35] Martin H. Redish, *The First Amendment in the Marketplace: Commercial Speech and the Values of Free Expression*, 39 Geo. Wash. L. Rev. 429 (1971).

human flourishing and, simultaneously, the dangers of the dark side of the human personality.[36] Humans can develop their intellectual and moral faculties by participating in the control of their lives.[37] This perspective also simultaneously recognizes the never-ending danger of tyranny that would crudely and inevitably disrupt the benefits of a liberal democratic system. This paradoxical belief led the Constitution's Framers to diffuse political power to deter the creation of tyranny.[38] They divided power both laterally, within the three branches of the federal government, and vertically, between the federal and state governments, to deter or disrupt its concentration in the hands of one individual, group, or faction.

The regulatory-centric perspective is essential to the First Amendment's guarantee of free expression. Tyranny is likely to begin once those in power suppress views counter to their own. Thus, the Supreme Court has looked for red flags when expression is restricted. For example, the First Amendment categorically prohibits suppressing speech because a viewpoint is offensive.

The rationalist-centric perspective, in contrast, is best seen as a means to deter or prevent such regulatory-centric pathologies of government. This perspective provides a check on the rationales for offering different levels of First Amendment protection to various expressive categories. In a sense, this perspective can be seen as a type of policeman, designed to ensure that the differences between levels of protection are neither under- nor overinclusive and are not merely guises for regulatory hostility to the ideology or viewpoint of the suppressed expression.

The same logic applies to selective protection of expression. If a court chooses to extend First Amendment protection to picketing on the part of socialists, it cannot deny the same to anti-socialist demonstrators absent some nonideological, principled basis for the distinction. Finally, the regulatory-centric model prohibits government from imposing restrictions on the expression of truthful information or advocacy to adult recipients for fear that those recipients might make the "wrong" decision – at least when that ensuing decision is lawful.[39] Such paternalistic motivations are inherently inconsistent with the notion of free citizens, who are worthy of dignity and respect.

---

[36] Martin H. Redish, *Fear, Loathing, and the First Amendment: Optimistic Skepticism and the Theory of Free Expression*, 76 Ohio St. L. J. 691 (2015).
[37] See generally Martin H. Redish, *The Value of Free Speech*, 130 U. Pa. L. Rev. 591 (1982).
[38] See Martin H. Redish, *The Constitution as Political Structure* (1995), pp. 99–134.
[39] When the speech advocates criminal behavior, different considerations may apply. See *Brandenburg v. Ohio*, 395 U.S. 444 (1969). However, those considerations are beyond the scope of this policy analysis.

For these reasons the Supreme Court has said that underinclusive regulation of expression violates the First Amendment.[40] Government cannot, for example, suppress burning of the American flag in order to prevent fires when burning the flag of any other nation gives rise to the very same danger. Such nonideological rationales for suppression thus mask what is in reality an ideologically driven selectivity that is anathema to the foundations of free expression in a democratic society. The rationalist-centric perspective enables a reviewing court to free constitutional analysis from ideologically driven disingenuousness and manipulation.

I will now apply the four perspectives to consider whether commercial speech should receive either full protection, less constitutional protection than more traditionally protected categories, or no protection at all.

THE SPEAKER-CENTRIC PERSPECTIVE AND COMMERCIAL SPEECH

Many observers believe commercial speech should be denied the protections accorded other expression because the speaker derives none of the benefits the First Amendment is designed to protect. Even if this were true, it would not necessarily follow that protection for commercial speech should be reduced or denied. Protecting commercial speech serves numerous other values apart from those of the speaker. We should see the various perspectives discussed here not as necessary, but as sufficient, conditions to trigger constitutional protection. Thus, even if expression does not advance the values underlying the speaker-centric perspective, it still deserves full protection if, for example, it fosters the values advanced by either the listener-centric or regulatory-centric perspectives. Indeed, one of the leading free speech scholars of all time, Alexander Meiklejohn, grounded First Amendment rights of free expression normatively in the listener's interest in receiving information and opinion so as to participate in self-government.[41] The Supreme Court has often echoed Meiklejohn's thinking.[42] Although perhaps unduly limited, this argument shows that even in the absence of First Amendment value to the speaker, expression may often serve valuable First Amendment interests. If any of the values underlying the First Amendment are threatened or undermined by

---

[40] R.A.V. v. City of St. Paul, 504 U.S. 377 (1992) (plurality opinion).
[41] See generally Alexander Meiklejohn, *Political Freedom*.
[42] See, for example, New York Times Co. v. Sullivan, 376 U.S. 254, 297 (1964) (Black, J., concurring); and Red Lion Broadcasting Co. v. F.C.C., 395 U.S. 367, 390 (1969). See generally, William J. Brennan, *The Supreme Court and the Meiklejohn Interpretation of the First Amendment*, 79 Harv. L. Rev. 1 (1965).

governmental suppression of expression, the First Amendment will have been violated. That said, commercial speech does foster speaker-centric values.

Scholars have suggested two reasons why commercial speech fails to advance speaker-centric values. Initially, Professor C. Edwin Baker long ago suggested that the underlying value of free speech protection is the exercise of liberty, and that when corporations speak they are not exercising their free will to speak because corporations are nothing more than robotic profit-maximizers.[43] Assuming for the moment the accuracy of Baker's unduly truncated version of the First Amendment's purpose,[44] he fails to understand the catalytic role that the corporate form plays in fostering individual self-realization.[45] Corporations are instruments created by the law so that citizens may achieve their personal economic or social goals. Indeed, the modern corporation finds its roots in Jacksonian democracy, as a device designed, through its limitation of liability, to enable the common person to combat New England industrialists and Southern landed gentry.[46] Thus, to divorce the corporate form from its roots in democratic theory incorrectly ignores the theoretical link between the corporation and the liberal democratic values fostered by the First Amendment's guarantee of free expression.

Robert Post articulated the second reason why commercial speech supposedly fails to advance the First Amendment speaker-centric value.[47] Post presumes that the First Amendment seeks to "safeguard public discourse from regulations that are inconsistent with democratic legitimacy."[48] He therefore

---

[43] C. Edwin Baker, *Scope of the First Amendment Freedom of Speech*, 25 UCLA L. Rev. 964 (1978).

[44] See Redish, *The Value of Free Speech*.

[45] This theory of catalytic self-realization and its relevance to corporate speech is explored in detail in Martin H. Redish and Howard M. Wasserman, *What's Good for General Motors: Corporate Speech and the Theory of Free Expression*, 66 Geo. Wash. L. Rev. 235 (1998).

[46] Herbert Hovenkamp, *Enterprise and American Law, 1836–1937* (Cambridge, MA: Harvard University Press, 1991), p. 3; Bray Hammond, *Sovereignty and an Empty Purse: Banks and Politics in the Civil War* (1970) reprinted in *Conflict and Consensus in Early American History*, 6th ed., eds. Allen F. Davis and Harold D. Woodman (Lexington, MA: D.C. Heath, 1984), pp. 216, 218; Ronald Seavoy, *The Origins of the American Business Corporation, 1784–1855* (Westport, CT: Greenwood Press, 1982), p. 256; and Alexis de Tocqueville, *Democracy in America*, trans. Henry Reeve (Cambridge, MA: Sever and Francis, 1862), pp. 129–30, 132, 140–41.

[47] I should note that Post does not totally exclude commercial speech from the scope of First Amendment protection because he recognizes a listener-centric informational value of such expression. See Robert C. Post, *The Constitutional Status of Commercial Speech*, 48 UCLA L. Rev. 1, 32 (2000). However, Post extends a significantly lower level of protection than he does to speech that fosters speaker-centric related values. See Redish, *The Adversary First Amendment*.

[48] Robert C. Post, *Reconciling Theory and Doctrine in the First Amendment*, 88 Cal. L. Rev. 2353, 2373 (2000).

reasons that to deserve the highest level of protection, under his participatory theory, the purpose of the expression must be to contribute to public discourse. Post summarily assumes that with commercial advertising, the expression's purpose is not to contribute to public discourse or communicative interchange, but rather to advance the economic interest of the speaker.[49] The commercial advertiser, according to Post, neither seeks nor derives the sort of public benefits that legitimize freedom of speech.

There is much that is troubling about Post's analysis. He is unable or unwilling to recognize the potentially complex, multilayered motivations of most expression. Speakers usually do not speak solely to contribute to public discourse or solely for purposes of narrow personal economic gain. For example, lobbyists working on behalf of labor unions seeking to engender political support for higher tariffs or the repeal of the North American Free Trade Agreement (NAFTA) may, on one level, truly believe in the political merits and morality of their position. Yet simultaneously their expression is undoubtedly influenced by economic motivation, both personally and on behalf of their clients. In this instance, presumably, Post would focus exclusively on the effort to contribute to public discourse. In contrast, in the case of commercial advertisers – who also may well have mixed motivations for their expression – Post assumes exclusively a personal economic motivation and therefore rejects any protection founded on speaker-centric values.

In any event, Post's use of commercial advertising as an unwavering surrogate for economic motivation forces us to draw technical, formalistic distinctions that effectively render his entire conceptual framework incoherent. Consider the following example: a beekeeper firmly believes – contrary to accepted scientific thought – that bee pollen possesses scientifically provable health benefits. He wishes to publish an op-ed article that asserts such benefits and mentions his own product. Regulatory authorities, believing that the beekeeper's assertion is scientifically incorrect, or at the very least, unproven, seek to suppress publication. Post would likely characterize such expression as a contribution to public discourse and therefore fully protected by the First Amendment, regardless of its accuracy. This is so, even though the beekeeper obviously possesses a strong economic interest in listeners accepting his viewpoint. Yet if, instead of writing an op-ed article, the beekeeper takes out an advertisement making the exact same claim about the product, Post would presumably deem the advertisement not a contribution to public discourse but rather pure commercial speech. To thus distinguish the two expressions represents the height of mindless formalism.

[49] See the discussion in Redish, *The Adversary First Amendment*, pp. 60–62.

It makes no difference whether one agrees that commercial speech fully serves the speaker-centric perspective of First Amendment analysis. One can reject that claim and still conclude that commercial speech unambiguously serves the interests fostered by the listener-centric perspective of First Amendment analysis, as I will show in the next section.

THE LISTENER-CENTRIC PERSPECTIVE AND COMMERCIAL SPEECH

Famed free speech theorist Alexander Meiklejohn argued that the First Amendment served democracy by fostering self-governance by citizens.[50] By receiving information and opinion, he reasoned, citizens become better "governors." Meiklejohn went too far in denying any First Amendment value to the speaker. However, he was surely correct to recognize the important First Amendment value of expression to listeners. Individuals' faculties may be developed just as much by receiving expression as by expressing themselves.

Meiklejohn believed that his theory logically implied that only speech relevant to the political process deserved First Amendment protection (though he defined that concept broadly).[51] But his theory implies the opposite. Just as individuals need free and open communication of information and opinion to participate in the collective self-governing process, so, too, do they require a similar uninhibited flow of information and opinion to govern themselves. Indeed, it is illogical to value expression that facilitates collective self-governance (where listeners have limited say in how they are governed), while simultaneously denying protection to expression that aids in the private self-governing (where an individual possesses 100 percent of the decision-making power). Commercial speech assists private self-governance. Advertising provides information and opinion, assisting individuals in making life-affecting choices that impact their lives and those of their families.

Listeners derive value from receiving information and opinion on commercial products and services when that information and opinion comes in some form other than commercial advertising. For example, *Consumer Reports* magazine's comments on commercial products and services receives full First Amendment protection.[52] Similarly, press reports on manufacturers and the relative merits of their products are presumably fully protected by

---

[50] Redish, *The Value of Free Speech*, pp. 604–05.
[51] Ibid., pp. 601–02.
[52] *Bose Corp. v. Consumers Union of U.S., Inc.*, 466 U.S. 485 (1984).

the First Amendment. The benefit to the reader or listener in making private choices justifies such protection. Yet those who would deny or reduce protection for commercial advertising overlook such benefits when they arise from advertising.

It is true, of course, that advertising is by no means objective. The speaker clearly has an economic interest in persuading listeners. Advertising is generally a form of advocacy, not purely the description of objective fact. But it does not follow that the information provided by an advocate has no value to the listener or reader. Speakers who contribute to political debate usually have their own personal, economic, or ideological agendas behind their expression. Their expression, like commercial advertising, is advocacy, not objective fact. Moreover, much like commercial advertising, political advertising may be more persuasion than pure information. Commercial speech functions much like political speech. Scholars and jurists should recognize that such speech deserves full First Amendment protection.

THE REGULATORY-CENTRIC PERSPECTIVE AND COMMERCIAL SPEECH

One conceivable justification for downgrading First Amendment protection for commercial speech is that there is no reason to fear the possibility of improper or ideologically driven motivation for the regulation or suppression of commercial speech. The same is, of course, untrue of suppression of political speech. Continuing this line of argument, we might say that the regulation of commercial speech poses no threats to democratic values. Nothing could be further from the truth.

Even if commercial speech were never improperly suppressed, there may still be reason to have the courts act as a watchdog. The very real danger of overzealous regulation that fails to demonstrate proper reverence for First Amendment values gives rise to legitimate concern. It is, after all, the judiciary that has primary responsibility for protecting and enforcing counter-majoritarian constitutional guarantees. This is particularly true of regulatory agencies, whose very reason for existence is to regulate and for whom the First Amendment is little more than an obstacle to attaining their goals. But the basis for concern extends far beyond this consideration.

There are at least three ways in which regulation of commercial speech could conceivably threaten the core values of the regulatory-centric perspective. First, as the public-choice literature teaches us, government is often vulnerable to capture by powerful economic interests.[53] It is certainly conceivable that a business could seek to have government suppress the advertising of its competitor. Second, government could choose to draw a regulatory distinction between commercial and noncommercial expression because of anti-capitalistic prejudice or hostility. Indeed, it was just such a suspicion that led the Supreme Court in *Sorrell v. IMS Health, Inc.* to impose strict scrutiny on a state's selective suppression of commercial but not noncommercial speech.[54] Finally, government could regulate truthful commercial speech out of fear that listeners either are incapable of comprehending the complexities of the information conveyed or will make unwise – even if perfectly lawful – decisions on the basis of it. In his 1996 opinion announcing the judgment of the Court in *44 Liquormart v. Rhode Island*,[55] Justice Stevens explained how such governmental paternalism is pathological:

> [B]ans against truthful, nonmisleading commercial speech ... usually rest solely on the offensive assumption that the public will respond 'irrationally' to the truth. The First Amendment directs us to be especially skeptical of regulations that seek to keep people in the dark for what the government perceives to be their own good. That teaching applies equally to state attempts to deprive consumers of accurate information about their chosen products.[56]

All of these concerns involve the regulatory-centric perspective.

THE RATIONALIST-CENTRIC PERSPECTIVE AND COMMERCIAL SPEECH

Our constitutional system and the dictates of the rule of law demand that the courts interpret and apply the law in a rational manner. Distinctions drawn by the political branches and the courts must be grounded in precepts of rationality. Otherwise, asserted distinctions are nothing more than cynical disguises

---

[53] Martin H. Redish, *Commercial Speech, First Amendment Intuitionism and the Twilight Zone of Viewpoint Discrimination*, 41 Loy. L. A. L. Rev 67 (2007); and Cass R. Sunstein, *The Republican Civic Tradition: Beyond the Republican Revival*, 97 Yale L. J. 1539 (1988).

[54] In *Sorrell*, the Supreme Court struck down a state law prohibiting drug manufacturers from obtaining data-mined information about doctors' prescription patterns but imposed no such restriction on academic researchers. The Court imposed strict scrutiny because it deemed the dichotomy to constitute a viewpoint-based discrimination. For a more detailed discussion of what I have labeled the "twilight zone" version of commercial speech regulation, see Redish, *Commercial Speech, First Amendment Intuitionism and the Twilight Zone of Viewpoint Discrimination, supra.*

[55] U.S. 484 (1996).

[56] id. at 503.

designed to obscure assertions of naked power and suppression. This is especially true of both judicial and governmental discriminations that impact expression. The regulatory-centric perspective tells us why this is such a concern.

Throughout this chapter, we have seen a number of puzzlingly and troublingly irrational distinctions in the arguments opposing significant protection for commercial speech. On the one hand, some people suggest that commercial speech does not deserve protection because it does not concern the political process, yet at the same time they have no trouble protecting *Consumer Reports* magazine, which focuses on the very same commercial products and services that are the subject of commercial speech. Others distinguish commercial speech because of the economic self-interest of the speaker, while at the same time wanting to fully protect the free speech rights of self-interested political actors. Still others would distinguish commercial speakers because of their corporate status, while having no problem protecting the First Amendment rights of media corporations.[57] It is difficult to understand how such irrational distinctions could be drawn absent some degree of underlying ideological hostility – conscious or subconscious – toward commercial advertising. The rationalist-centric perspective alerts us to the existence and dangers of such logically dubious distinctions and thereby enables us to invoke protections inherent in the regulatory-centric perspective.

THE PROBLEM OF FALSE COMMERCIAL SPEECH

Up to this point, my analysis has focused on the regulation of what is assumed to be truthful commercial speech. How would my approach deal with the problem of false commercial speech?

Under long-established doctrine, false or misleading commercial speech is automatically excluded from First Amendment protection. Even as protection for truthful commercial speech has dramatically expanded, the categorical exclusion of false commercial speech has remained firm. One could conceivably conclude, purely as a theoretical matter, that truthful commercial speech is deserving of full First Amendment protection, while false or misleading commercial is not. The fact that false speech is denied protection logically says nothing about whether comparable truthful speech should be protected. But

---

[57] The argument that media corporations are distinguishable because they are protected by the separate guarantee of freedom of the press is specious. No compelling reason has been given as to why the corporate nature of a speaker matters for freedom of speech but not for freedom of the press. In any event, the Supreme Court has always treated the two First Amendment guarantees fungibly.

the issue of protection for false commercial speech is far more complex than courts or commentators have to this point recognized.

False speech that is assumed by the listener to be truthful is never of societal value. The Court has chosen to protect certain forms of false speech about matters of public concern, not because of the inherent value of such expression, but because of the incidentally harmful impact of this form of regulation on truthful expression. In *New York Times Co. v. Sullivan*, the Court protected all but knowingly or recklessly false defamatory speech about public officials, because of the chill on truthful commentary arising from fear that the speech would later be deemed to be false.[58] The goal, then, was to avoid a chill on truthful speech by protecting false speech.

It has been argued that the danger of such a chill is nonexistent in the context of commercial speech, due to the speaker's profit incentive to communicate about its products. But surely many noncommercial speakers have similar self-interested motivations for their speech, yet they are uniformly protected to avoid chilling speech. In any event, there is no reason to assume that the existence of a profit incentive prevents chilling speech. Commercial enterprises will often be risk-averse about possible negative legal consequences of their actions in their commercial decision-making, and this applies to their advertising choices as well as to other economic decisions.

It does not follow that *all* false advertising should receive First Amendment protection. Knowingly false statements about commercial products amount to fraud, and there is no reason to believe that the First Amendment protects such activity. It follows only that false commercial speech receive the same protection as false and defamatory political speech: such expression is not to be protected when, and only when, it is determined to have been uttered with knowledge of falsity or reckless disregard of the statement's truth.[59]

THE DILUTION DANGER

Some worry that if commercial speech receives a level of First Amendment protection comparable to that given to traditionally protected categories of expression, the result will not be the expansion of the reach of First Amendment protection, but rather a dramatic pull-back of protection in those traditionally protected areas. Those who express this concern reason in the following manner: Whatever degree of protection is purportedly extended to commercial speech, under no circumstances will the courts protect many

---

[58] 376 U.S. 429 (1964).
[59] See Chapter 2 *infra*.

types of harmful expression that fall within this category. The danger of harm is simply too great. Therefore, if we demand at the outset that commercial speech should receive the exact same level of protection as traditionally protected expression does, then the inevitable result will be a reduction in the degree of protection extended to those traditional categories.

There are two responses to this concern. First, the argument begs the very question that is the subject of debate – namely, whether commercial speech and traditionally protected categories of expression should be deemed to be of equivalent First Amendment value. If the answer is yes, then there is no basis for drawing the distinction in the first place. For example, if a manufacturer is prohibited from advertising the benefits of a product found by the government to be harmful, it is unclear why journalists or scholars should have any greater right to communicate the very same harmful information and opinion. Second, the real danger is not of dilution of traditional protection, but rather of what can be called *reverse* dilution. Once it is accepted that government may paternalistically suppress the general dissemination of truthful information about commercial products and services on the grounds that the public will not be able to make the "right" decision from that information, we will have irretrievably contravened the values of the regulatory-centric framework. People are either sheep, or they are not: if they cannot be trusted to make the "correct" commercial purchasing decision on the basis of free and open debate, how can they logically be trusted to make political choices on the basis of such debate? Once it is established that government can selectively suppress information and opinion because the citizens are effectively children, the result will be a real threat to the foundations of the liberal democratic social contract between government and citizen. Hence, it is simply wrong to put commercial speech and noncommercial speech into hermetically sealed expressive categories. Excluding commercial speech from the First Amendment's protection will have negative consequences for the foundations of free expression and our democratic system.

CONCLUSION

Commercial speech has come a long way since the days before *Virginia Board* in 1976. Before that decision, due either to the absence of careful thought or disguised ideological hostility, both the Supreme Court and constitutional scholars gave short shrift to First Amendment protection to commercial speech. This was so, even though both court and scholars took for granted that other forms of expression about the relative merits of commercial products or services should receive full First Amendment protection.

Yet in no other area of First Amendment jurisprudence are speakers' constitutional protections reduced because of their self-interest, economic or otherwise. It is widely assumed that our democratic system is designed to protect the rights of citizens to advance their personal or economic interests by seeking to persuade others to accept their arguments. There exists no rational basis on which to categorically set commercial speakers apart, other than the ideologically driven desire to penalize those who benefit from the capitalistic system. Such justification is pathologically inconsistent with the very foundations of the First Amendment the argument purports to implement.

Fortunately, the trend in the Court has been to extend commercial speech protection to the point that it is rapidly approaching a level of constitutional insulation similar, if not yet identical, to that given more traditionally protected categories of speech. The perspective framework I have fashioned in this policy analysis clearly demonstrates the important constitutional values served by commercial speech. It is time for the Court to expressly acknowledge that commercial speech properly stands on an equal footing with all other kinds of expression given full protection by the First Amendment.

In the chapters that follow, I will apply the analysis and conclusions developed here to a variety of specific doctrinal areas of commercial speech protection: false advertising, the right of publicity, compelled expression, and scientific speech. In each area, I will demonstrate that the analytical framework shaped in this chapter logically dictates application of the equivalency principle to each of these areas. My conclusions are likely to be counterintuitive to many. In most of the areas discussed, no one has ever seriously suggested that commercial and noncommercial speech be judged under the same constitutional standard. It is about time that this long-held understanding be reconsidered.

2

False Commercial Speech and the First Amendment

INTRODUCTION

In the late 1960s, the Phillip Morris Company introduced a cigarette known as Virginia Slims.[1] In an effort to give the cigarette a marketing personality, the company advertised it as a cigarette for women, apparently attempting to tie the brand to the burgeoning women's liberation movement.[2] Its highly successful slogan was, "You've come a long way, baby."[3] The slogan was designed to get women to realize how far they had come in terms of independence in what had previously been a man's world, and identify that independence with the cigarette made especially for them.[4] One can debate the morality of such an advertising campaign, but however one feels about its merits or demerits, there is no doubt that the campaign's slogan could easily be applied to commercial speech itself. Although it took almost seventy years, commercial speech went from being outside the First Amendment looking in to a status almost equivalent to that of the most protected forms of expression.[5]

As explained in Chapter 1, for many years commercial speech was summarily excluded from any meaningful level of constitutional protection under the First Amendment right of free speech.[6] In its 1976 decision in *Virginia State Board of*

---

[1] Ruth Rosen, *You've Come a Long Way Baby (Or Have You?)*, Huffington Post Blog (February 21, 2013, 10:52 AM), www.huffingtonpost.com/ruth-rosen/womens-movement_b_2733469.html [https://perma.cc/ZD2B-VY4U].

[2] Cathryn Jakobson, *Why They Stretched the Slims*, N.Y. Times (June 8, 1986), www.nytimes.com/1986/06/08/magazine/why-they-stretched-the-slims.html?pagewanted=all [https://perma.cc/3NV8-M5UU].

[3] Rosen, *supra* note 1.

[4] See Jakobson, *supra* note 2; Rosen, *supra* note 1.

[5] See *Sorrell v. IMS Health Inc.*, 564 U.S. 552, 557 (2011) (holding that "[s]peech in aid of pharmaceutical marketing" is subject to "heightened judicial scrutiny"); *Valentine v. Chrestensen*, 316 U.S. 52, 54 (1942) (stating that "purely commercial advertising" does not enjoy the same safeguards as other types of speech).

[6] See *Breard v. City of Alexandria*, 341 U.S. 622, 645 (1951); *Valentine*, 316 U.S. at 54.

Pharmacy v. *Virginia Citizens Consumer Council, Inc.*,[7] the Court changed all of that by extending a not-insignificant level of constitutional protection to commercial speech.[8] However, the Court quickly made clear that commercial speech is "afforded ... a limited measure of protection, commensurate with its subordinate position in the scale of First Amendment values."[9] As a result, the Court deemed itself free to uphold regulation of commercial speech when the regulatory authority established merely that damage "may" occur,[10] or that there is a "possibility" of harm resulting from the speech in question.[11] This degree of protection was far less than that given most categories of noncommercial speech, for which the showing of a "compelling interest" was usually required to justify suppression.[12]

The famed four-pronged test from *Central Hudson Gas & Electric Corp.* v. *Public Service Commission*,[13] adopted by the Court in 1980, at best appeared to extend commercial speech a form of intermediate scrutiny protection, still far below the strict scrutiny/compelling interest protection given more traditionally protected categories of noncommercial expression.[14] The Court purports to continue to apply that test to this very day.[15] Beginning in 1993, however, both the Court's rhetoric and decisions began to change.[16] Since that year, it is difficult to find a Supreme Court decision upholding the suppression of truthful commercial speech. As a practical, if not a formal, matter, then, it could reasonably be said that today, truthful commercial speech receives a level of protection approaching, if not actually reaching, the level of protection received by noncommercial speech.[17] In fact, in recent years the Court appears to have adopted the principle that, contrary to statements in its decisions during the early years of the commercial speech

---

[7] 425 U.S. 748 (1976).
[8] See id. at 762–65.
[9] *Ohralik* v. *Ohio State Bar Ass'n*, 436 U.S. 447, 456 (1978).
[10] See id. at 457, 464–68.
[11] See *Friedman* v. *Rogers*, 440 U.S. 1, 13–16 (1979).
[12] See Martin H. Redish & Kelsey B. Shust, *The Right of Publicity and the First Amendment in the Modern Age of Commercial Speech*, 56 Wm. & Mary L. Rev. 1443, 1489 (2015).
[13] 447 U.S. 557, 566 (1980).
[14] See id. at 564–66.
[15] See, e.g., *Sorrell* v. *IMS Health Inc.*, 564 U.S. 552, 572 (2011).
[16] See *City of Cincinnati* v. *Discovery Network, Inc.*, 507 U.S. 410, 417 (1993) (holding that the City's restriction on commercial speech was not a "reasonable fit" between the government's interest and means).
[17] See, e.g., *Greater New Orleans Broad. Ass'n* v. *United States*, 527 U.S. 173, 176 (1999) (holding that a prohibition on broadcasts concerning legal gambling was a violation of the First Amendment); *44 Liquormart, Inc.* v. *Rhode Island*, 517 U.S. 484, 489 (1996) (plurality opinion) (holding "that Rhode Island's statutory prohibition against advertisements that provide the public with accurate information about retail prices of alcoholic beverages [was] ... invalid").

doctrine, in the broad scheme of the First Amendment truthful commercial speech is deemed to have value roughly equivalent to that of noncommercial speech.[18] To the extent commercial speech can be suppressed in situations where noncommercial speech would be protected, it must be because of a showing of harm uniquely associated with commercial speech.[19] As explained in Chapter 1, this judicial assumption of equivalent value of commercial and noncommercial speech can properly be described as the "equivalency principle." This does not mean that the Supreme Court has, at this point, fully recognized the inexorable doctrinal implications of its own equivalency principle.[20] But there can be no doubt that the Court has in fact adopted the principle, at least in most situations. Indeed, in its most recent statements on the issue, the Court has held that governmental regulation providing noncommercial speakers better treatment than comparably situated commercial speakers is deserving of strict scrutiny.[21]

One of the most glaring exceptions to application of this equivalency principle is false commercial speech, which has long been categorically excluded from the protective reach of the First Amendment.[22] At first blush this categorical exclusion might seem understandable. False commercial speech, of course, serves no value in and of itself; indeed, it is reasonable to believe that it can only be harmful to society and the individuals who populate it, in a variety of ways. But in the abstract, at least, the same could be said of false noncommercial speech as well: Listeners or readers who base life-affecting decisions – either political or personal – in reliance on false information or opinion may suffer great harm. Moreover, false speech may unjustly injure the reputations of innocent individuals. Yet the Supreme Court has long recognized, at least in the context of noncommercial speech, that the relevant constitutional analysis is far more complex than this simplistic description might suggest.[23] Even though false speech in and of itself serves

---

[18] See discussion *infra* at 27–34.
[19] *Sorrell*, 564 U.S. at 579; *Discovery Network, Inc.*, 507 U.S. at 426.
[20] See, e.g., Redish & Shust, *supra* note 12 (criticizing preferential protection of traditional media over commercial advertisers in response to suits for violation of the right of publicity).
[21] See *Reed v. Town of Gilbert*, 135 S. Ct. 2218, 2224 (2015) (holding that Gilbert's sign code imposing content-based restrictions on speech was subject to strict scrutiny); *Sorrell*, 564 U.S. at 557 (holding that "[s]peech in aid of pharmaceutical marketing ... is a form of expression protected by the Free Speech Clause of the First Amendment" and thus "must be subjected to heightened judicial scrutiny").
[22] *Cent. Hudson Gas & Elec. Corp. v. Pub. Serv. Comm'n*, 447 U.S. 557, 566 (1980) (holding that for commercial speech to be protected by the First Amendment, it "must ... not be misleading").
[23] See, e.g., *N.Y. Times Co. v. Sullivan*, 376 U.S. 254, 279–80 (1964) (requiring "actual malice" for a false statement about a public official to fall into a free speech exception).

no value and often causes harm, occasions will arise in which false speech must be protected in order to foster broader values and societal needs.[24]

The question then arises: Why has the equivalency principle, which has played such an important doctrinal role in the recent shaping of modern commercial speech doctrine, not played an equally important role in the context of the regulation of false commercial speech? There may well be a satisfactory answer to this question, but there can be no doubt that the Supreme Court has failed even to devote sufficient attention to the question to determine whether such an answer exists.

The thesis asserted here is that the logic underlying the equivalency principle, which now appears to play so important a role in the context of First Amendment protection for truthful commercial speech, applies with equal force to the regulation of false commercial speech. In other words, to the extent false noncommercial speech is deemed to have value, if only indirectly, false commercial speech should be seen as serving the very same values. In every instance it is important to note, however, that this does not mean that the actual protection extended to false commercial speech needs to be equivalent to that received by false noncommercial speech in order to satisfy the equivalency principle. That principle, it should be recalled, does not require that regulators always provide identical treatment to commercial and noncommercial speech. Rather, all it demands is that to the extent the two categories of expression are to be distinguished in the level of First Amendment protection they receive, it must be because the harm caused by one is uniquely greater than the harm caused by the other, not because the value of one of the categories of expression is deemed to be greater than that of the other.[25] In short, the equivalency principle demands an assumption of equivalent *value*, not necessarily equivalent *consequences* or equivalent *protection*.

When the dust settles, then, a proper analysis will reveal that the result of the application of the equivalency principle in the context of false commercial speech regulation should in some important respects differ little, if at all, from the way that false noncommercial speech is treated today.[26] But that will not be true in all cases as either a doctrinal or theoretical matter, and in any event the constitutional stakes involved extend well beyond the principle's doctrinal implications for the regulation of false commercial speech. That is because those who oppose the idea that commercial and noncommercial speech are equivalent as a matter of First Amendment value can today simply point to the

---

[24] See, e.g., id.
[25] See discussion *infra* at 51–56.
[26] See discussion *infra* at 32–56.

significant doctrinal difference in the level of protection received by false commercial and noncommercial speech as persuasive evidence that the equivalency principle is nothing more than a doctrinal mirage.[27] In reality, the argument proceeds, by refusing to protect false commercial speech while simultaneously protecting most false noncommercial speech, the Court properly recognizes that commercial speech does not possess value equivalent to noncommercial speech.

The goal of this chapter, then, is twofold. First, it is designed to demonstrate that the logic of the equivalency principle that the Court has effectively developed for most truthful commercial speech is logically as applicable to the context of false speech as it is in the context of truthful speech.[28] Second, it is designed to demonstrate that to the extent false commercial and noncommercial speech are to be treated differently in specific contexts, it is not because of variance in value of the two forms of speech, but rather because of variance in the nature and degree of harm caused by the two categories of speech.[29] In this way, the chapter will have accomplished two goals. First, it will have shown how and why First Amendment doctrine needs to be adjusted to take account of the proper application of the equivalency principle to false speech. Second, it will have disposed of the argument that the different treatment given false commercial speech demonstrates the invalidity of the equivalency principle when applied to truthful commercial speech.[30]

The first section of this chapter explores both the doctrinal evolution and theoretical merits of the equivalency principle.[31] It concludes first that the Supreme Court's commercial speech doctrine has evolved to the point where government is no longer permitted to regulate truthful commercial speech in a manner differently from its regulation of noncommercial speech solely on the grounds that commercial speech is of lesser value to the interests fostered by the First Amendment.[32] To the extent commercial speech may be subjected to more invasive regulation than noncommercial speech, it must be due to government's efforts to prevent harms caused by commercial speech but not caused by comparable false noncommercial speech.[33] The part then concludes that the

---

[27] See discussion *infra* at 27–31.
[28] See discussion *infra* at 34–39.
[29] See discussion *infra* at 53–56.
[30] See discussion *infra* at 29–30.
[31] See discussion *infra* at 27–31.
[32] See discussion *infra* at 31–34.
[33] See discussion *infra* at 39–41.

Court's current approach is not only fully justified but actually dictated by a proper understanding of the theory of free expression.[34]

In the following section, this chapter explores the implications of the equivalency principle for regulation of false commercial speech.[35] On the basis of an analysis of First Amendment theory, I conclude that the equivalency principle logically applies to false, as well as truthful commercial speech.[36] In the case of *unknowingly* false commercial speech, the equivalency principle dictates that even in the face of potentially substantial harm, the speech must be protected.[37] The Court has reached this conclusion for unknowingly false defamatory speech of public figures, even though such speech may give rise to serious and unique harm to victims' reputations.[38] There is absolutely no principled basis on which to distinguish these two situations.[39] In the case of knowingly false commercial speech, however, I conclude that – as is the case for knowingly false defamation of public figures – the harm is sufficiently severe to justify the loss of constitutional protection.[40] As a doctrinal matter, this would differ from the constitutional treatment given most knowingly false non-defamatory noncommercial speech.[41] But that difference is justified not by a difference in First Amendment value but rather by a significant difference in the nature and intensity of the harm caused by the different forms of knowingly false speech.

Thus, while as a practical matter knowingly false commercial speech would, under the framework suggested here, generally be subject to more pervasive regulation than knowingly false noncommercial speech, this is not because it possesses lower First Amendment value than noncommercial speech. Rather, it is because the nature, intensity, and immediacy of the harm it causes justifies the distinction in First Amendment protection. Avoidance of the harm constitutes a sufficiently compelling interest to justify suppression of knowingly false commercial speech while in most (though not all) cases the harm caused by knowingly false noncommercial speech does not. However, to the extent that false noncommercial speech does, in fact, give

---

[34] See discussion *infra* at 34–41.
[35] See discussion *infra* at 41–47.
[36] See discussion *infra* at 34–41.
[37] One might suggest that even unknowingly false speech may cause serious harm. But the same could be said of defamatory harm. In any event, once it is unambiguously established that the expression is in fact false, the speaker's continued expression of the same information would at that point constitute knowingly false speech.
[38] See discussion *infra* at 42–47.
[39] See discussion *infra* at 34–42.
[40] See discussion *infra* at 54.
[41] See discussion *infra* at 53–55.

rise to dangers of harm identical to those caused by false commercial speech, such speech should be (and, to a certain extent, already is) subject to the same regulatory regime constitutionally permitted for false commercial speech.[42] The difference, in other words, is based on the nature and severity of the harm, not on the commercial nature of the expression.

COMMERCIAL SPEECH AND THE EVOLUTION OF THE EQUIVALENCY PRINCIPLE

The Doctrinal Evolution of the Equivalency Principle

Early Protection for Commercial Speech

For many years, commercial speech received no First Amendment protection. Most famously, the Court in *Valentine v. Chrestensen*[43] stated that "[w]hether, and to what extent, one may promote or pursue a gainful occupation in the streets, to what extent such activity shall be adjudged a derogation of the public right of user, are matters for legislative judgment."[44] Although the Court held that while the Constitution demands that government restrictions of free speech must not be "unduly burden[some]," it stated explicitly that "the Constitution imposes no such restraint on government as respects purely commercial advertising."[45]

Matters stood this way for more than thirty years. However, in *Virginia State Board of Pharmacy v. Virginia Citizens Consumer Council, Inc.*, the Court dramatically altered the state of First Amendment doctrine, picking up where it left off in *Bigelow v. Virginia*.[46] While the Court had previously extended protection to an advertisement that "did more than simply propose a commercial transaction,"[47] the Court in *Virginia Board* extended First Amendment protection to pure commercial speech.[48] The *Virginia Board* Court first expounded on *Bigelow*, stating that the First Amendment protects speech even though "money is spent to project it . . . [, and] even though it is carried in a form that is 'sold' for profit."[49] The Court, in holding that commercial speech is protected by the First Amendment, emphasized the

---

[42] See discussion *infra* at 41–57.
[43] 316 U.S. 52 (1942).
[44] id. at 54.
[45] id.
[46] See generally *Va. State Bd. of Pharmacy v. Va. Citizens Consumer Council, Inc.*, 425 U.S. 748 (1976); *Bigelow v. Virginia*, 421 U.S. 809 (1975).
[47] *Bigelow*, 421 U.S. at 822.
[48] 425 U.S. at 762.
[49] id. at 761 (citations omitted).

importance of the "free flow of commercial information" to both individuals and society more generally.[50] Because private economic decisions abound in individuals' lives, there is both a societal and individual interest in ensuring those decisions are "intelligent and well informed."[51] Indeed, even if a speaker's motivation is purely economic, "[t]hat hardly disqualifies him from protection under the First Amendment."[52] Commercial speech therefore deserves protection even if it only proposes a transaction.[53] While *Virginia Board* was the first decision to explicitly extend First Amendment protection to "pure" commercial speech, it did not extend entirely the same degree of protection to commercial speech as it had to noncommercial speech.[54] Instead, the Court pointed to "commonsense differences" between commercial and noncommercial speech that might justify greater restriction of the former.[55] Most importantly, the Court regarded commercial speech's "greater objectivity and hardiness," in comparison to noncommercial speech, as reducing the need to tolerate false or misleading commercial speech.[56]

The Supreme Court has held that the First Amendment protects several categories of false noncommercial statements of fact, because such speech is "inevitable in free debate" and strict punishment of all such speech therefore "runs the risk of inducing a cautious and restrictive exercise of the constitutionally guaranteed freedoms of speech and press."[57] In *Virginia Board*, however, the Court reasoned that commercial speakers are unlikely to similarly fear inadvertently violating false commercial speech regulations and thus refrain from engaging in commercial speech, because commercial speech's greater objectivity allows speakers to "more easily verif[y]" its accuracy before they speak.[58] The Court further reasoned that truthful commercial speech is hardier, or "more durable," than noncommercial speech, because commercial speech is necessarily required in order to make profits.[59] Insofar as speakers are profit driven, then, they are unlikely to be "chilled by proper

---

[50] id. at 764–65 (remarking that some commercial advertisements "may be of general public interest").
[51] id. at 765.
[52] id. at 762.
[53] id.
[54] id. at 771–72 n.24.
[55] id.
[56] id.; see, e.g., *Friedman v. Rogers*, 440 U.S. 1, 13, 15–16 (1979) (upholding a law preventing optometrists from practicing under trade names because "there is a significant possibility that trade names will be used to mislead the public").
[57] *Gertz v. Robert Welch, Inc.*, 418 U.S. 323, 340 (1974).
[58] *Va. State Bd. of Pharmacy*, 425 U.S. at 771–72 n.24.
[59] id.

regulation" of false commercial speech.[60] In sum, the *Virginia Board* Court, relying on these so-called differences between commercial and noncommercial speech as justification,[61] held that while the First Amendment must in some instances protect false noncommercial speech, under no circumstances does it protect false commercial speech.[62]

While *Virginia Board* and its early progeny seemed to suggest only that some particular features of commercial speech might permit heavier restrictions, the Court's decision in *Ohralik v. Ohio State Bar Ass'n*[63] broadly restricted the First Amendment protections for both truthful and false commercial speech.[64] According to the *Ohralik* Court, *Virginia Board* acknowledged "the 'common sense' distinction" between commercial and noncommercial speech,[65] namely that commercial speech "occurs in an area traditionally subject to government regulation."[66] Ignoring that distinction and providing equal First Amendment protection to commercial and noncommercial speech, the Court reasoned, "could invite dilution, simply by a leveling process, of the force of the Amendment's guarantee with respect to the latter kind of speech."[67] To invite that dilution and "subject the First Amendment to such a devitalization"[68] all for the sake of commercial speech, which the Court stated has a "subordinate position in the scale of First Amendment values," would simply be too risky.[69] Accordingly, the Court stated instead that commercial speech has "a limited measure of protection," thus "allowing modes of regulation that might be impermissible in the realm of noncommercial expression" but also preserving the heightened protection

---

[60] id.
[61] See discussion *infra* at 47–51.
[62] 425 U.S. 771–73. Although *Virginia Board* was an obvious success for commercial speech advocates, the Court, in the years immediately following *Virginia Board*, solidified its position that false commercial speech could be more heavily restricted than false noncommercial speech. See, e.g., *Bates v. State Bar of Ariz.*, 433 U.S. 350, 383 (1977) (holding that "leeway for untruthful or misleading expression that has been allowed in other contexts has little force in the commercial arena" (citations omitted)).
[63] 436 U.S. 447 (1978).
[64] id. at 455–56.
[65] id. (quoting *Va. State Bd. of Pharmacy*, 425 U.S. at 771 n.24).
[66] id. at 456 (citing *Va. State Bd. of Pharmacy*, 425 U.S. at 771 n.24).
[67] id.
[68] id.
[69] See id. But see *City of Cincinnati v. Discovery Network, Inc.*, 507 U.S. 410, 434 n.2 (1993) (Blackmun, J., concurring) ("[T]he 'limited measure of protection' our cases had afforded commercial speech reflected the fact that we had allowed 'modes of regulation that might be impermissible in the realm of noncommercial expression' and not that we had relegated commercial speech to a 'subordinate position in the scale of First Amendment values.'").

for noncommercial speech.[70] *Ohralik* thus continued the Court's practice of allowing much more pervasive regulation of commercial speech than of noncommercial speech. The Court's subsequent decision in *Central Hudson* enshrined in doctrine a method to ensure that commercial speech, regardless of falsity, is entitled to noticeably less First Amendment protection than noncommercial speech.

After reinforcing *Ohralik*'s justifications for affording commercial speech less First Amendment protection, the Court in *Central Hudson* adopted a four-part analysis for determining whether particular government regulations of commercial speech are unwarranted.[71] Such an approach ensures that commercial speech receives First Amendment protection only in appropriate cases and that, in those cases, commercial speech receives only the appropriate amount of protection against unjustified speech restrictions.

The first step of *Central Hudson*'s four-part analysis concerns whether the commercial speech affected by some government regulation is protected by the First Amendment at all.[72] Given the Court's view that the First Amendment protects commercial speech only because of the "informational function of advertising," the First Amendment protects commercial speech only if it "accurately inform[s] the public about lawful activity."[73] The First Amendment does not protect, and the government may thus freely suppress, any commercial speech that (1) provides false information to the public, (2) is "more likely to deceive the public than to inform it," and (3) concerns unlawful activities.[74] While acknowledging that, "[i]n most other contexts, the First Amendment prohibits" content-based speech regulations such as these, the Court justified content-based regulation of commercial speech because its greater objectivity and hardiness protect it from the suffocation of overbroad regulation.[75]

If, however, the First Amendment applies because the commercial speech in question is "neither misleading nor related to unlawful activity,"[76] the government must then show that its regulation satisfies the final three parts of the *Central Hudson* test,[77] which essentially amounts to surviving

---

[70] *Ohralik*, 436 U.S. at 456.
[71] 447 U.S. 557, 566 (1980).
[72] id.
[73] id. at 563.
[74] id. at 563–64 (citations omitted).
[75] id. at 564 n.6 (citing *Consol. Edison Co. v. Pub. Serv. Comm'n of N.Y.*, 447 U.S. 530, 537–40 (1980); *Bates v. State Bar of Ariz.*, 433 U.S. 350, 381 (1977)).
[76] id. at 564.
[77] id. at 566.

intermediate scrutiny.[78] *Central Hudson's* second part requires that the government "assert a substantial interest to be achieved by restrictions on commercial speech."[79] Third, *Central Hudson* requires that the government's commercial speech regulation "directly advance[s] the state interest," thus prohibiting regulations that "provide only ineffective or remote support for the government's purpose."[80] Fourth, and finally, the test requires that commercial speech regulations are "narrowly drawn" to restrict only as much speech as necessary to advance or protect the state's interest.[81]

CONTEMPORARY COMMERCIAL SPEECH PROTECTION

While *Central Hudson* has never been overruled, several post-*Central Hudson* cases seem to afford commercial speech more protection than the *Central Hudson* test originally contemplated. Indeed, it seems that, in almost all facets, the Court now affords truthful commercial speech virtually as much First Amendment protection as it does noncommercial speech. The Supreme Court has not upheld governmental suppression of truthful commercial speech in more than twenty years. As Chapter 1 established, the Supreme Court now holds that the value of truthful commercial speech is fungible with that of truthful noncommercial speech.[82]

The Court's refusal to allow commercial speech to be restricted merely because it is of purportedly lower value than noncommercial speech represents an important insight about the essence of commercial speech protection. The Court has stated that "an interest in preventing commercial harms ... [is] the typical reason why commercial speech can be subject to greater governmental regulation than noncommercial speech."[83] This

---

[78] See id. at 573 (Blackmun, J., concurring) (asserting that, while intermediate scrutiny might be appropriate for restrictions on false or misleading commercial speech, restrictions on truthful and lawful commercial speech must survive heightened scrutiny).

[79] id. at 564. But see Bolger v. Youngs Drug Prods. Corp., 463 U.S. 60, 74-75 (1983) (citing Linmark Assocs., Inc. v. Twp. of Willingboro, 431 U.S. 85, 95–96 (1977)) (suggesting that some commercial speech provides information of such great import, e.g., truthful information that aids parents in giving informed parental guidance, that the restriction of that information "constitutes a 'basic' constitutional defect regardless of the strength of the government's interest").

[80] *Cent. Hudson*, 447 U.S. at 564; See, e.g., *Va. State Bd. of Pharmacy v. Va. Citizens Consumer Council, Inc.*, 425 U.S. 748, 769 (1976) ("The advertising ban does not directly affect professional standards one way or the other. It affects them only through the reactions it is assumed people will have to the free flow of drug price information.").

[81] *Cent. Hudson*, 447 U.S. at 565 (footnote omitted) (quoting *In re Primus*, 436 U.S. 412, 438 (1978)).

[82] See Chapter 1, *supra*.

[83] 447 U.S. at 426 (citations omitted).

statement strongly suggests that the Court now affords more protection to commercial speech than "a limited measure of protection, commensurate with its subordinate position in the scale of First Amendment values."[84] Instead, the Court's later commercial speech decisions suggest that commercial speech enjoys just as much protection as any other form of speech.[85] That is a long way from the *Central Hudson* position that all commercial speech, regardless of context, is afforded less First Amendment protection than noncommercial speech.[86] Indeed, in one case, the Court's willingness to consider, after moving past the reasonable fit discussion, whether the city's regulation of commercial speech was "justified as a legitimate time, place, or manner restriction on protected speech", signals that it was willing to consider commercial speech as fully protected speech that may sometimes be subjected to more severe restrictions because of its unique harms.[87]

Indeed, the Court effectively adopted the equivalency principle, extending full First Amendment protection to truthful commercial speech in *Sorrell v. IMS Health Inc.*[88] The case concerned a First Amendment challenge to a Vermont law that restricted the sale or use of pharmaceutical data for marketing purposes.[89] The law was designed to prevent pharmaceutical companies from making use of data concerning the prescribing history of individual doctors in order to shape their advertising appeals to those doctors.[90] However, the state statute was construed not to bar the use of the very same data by academic researchers.[91] The Court found the law to be a "content- and speaker-based" restriction on protected speech,[92] and thus required "heightened judicial scrutiny."[93] The Court further held that "[c]ommercial speech is no exception" to the required heightened judicial scrutiny of content-based speech restrictions.[94] This application of heightened scrutiny to content- or speaker-based restrictions on commercial speech was a remarkable step forward for commercial speech protection, because, as Justice Breyer correctly noted in dissent, no such restriction of commercial speech "ha[d] ever before justified greater scrutiny when regulatory activity affects commercial

---

[84] *Ohralik v. Ohio State Bar Ass'n*, 436 U.S. 447, 456 (1978).
[85] *Discovery Network*, 507 U.S. at 426.
[86] See *Cent. Hudson Gas & Elec. Corp. v. Pub. Serv. Comm'n*, 447 U.S. 557, 563 (1980).
[87] *Discovery Network*, 507 U.S. at 430.
[88] 564 U.S. 552 (2011).
[89] id. at 557, 561.
[90] See id. at 558–59.
[91] id. at 563.
[92] id.
[93] id. at 565.
[94] id. at 566.

speech."[95] In fact, wasn't the inescapable consequence of the reduced protection for commercial speech that there would be discrimination between commercial and noncommercial speakers? By the Court's reasoning in *Sorrell*, then, the Court's own commercial speech doctrine amounts to a discrimination deserving of strict scrutiny.

While the *Sorrell* Court reaffirmed that "the government's legitimate interest in protecting consumers from 'commercial harms' explains 'why commercial speech can be subject to greater governmental regulation than noncommercial speech,'"[96] the Court found that Vermont had failed to tie its restriction to any unique commercial harm.[97] Further, Vermont did not assert that pharmaceutical "detailing" was false or misleading, nor that the law would proactively reduce some risk of false or misleading commercial speech.[98] Finally, while the Court did state that under the *Central Hudson* test the regulation would have to "show at least that the statute directly advance[d] a substantial governmental interest" and that there was a reasonable fit between the regulation and that interest, it apparently did so only to show that "the outcome is the same whether a special commercial speech inquiry or a stricter form of judicial scrutiny is applied."[99] Thus, the Court found the content- and speaker-based Vermont law to violate the First Amendment.[100]

Sorrell represents a capstone of sorts on the Court's move toward acceptance of the equivalency principle. At the very least, a synthesis of modern commercial speech cases and *Sorrell* strongly suggests that more invasive regulations of commercial speech can be justified only by uniquely commercial harms, not by the precept that commercial speech is inherently less valuable than noncommercial speech and thus receives less First Amendment protection. In that manner, *Sorrell* suggests that commercial speech regulations are subject to "a standard yet stricter than *Central Hudson*."[101] Indeed, at least one Justice

---

[95] id. at 588 (Breyer, J., dissenting) (citations omitted).
[96] id. at 579 (majority opinion) (quoting *City of Cincinnati v. Discovery Network, Inc.*, 507 U.S. 410, 426 (1993); then citing *44 Liquormart, Inc. v. Rhode Island*, 517 U.S. 484, 502 (1996) (plurality opinion)).
[97] id.; "[F]or example ... 'a State may choose to regulate price advertising in one industry but not in others, because the risk of fraud ... is in its view greater there.'" id. (third alteration in original) (quoting *R. A. V. v. City of St. Paul*, 505 U.S. 377, 388–89 (1992) then citing *Va. State Bd. of Pharmacy v. Va. Citizens Consumer Council, Inc.*, 425 U.S. 748, 771–72 (1976)).
[98] id.
[99] id. at 571–72 (citations omitted).
[100] id. at 578–80.
[101] id. at 588 (Breyer, J., dissenting).

openly regards *Sorrell's* majority opinion as an application of strict scrutiny to commercial speech.[102]

The Theoretical Case for the Equivalency Principle

As explained in Chapter 1,[103] while it is certainly valuable and informative to understand how the Supreme Court's doctrine has evolved over the years, legal scholars generally give at best limited force to purely doctrinal arguments. In this instance, however, analysis of the underlying purposes of the First Amendment protection of free expression only reinforces the Court's current doctrinal stance.

In undertaking this analysis, it is important to recall the Court's definition of commercial speech: speech that does no "more than propose a commercial transaction."[104] Expression either objecting to a commercial transaction or speech neutrally describing or commenting on commercial products or services, in contrast, are deemed fully protected noncommercial speech.[105] In light of this well-established distinction, none of the scholarly arguments employed to reduce the level of First Amendment protection for commercial speech on the basis of its lesser value to the goals of free speech protection has any merit.

Initially, it should be noted that the argument that commercial speech is deserving of a lower level of First Amendment protection because it does not concern the political process, which is the type of speech thought by many to be most closely aligned with the values fostered by that provision,[106] proves far too much. Most commentators would readily concede that full First Amendment protection extends to many more expressive categories than speech intertwined with the political process – for example, art, music, and literature. Of course, the response might be made that speech about the relative merits of commercial products and services is a far cry from art, music, or literature as a means of fostering the underlying value of personal and intellectual self-realization. Many years ago, I sought to respond to this argument by pointing out that speech about the relative

---

[102] See *Reed v. Town of Gilbert*, 135 S. Ct. 2218, 2235 (2015) (Breyer, J., concurring).
[103] See Chapter 1, *supra*.
[104] See discussion *supra* at 6.
[105] See *Bigelow v. Virginia*, 421 U.S. 809, 821–22 (1975).
[106] See generally Alexander Meikeljohn, *Political Freedom* (1960) (discussing First Amendment freedom of speech as a tool for self-governance); Robert H. Bork, *Neutral Principles and Some First Amendment Problems*, 47 Ind. L.J. 1 (1971) (arguing that "Constitutional protection should be accorded only to speech that is explicitly political").

merits of commercial products and services facilitates individual self-realization by providing information and opinion relevant to an individual's *private* self-governing decisions.[107] The argument was made that it would make little sense to protect political speech on the grounds that such speech facilitates collective self-government when the individual's role in making those self-governing decisions represents only a tiny fraction of the whole, but simultaneously deny protection to commercial expression when such communications facilitate the making of life-affecting decisions that belong – both in terms of choice and consequences – entirely to the individual.[108] In a fundamental sense, it was argued, *both* forms of expression facilitate the making of the individual's life-affecting, self-governing decisions, and therefore equally foster the key value underlying the constitutional protection of free expression – namely, realization of both the individual's personal goals and personal potential.[109]

In light of the Supreme Court's subsequent definition of commercial speech, however, it is unnecessary to delve into possible differences or similarities between speech that facilitates the recipient's private and collective self-government. While the Court has on occasion wavered in its definition[110] and has complicated that definition with multi-factor tests of limited clarity and coherence,[111] reduced to its core, the definition of "commercial speech" generally employed by the Court is speech that does no more than "propose a commercial transaction."[112] As a result, speech concerning the relative merits of commercial products and services that does something other than propose a commercial transaction – for example, *Consumer Reports* magazine,[113] Ralph Nader's criticism of the safety of the Chevrolet Corvair,[114] or media revelations that Nike allegedly employed "sweat shop" labor in foreign

---

[107] See Martin H. Redish, *The First Amendment in the Marketplace: Commercial Speech and the Values of Free Expression*, 39 Geo. Wash. L. Rev. 429, 438–43 (1971).
[108] See generally id.
[109] id. at 438–48.
[110] *Cent. Hudson Gas & Elec. Corp. v. Pub. Serv. Comm'n*, 447 U.S. 557, 561–62 (1980) ("Commercial expression not only serves the economic interest of the speaker, but also assists consumers and furthers the societal interest in the fullest possible dissemination of information.").
[111] See *Bolger v. Youngs Drug Prods. Corp.*, 463 U.S. 60, 68–69 (1983) (citing *Cent. Hudson*, 447 U.S. at 566).
[112] See, e.g., *Lorillard Tobacco Co. v. Reilly*, 533 U.S. 525, 553–54 (2001) (referring to "speech proposing a commercial transaction").
[113] See, e.g., *Bose Corp. v. Consumers Union of U.S., Inc.*, 466 U.S. 485, 513 (1984) (extending full First Amendment protection to *Consumer Reports*).
[114] See generally Ralph Nader, *Unsafe at Any Speed: The Designed-In Dangers of the American Automobile* (1965).

countries to produce its shoes[115] – receives full First Amendment protection. In stark contrast, speech about the very same subjects disseminated to the very same audience is characterized as traditionally less protected "commercial speech" when it is expressed by the manufacturer or seller.[116] Purely as a logical matter, then, commercial speech protection cannot be distinguished from fully protected noncommercial speech solely on the grounds that it deals with such mundane matters as the relative merits of commercial purchases. Speech that receives full First Amendment protection deals with the very same issues. Indeed, if a commercial seller did no more than reproduce the very same words said about its product in *Consumer Reports*, under the Court's definition of commercial speech, those exact same words would receive a considerably lower level of protection, for no reason other than the commercial motivation of the party uttering the expression in question. When one adds a listener-centric perspective to First Amendment theory, then, the Court's asserted distinction between speech proposing a commercial transaction and speech neutral about or opposing commercial transactions makes absolutely no sense.

Some would no doubt respond that it is the very fact of the speaker's commercial motivation that properly distinguishes the two types of expression, even though they deal with the exact same subject (and, indeed, may even say the exact same thing). Two different grounds have, over the years, been suggested to support this speaker-based distinction. First, it has been suggested that commercial promotion of sale is effectively part of the process of commercial sale and therefore is "linked inextricably" to the commercial transactions themselves.[117] Therefore, the argument proceeds, commercial speech constitutes a form of conduct, rather than expression. As I argued a number of years ago, however, "[i]t is only at the point of sale that commercial advocacy is even arguably so temporally linked to the acts of purchase and sale that it can realistically be deemed an element of these acts."[118] The mere fact that speech *advocates* action does not make the speech *part of* that action.

The second argument designed to distinguish speech *about* or *opposing the sale* of commercial products and services from speech *advocating purchase* of commercial products and services is the theory, associated primarily with

---

[115] See generally *Kasky v. Nike, Inc.*, 45 P.3d 243 (Cal. 2002), *cert. granted*, 539 U.S. 1099 (2003), and *cert. dismissed as improvidently granted*, 537 U.S. 654 (2003).
[116] See Daniel A. Farber, *Commercial Speech and First Amendment Theory*, 74 Nw. U. L. Rev. 372, 372–73 (1979).
[117] *Friedman v. Rogers*, 440 U.S. 1, 10–11 n.9 (1979).
[118] Martin H. Redish, *Money Talks: Speech, Economic Power and the Values of Democracy* 33 (2001).

Robert Post,[119] that speech designed for the purpose of commercial profit is automatically not speech designed to contribute to public discourse, and it is only the latter type of expression that is deserving of full First Amendment protection.[120] There is no need to rehash all of the arguments pointing out the serious flaws in this theory, because the issue has already been thoroughly discussed in earlier portions of the book.[121] Suffice it to say at this point that while Post has on occasion suggested that a court should engage in a case-by-case evaluation of speech and its speaker to determine whether the speech represents "an effort to engage in public opinion,"[122] an "engagement ... in the public life of the nation,"[123] or an individual's "attempt to render the state responsive to [her] views,"[124] it is certainly true that, as I have previously noted, "[a] good deal of speech, not just commercial speech, would be excluded from public discourse if Post applied this approach consistently."[125]

In any event, it is not immediately clear why commercial speech does not qualify as a contribution to public discourse. The speech is certainly not distributed privately or secretly to only a limited audience. Nor is it clear why – as is true of most speakers – commercial speakers may not have multiple motives for their expression. It is by no means obvious why expression cannot be intended simultaneously for purposes of personal gain and for purposes of contributing to public discourse. Post's assumption of mutual exclusivity has no basis in logic or reality.

The most troublesome aspect of such a speaker-oriented approach is that it ignores the simple fact that free expression is as much about the *listener* as it is about the *speaker*. Indeed, as explained earlier, at least one leading free speech theorist, Alexander Meiklejohn, actually argued that the *only* legitimate value served by free expression is to the listener.[126] While this viewpoint is fatally incomplete, it is certainly true that free and open expression provides potentially valuable information and opinion to the listener that enables her to make life-affecting choices, and in so doing facilitate realization of her life goals.[127]

---

[119] See generally Robert Post, *The Constitutional Status of Commercial Speech*, 48 UCLA L. Rev. 1 (2000).
[120] See id. at 14–15.
[121] See Chapter 1, *supra*.
[122] Post, *supra* note 119, at 18.
[123] id. at 20.
[124] id. at 27.
[125] Martin H. Redish, *The Adversary First Amendment: Free Expression and the Foundations of American Democracy* 66 (Stanford: Stanford Law Books, 2013).
[126] See generally Meikeljohn, *supra* note 106.
[127] For a more detailed description of this self-realization theory, see generally Martin H. Redish, *The Value of Free Speech*, 130 U. Pa. L. Rev. 591 (1982).

In facilitating individual self-realization, the listener's receipt of communication fosters First Amendment values, regardless of its impact on the speaker. But if this is so, what possible difference, in terms of the values fostered by the expression, does the motivation of the speaker make? The speaker can be motivated solely by purposes of private gain, and the expression may nevertheless make an important contribution to public discourse. In any event, numerous speakers have an agenda of personal gain – hidden or open – for their expression and in no other area of First Amendment protection is the level of protection reduced because of this fact.[128] There is therefore no principled reason for categorically reducing the level of First Amendment protection to commercial speech on the basis of the speaker's profit incentive.

The greatest concern with defining the less-protected category of commercial speech solely on the basis of the speaker's profit motivation is that it inevitably leads to blatant viewpoint-based stratification in the level of free speech expression. A speaker who argues *against* commercial purchase is extended full First Amendment protection, while a speaker who seeks to respond to that argument by *advocating* commercial purchase is denied full First Amendment protection. Examples, as already noted, include Ralph Nader receiving full First Amendment protection for his attack on the Chevrolet Corvair while General Motors receives a significantly lower level of protection of its responsive defense, or media commentators receiving full First Amendment protection for their allegations that Nike uses sweat shops, while Nike receives a much lower level of protection for its counter-speech.[129] Surely, the First Amendment cannot be satisfied by such a blatantly selective disparity in First Amendment protection.[130]

Finally, it might be argued that commercial speech is deserving of a lower level of protection because there is greater concern about the motivation of the regulator in the context of noncommercial speech. When government regulates political speech, the argument could be made that there is always a real concern that the regulators are motivated by political hostility – a concern generally assumed to be irrelevant in the case of commercial speech regulation. But this argument once again proves too much, because the relevant dichotomy is not between commercial and *political* speech, but rather between commercial and noncommercial speech. As previously explained,

---

[128] See generally Redish, *supra* note 125 (discussing First Amendment speech in American democracy).
[129] See Chapter 1, *supra*.
[130] R. A. V. v. City of St. Paul, 505 U.S. 377, 392 (1992) ("St. Paul has no such authority to license one side of a debate to fight freestyle, while requiring the other to follow Marquis [sic] of Queensberry rules.").

the latter category includes far more than political speech.[131] Indeed, as already shown, it includes all speech about the relative merits of commercial products and services communicated by any speaker who is not seeking to engage in commercial sale.[132] If anything, there is a stronger basis of suspicion of regulatory motives for suppressing speech when speech about commercial products is made by the seller, since there always exists the danger that competitors have enlisted the help of the regulators to take away the speaker's competitive advantage. Lastly, excessive regulatory zeal, which fails to take into account the fundamentally important value of free expression, is as likely a basis for pathological suppression of expression as is political motivation.

The Equivalency Principle and the Danger of Dilution

It might be suggested that use of the equivalency principle to assume value fungibility between commercial and noncommercial speech gives rise to the serious danger of dilution. In other words, because it is generally assumed that commercial speech must be extensively regulated, the assumption that commercial and noncommercial speech are on some level fungible would require us to allow far more extensive regulation of noncommercial speech than is generally deemed acceptable.[133] As a result, in the hope of expanding the reach of First Amendment protection, we will have counterproductively reduced the scope of such protection. Simply put, this is known as the danger of dilution.

The first point to note in response is that, as will be shown in subsequent discussions, the mere fact that commercial speech is assumed to serve First Amendment values in the same manner as noncommercial speech does not necessarily mean that the two are always to be treated identically for First Amendment purposes.[134] Where commercial speech gives rise to significantly greater risks of serious harm than would most noncommercial speech, such expression may logically be regulated more intensively than noncommercial speech, despite the assumption of value equivalency.[135] But wholly beyond that point, the greatest flaw in the dilution argument is that it is, at its core, question begging: it assumes the answer to the issue in dispute – that is,

---

[131] See Chapter 1, *supra*.
[132] See Chapter 1, *supra*.
[133] See, e.g., Vincent Blasi, *The Pathological Perspective and the First Amendment*, 85 Colum. L. Rev. 449, 451 (1985) (arguing "that continually applicable doctrines be formulated with emphasis on how well they would serve in the worst of times").
[134] See discussion *infra* at 51–56.
[135] See id.

whether commercial speech should be deemed to serve the same values as noncommercial speech. One cannot logically answer that question by saying we should not treat them identically, because noncommercial speech has greater value. That is the very question at issue. If one ultimately decides that commercial speech is in fact value-equivalent to noncommercial speech, then any dilution that might result is totally proper. In short, the dilution argument ignores the key question subject to debate.

To be sure, there may be instances in which noncommercial speech gives rise to the very same harm as commercial speech. For example, imagine two situations: (1) a commercial advertiser, with knowledge of his statement's falsity, makes a false claim about his product's scientific qualities. For a variety of reasons discussed subsequently,[136] such expression should be deemed to give rise to harm of such intensity as to justify suppression; (2) a scientist, for whatever reason, writes an article in a popularly distributed magazine making the exact same claim for the product's scientific properties, with full knowledge of the claim's falsity. Under the equivalency principle, the expression in both hypotheticals serves the very same First Amendment value, and both give rise to the same potential for harm. Therefore, logically, the two examples of expression are deserving of identical treatment, even though one is classified as commercial and the other as noncommercial.

Another key point missed by the dilution argument is that an important concern underlying the equivalency principle concerns the impact of suppression on the nature of the relationship between government and citizen. In the noncommercial setting, government is denied power to suppress truthful speech out of a fear that citizens will make "wrong" choices, because such paternalism on the part of government is inconsistent with the fundamental premises of liberal democracy: government may not manipulate citizens' lawful choices by selective suppression of free expression. But if this fundamental precept of democratic thought applies in the context of noncommercial speech, there is no reason to deem it automatically inapplicable to commercial speech. Citizens are either sheep, or they are not. We cannot rationally deem selective suppression of speech designed to manipulate lawful behavior by citizens politically pathological in one context but benign in the others. Thus, rejection of the equivalency principle gives rise to a serious danger of what can be called *reverse* dilution. If one rejects the equivalency principle, government is allowed to suppress even truthful commercial speech for fear that the recipients of the information will make the wrong decision on the basis of it. But people cannot be deemed too ignorant to process truthful

---

[136] See discussion *infra* at 42–56.

information advocating lawful activity in the commercial realm yet sufficiently trustworthy to do so in the political realm. Thus, if one accepts the initial premise that citizens cannot be trusted to make *commercial* decisions on the basis of truthful advocacy and debate, one could quite easily transfer that skepticism about citizen capability to *political* judgments, thereby justifying widespread selective suppression of political debate.

Most importantly, the fundamental concern of the dilution argument is undermined by the definition of commercial speech that the Court has adopted. Recall once again that the category has been defined not by the subject of the expression but rather by the motivation of the speaker.[137] The result, as already shown, is a pathological viewpoint-based dichotomy of protection in important public debates, grounded in nothing more than distaste for the motivation of the speaker.[138]

FALSE COMMERCIAL SPEECH AND THE EQUIVALENCY PRINCIPLE

The preceding discussion explored the equivalency principle's application, both doctrinally and normatively, to the regulation of truthful commercial speech. In an important sense that discussion served as a prelude to the issue at hand: the extent to which the equivalency principle should similarly be applied to false commercial speech. It is important to understand that we are not asking whether false commercial speech should receive absolute protection. False noncommercial speech in no way receives absolute protection; indeed, in certain situations it receives no constitutional protection at all. The equivalency principle demands only a relative judgment, requiring that however noncommercial speech is treated, commercial speech is deemed to be of equivalent First Amendment value. In other words, the equivalency principle demands a type of "most favored nation" status for commercial speech.

It is important to note that application of the equivalency principle would not dictate that in all instances commercial speech would be protected as often as false noncommercial speech would be protected. It means, simply, that if commercial speech is not to be protected when parallel noncommercial speech would be protected, that difference in constitutional treatment is due not to a judgment about the relative value of the speech in question to the purposes served by the First Amendment right of free expression, but rather because commercial speech will more often give rise to the danger of

---

[137] See Chapter 1, *supra*.
[138] See id.

significant harm than does the similarly situated noncommercial speech. There can be no doubt, however, that, at least purely as a doctrinal matter, the equivalency principle has never been applied to false commercial speech. This is so, despite the fact that a strong doctrinal case can be made for the proposition that this principle has been doctrinally adopted by the Court for truthful commercial speech.[139]

Recall that the very first prong of the *Central Hudson* test involves an inquiry into whether the commercial speech in question is false or misleading, or uttered on behalf of an illegal product or activity.[140] If the answer to either of those inquiries is in the affirmative, the speech is automatically and categorically excluded from the scope of First Amendment protection.[141] The level of awareness on behalf of the commercial speaker of the speech's falsity, under the *Central Hudson* test, was wholly irrelevant.[142] Rather, the *Central Hudson* standard is one of strict liability.[143] While as already shown, the level of First Amendment protection for truthful commercial speech has changed dramatically since the Court's adoption of the *Central Hudson* test in 1980,[144] the categorical exclusion of First Amendment protection for false commercial speech has budged not an inch.[145] As the following discussion shows, this categorical exclusion of First Amendment protection differs dramatically from the level of First Amendment protection given to false noncommercial speech.

False Noncommercial Speech and the Equivalency Principle

As the middle of the twentieth century approached, it would probably have been safe to say that at least most forms of false expression were categorically excluded from the First Amendment's protective scope.[146] This was particularly true of defamatory speech – false expression that damaged an individual's

---

[139] See discussion *supra* at 31–34.
[140] *Cent. Hudson Gas & Elec. Corp.* v. *Pub. Serv. Comm'n*, 447 U.S. 557, 563–64 (1980).
[141] See id.
[142] See id. at 563–66.
[143] See id.
[144] See discussion *supra* at 31–34.
[145] See discussion *supra* at 30.
[146] See, e.g., *Chaplinsky* v. *New Hampshire*, 315 U.S. 568, 571 (1942) ("There are certain well-defined and narrowly limited classes of speech, the prevention and punishment of which have never been thought to raise any Constitutional problem. These include the lewd and obscene, the profane, the libelous, and the insulting or 'fighting' words – those which by their very utterance inflict injury or tend to incite an immediate breach of the peace." (footnote omitted)); See also *Beauharnais* v. *Illinois*, 343 U.S. 250, 266–67 (1952) (holding that a prohibition on group defamation did not violate the First Amendment).

reputation.[147] In subsequent years, however, the Court recognized that the issue is far more complex than the simple categorical rejection of First Amendment protection for false speech assumed. In *New York Times Co. v. Sullivan*,[148] the Court held that the First Amendment precludes imposition of liability for defamation of a public official unless the plaintiff proves by the heavier-than-normal burden of clear and convincing evidence that the defendant acted with "actual malice."[149] The Court reasoned that the First Amendment requires that debate about public officials be "uninhibited, robust, and wide-open."[150] The Court recognized "[t]hat erroneous statement is inevitable in free debate, and ... it must be protected if the freedoms of expression are to have the 'breathing space' that they 'need ... to survive.'"[151]

Although several of the Justices believed that such defamatory expression deserved absolute protection regardless of the speaker's awareness of falsity,[152] a majority was unwilling to go that far. While the majority was willing to extend First Amendment protection even to negligently false defamation, it drew the line at outright lying. It therefore recognized an exception for defamation that constituted "actual malice."[153] Despite its name, that phrase has never had anything to do with ill will or malicious intent. Rather, it refers exclusively to knowledge of falsity or reckless disregard of the statement's truth or falsity.[154] "Reckless disregard" has been given an extremely narrow definition, requiring a showing that a false publication was made with a "high degree of awareness of ... probable falsity."[155] For recklessness to be established, the Court has stated, "[t]here must be sufficient evidence to permit the conclusion that the defendant in fact entertained serious doubts as to the truth of his publication."[156]

---

[147] N.Y. Times Co. v. Sullivan, 376 U.S. 254, 268–69 (1964) (recognizing its own precedent of not protecting libelous speech).
[148] 376 U.S. 254 (1964).
[149] id. at 279-80, 285–86.
[150] id. at 270.
[151] id. at 271–72 (third alteration in original) (quoting NAACP v. Button, 371 U.S. 415, 433 (1963)).
[152] id. at 293-97 (Black, J., concurring); id. at 297–305 (Goldberg, J., concurring).
[153] See id. at 279–80 (majority opinion).
[154] id. at 280.
[155] Garrison v. Louisiana, 379 U.S. 64, 74 (1964).
[156] St. Amant v. Thompson, 390 U.S. 727, 731 (1968); See also id. at 732 (showing of reckless disregard requires proof that "allegations are so inherently improbable that only a reckless man would have put them in circulation. Likewise, recklessness may be found where there are obvious reasons to doubt the veracity of the informant or the accuracy of his reports." (footnote omitted)). In St. Amant, according to a subsequent lower court decision, the record did not support a finding of reckless disregard for the accuracy of statements even though the defendant had no personal knowledge of the plaintiff's activities, relied solely on an affidavit,

That the Court has drawn a clear distinction between recklessness and negligence of any kind – even gross negligence – was underscored in the Court's subsequent decision in *Harte-Hanks Communications, Inc. v. Connaughton*.[157] The Court there noted that the standard that Justice Harlan had advocated in his plurality opinion in *Curtis Publishing Co. v. Butts*,[158] where he had suggested that a public figure need only make "a showing of highly unreasonable conduct constituting an extreme departure from the standards of investigation and reporting ordinarily adhered to by responsible publishers[,]"[159] "was emphatically rejected by a majority of the [*Curtis*] Court in favor of the *stricter New York Times actual malice rule.*"[160] A synthesis of these decisions reveals that the Supreme Court has construed the First Amendment to impose a highly demanding showing in order to establish the reckless disregard sufficient to satisfy *New York Times*'s actual malice standard.[161] For purposes of the First Amendment, recklessness does not include the mere failure to investigate, even if such failure is appropriately characterized as grossly negligent.[162] Rather, recklessness demands a showing that the defendant inexplicably ignored a strong basis for suspicion of falsity.[163] This is not merely a difference in degree from any form of negligence. It is, rather, a difference in kind.

Though the *New York Times* doctrine was employed originally with regard to defamation of public officials, it was quickly expanded to include defamation of public figures, even if they did not hold governmental office.[164] In *Dun & Bradstreet, Inc. v. Greenmoss Builders, Inc.*,[165] which involved a suit against an information provider for an allegedly inaccurate report, the Court adopted as the central inquiry for the reach of the doctrine whether "matters of public concern" are involved.[166]

---

failed to verify the information by those who might have known the facts, did not consider whether the statements defamed the plaintiff, and mistakenly believed he was not responsible for the broadcast because he was merely quoting the affiant's words. *Campbell v. Citizens for an Honest Gov't*, 255 F.3d 560, 570 (8th Cir. 2001) (citation omitted).

[157] 491 U.S. 657 (1989).
[158] 388 U.S. 130 (1967) (plurality opinion).
[159] id. at 155.
[160] *Harte-Hanks*, 491 U.S. at 666 (emphasis added).
[161] See discussion *supra* at 42–43.
[162] See discussion *supra* at 43–44.
[163] See discussion *supra* at 42–43.
[164] See, e.g., *Curtis*, 388 U.S. at 155.
[165] 472 U.S. 749 (1985).
[166] id. at 751, 761; See also id. at 762 n.8 ("The protection to be accorded a particular credit report depends on whether the report's 'content, form, and context' indicate that it concerns a public matter.").

That the Court has extended the *New York Times* doctrine far and wide into the world of commerce is demonstrated by its decision in *Bose Corp. v. Consumers Union of United States, Inc.*[167] *Bose* involved a commercial disparagement suit brought by a corporation against the publisher of *Consumer Reports* for allegedly false critical comments about its speakers.[168] The magazine is designed to be an objective commentator on the relative merits of commercial products and services.[169] Without the slightest analysis, the Court simply assumed that the disparagement claim was limited by the First Amendment doctrine of *New York Times Co. v. Sullivan*, rendering the publisher liable only if the plaintiff could establish by clear and convincing evidence that the defendant uttered the false statements with "actual malice" – either knowledge of their falsity or reckless disregard of their truth or falsity.[170] However, as already noted, that doctrine has been held categorically inapplicable to regulation of commercial speech, defined not as speech *concerning* commercial sales and transactions but rather as speech *promoting* commercial sale.[171] In this context, the Court has consistently applied a strict liability standard, categorically excluding all false commercial speech from the scope of First Amendment protection.[172]

In certain noncommercial speech contexts, the Court appears to have held that even consciously false speech is protected by the First Amendment. In *United States v. Alvarez*,[173] the Court found unconstitutional the Stolen Valor Act, which made it a crime to falsely claim receipt of military decorations or medals and provided for enhanced penalties if the Congressional Medal of Honor is involved,[174] even when the defendant's falsehood was unambiguously uttered with knowledge of its falsity.[175] The plurality opinion by Justice Kennedy rejected the government's argument that false speech was inherently valueless and therefore undeserving of First Amendment protection.[176] The opinion distinguished the three examples of criminal punishment for false speech to which the government pointed on the grounds that each of those

---

[167] 466 U.S. 485 (1984).
[168] id. at 488.
[169] See Paul Hiebert, *Consumer Reports* in the Age of Amazon Review, Atlantic (April 13, 2016), www.theatlantic.com/business/archive/2016/04/consumer-reports-in-the-age-of-the-amazon-review/477108/ [https://perma.cc/74ZH-BEJF].
[170] *Bose*, 466 U.S. at 497–502.
[171] See Chapter 1, *supra*.
[172] See discussion *supra* at 30.
[173] 132 S. Ct. 2537 (2012) (plurality opinion).
[174] 18 U.S.C. § 704(b)–(c) (2006), *invalidated by United States v. Alvarez*, 132 S. Ct. 2537 (2012).
[175] *Alvarez*, 132 S. Ct. at 2551 (plurality opinion).
[176] id. at 2544–47.

instances inherently involved "legally cognizable" harm caused by the falsehoods.[177] In contrast, the plurality could find no harm caused by the false assertion that one was a Congressional Medal of Honor winner.[178]

One could well debate the validity of the plurality's cavalier dismissal of harm flowing from the defendant's false assertion. For one thing, the inherent value of the medal itself could arguably be diluted as a result of the defendant's false assertion. For another thing, the defendant in *Alvarez* made the knowingly false assertion while attending his first public meeting as a member of the local water district board, a government entity, arguably giving rise to a claim of fraud on the public.[179] But for present purposes, the correctness of the Court's conclusion under the specific facts of the case is irrelevant. The key point, rather, concerns where the Court chose to place the First Amendment inertia when it comes to knowingly false speech. Rather than begin analysis with the premise that speech is not protectable unless it can be shown to have value – that is, directly further the values served by the constitutional guarantee of free expression – it began with the completely opposite premise: Speech is protected, regardless of value, unless it can be shown to cause legally cognizable harm.[180]

The doctrinal disparity between the First Amendment treatment given to false commercial speech and false noncommercial speech should now be obvious. False commercial speech never receives protection, while the Court begins with a rebuttable presumption in favor of protection for false noncommercial speech.[181] To summarize the Court's approach to widely distributed false noncommercial speech: For the most part, unknowingly false noncommercial speech is protected against penalization even where the speech gives

---

[177] id. at 2545–47.
[178] See id. at 2545.
[179] See id. at 2542.
[180] See id. at 2545–47. Justice Kennedy's plurality opinion spoke for himself and three other Justices. Justice Breyer, joined by Justice Kagan, concurred in the judgment. Unlike the plurality, Justice Breyer did not rest his conclusion "upon a strict categorical analysis." id. at 2551 (Breyer, J., concurring). Rather, he found the Act unconstitutional by means of intermediate scrutiny. id. at 2551–52. He noted that "[f]alse factual statements can serve useful human objectives, for example: in social contexts, where they may prevent embarrassment, protect privacy, shield a person from prejudice, provide the sick with comfort, or preserve a child's innocence; in public contexts, where they may stop a panic or otherwise preserve calm in the face of danger; and even in technical, philosophical, and scientific contexts, where ... examination of a false statement (even if made deliberately to mislead) can promote a form of thought that ultimately helps realize the truth. id. at 2553 (citation omitted). None of these contexts, of course, was fostered by Alvarez's falsehood." See generally *Alvarez*, 132 S. Ct. 2537 (plurality opinion).
[181] See id. at 2544–45.

rise to serious and unique harm, such as reputational harm. However, knowingly false noncommercial speech that gives rise to serious and unique harm is unprotected. False noncommercial speech that gives rise to nothing more than general political harm to society caused by deception of the electorate is protected even if it is communicated with knowledge of falsity.[182] Thus, the Court's disparate treatment of false commercial speech clearly constitutes a stark aberration from the equivalency principle, which the Court appears to have recently adopted in the case of truthful commercial speech.[183] Whether this disparity can be rationally justified, however, is quite a different matter. It is to that question that the analysis now turns.

Can the Commercial/Noncommercial False Speech Distinction Be Justified?

Why is false commercial speech of any kind automatically excluded from the scope of First Amendment protection while the constitutional treatment of false noncommercial speech is far more complex? The answer the Court has given to that question, interestingly, was provided in a context in no way confined to the protection given to false commercial speech. Rather, the Court in *Virginia Board*, the decision that first extended significant First Amendment protection to commercial speech, sought to provide reasons why *all* commercial speech was inherently deserving of a lower level of First Amendment protection.[184] But in doing so, the Court at most provided arguable rationales for distinguishing *false* commercial and noncommercial speech.[185]

The Court suggested two grounds on which to distinguish commercial speech from other forms of speech protection: (1) that "[t]he truth of commercial speech ... may be more easily verifiable by its disseminator than ... news reporting or political commen-tary [sic],"[186] and (2) that "[s]ince advertising is

---

[182] It should be noted that in the special context of a one-on-one professional fiduciary relationship, such as doctor–patient, even negligently false speech will be unprotected. However, this is a situation of unique vulnerability on the part of the recipient of the information, and the special obligation imposed on the professional speaker due to the professional relationship between speaker and listener. In any event, it seems reasonable to conclude that such speech will usually go well beyond the "promotion" of a commercial transaction, and therefore it is not properly characterized as "commercial speech."
[183] See Chapter 1, *supra*.
[184] See discussion *supra* at 31–34.
[185] *See Va. State Bd. of Pharmacy v. Va. Citizens Consumer Council, Inc.*, 425 U.S. 748, 761–72 & n.24 (1976).
[186] id. at 772 n.24.

the *sine qua non* of commercial profits, there is little likelihood of its being chilled by proper regulation."[187] Justice Stewart, concurring, added that commercial advertisers do not suffer from the burdens on "the press, which must often attempt to assemble the true facts from sketchy and sometimes conflicting sources under the pressure of publication deadlines."[188]

Even if one were to accept – solely for purposes of argument – the validity of these distinctions, the equivalency principle would not necessarily be undermined. These distinctions in no way turn on a comparative assessment of the value of the expression itself, but rather on the basis of factors supposedly unique to commercial speech that reduce the harm to First Amendment values flowing from suppression. Nevertheless, there are serious reasons to doubt the validity of the asserted distinctions.

Initially, one may question whether as a general matter the truth of commercial claims is, in all instances, more easily verifiable than the truth of noncommercial assertions. Numerous statements made in the course of political debate involve simple assertions of fact, which are presumably verifiable with relative ease. Indeed, it is just such assertions whose accuracy political fact checkers measure regularly.[189] In contrast, many claims about commercial products involve scientific assertions that are often subject to complex and controversial debate.[190] Secondly, there is no reason to assume that commercial speech is inherently "hardier" because of the existence of the profit motive.[191] Numerous noncommercial publications are driven by profit motive as much as commercial speakers are. And countless contributors to public discourse have a personal interest – often financial – in acceptance of their public claims. If *commercial* speakers are assumed not to be deterred by penalization if their speech turns out to be false, it is unclear why self-interested *noncommercial* speakers are any more likely to be deterred. Logically, then, if any distinction is to be drawn it should be one between self-interested and non-self-interested speech, on the grounds that the category of self-interested speech is somehow inherently immune from deterrence. Whatever one thinks of such a distinction (and it is likely that virtually everyone would quite wisely reject it), it is by no means equivalent to the commercial/noncommercial distinction which the Supreme Court has adopted. Obviously, countless self-interested speakers engage in noncommercial

[187] id.
[188] id. at 777 (Stewart, J., concurring).
[189] See Martin H. Redish, *Freedom of Expression: A Critical Analysis* 64 (Michie Co., 1984).
[190] See id.
[191] See id.

speech.[192] Indeed, commercial speakers are often likely to be among the most risk-averse of speakers, always concerned about the possibility of government penalization for their actions.[193] The issue, for First Amendment purposes, should not be whether the speaker will be deterred from speaking *at all*; but rather, whether the speaker will be chilled from making specific statements for fear they will be deemed false when with perfect knowledge we would have understood that they are in fact true and quite relevant to the listeners' decision making.

Finally, one may legitimately question arguments based on deadline pressure. Noncommercial stories of long-range interest have no immediate deadline pressure.[194] In contrast, "some advertisers who ... attempt to defeat a competitor or to gain first entry into a new market" may find timing to be critical.[195] As a result they, much like many noncommercial speakers, face significant time pressure.[196] In any event, there is no reason to believe that the *New York Times Co.* "actual malice" test extends only to the commercial press. Rather, it extends to private speakers who face no deadline pressures.[197]

Some might seek to distinguish between false commercial and noncommercial speech on the grounds that the latter categorically constitutes a contribution to public discourse while the former categorically does not. Robert Post has made just such an argument.[198] But as already shown, the idea that commercial speech inherently makes no contribution to public discourse is grounded in nothing more than the conclusory assertion that it fails to do so.[199]

It might be argued that while *truthful* commercial speech could conceivably make legitimate contributions to public discourse, *false* commercial speech does not. Once again, however, it is important to note that logically, the same could be said of false noncommercial speech, which, in and of itself, fosters no First Amendment value. Of course, in *New York Times Co.*, the Court recognized this fact but nevertheless decided to protect certain forms of false political speech in order to avoid a chilling of potentially valuable truthful speech.[200] But for reasons just explained, there is no

---

[192] See generally Redish, *supra* note 125 (demonstrating that American government is an adversary democracy).
[193] See Redish, *supra* note 125, at 143–44.
[194] id. at 64.
[195] id.
[196] id.
[197] See id.
[198] See discussion *supra* at 36–38.
[199] See discussion *supra* at 37–38.
[200] See N.Y. Times Co. v. Sullivan, 376 U.S. 254, 266 (1964).

legitimate basis on which to assume that commercial speakers are not subject to a similar form of chill. While commercial speakers are always incentivized to promote their products and services due to their inherent profit incentive, as already noted, many noncommercial speakers are similarly motivated by speakers' self-interest.[201]

This does not mean that false commercial speech should always be protected when comparable false noncommercial speech is protected. To the extent the two situations differ, however, it is not due to the lower value of commercial speech in general or false commercial speech in particular. Rather, it is because of the varying intensity of harm caused by the different forms of false speech under the circumstances. For example, as will be discussed in more detail later in this book,[202] occasions may arise where a false scientific claim made in a commercial advertisement may cause more harm than the exact same scientific claim made in a scientific journal, due both to the larger audience it reaches and the lack of scientific background of that audience. But in both contexts, both the value of the expression and the degree of speaker risk-averseness must be viewed as identical.

To be sure, the approach to false commercial speech advocated here is by no means consistent with the current doctrinal framework as shaped by the Supreme Court. The *Central Hudson* test, it should be recalled, categorically excludes *all* false commercial speech from constitutional protection, regardless of the culpability or knowledge of the speaker. While over the years the *Central Hudson* test has become far more protective than it was at the outset,[203] its categorical exclusion of false commercial speech from the scope of the First Amendment has remained unchanged. However, if one examines the framework employed by the Court in setting the contours of First Amendment protection for false noncommercial speech, one can easily see how the equivalency principle would work when applied in the context of false commercial speech.

When one synthesizes the *New York Times Co. v. Sullivan* line of cases in the defamation context with the Court's more recent decision in *Alvarez*,[204] one is left with the following doctrinal structure for First Amendment protection of false noncommercial speech: While good faith and even negligent falsehoods are usually protected even when they cause harm,[205] conscious

---

[201] See discussion *supra* at 48–49.
[202] See generally Chapter 5, *infra*.
[203] See discussion *supra* at 31–34.
[204] See discussion *supra* at 45–47.
[205] Narrow exceptions may exist to this general rule. For example, when an individual is operating one-on-one in a professional relationship with another individual (e.g., a doctor–

falsehoods that cause serious harm are never protected. However, in the case of unintentionally false speech, protection is extended even in the face of such serious harm.[206] The Court, in drawing such a distinction, is motivated by its desire to avoid chilling valuable expression. In the case of conscious falsehood, the Court has concluded that where noticeable harm is caused, the expression loses its protection, because consciously false speech should be chilled.[207] However, where no such harm results, even consciously false speech is protected, because it is still "speech" and no reason exists to suppress it.[208]

What this synthesis shows is that the Court's treatment of consciously false speech turns not on an assessment of value but rather on an assessment of the nature and extent of the harm. It logically follows that application of the equivalency principle to false commercial speech does not mean that false commercial speech is to be no more refutable than false noncommercial speech, but rather simply that to the extent false commercial speech is to be suppressed more extensively than comparably false noncommercial speech, it will be as a result of the greater harm it causes, rather than its lesser value.

The best way to understand this harm-based dichotomy is by development of a taxonomy of categorical harms to which false speech may give rise, and then application of that taxonomy to the commercial/noncommercial distinction. In that way, we will be able to understand how one can simultaneously adhere to the equivalency principle yet, in certain contexts, still provide lesser protection to false commercial speech.

APPLYING THE EQUIVALENCY PRINCIPLE TO FALSE COMMERCIAL SPEECH: THE TAXONOMY OF HARMS

Recall that under the equivalency principle, commercial speech cannot receive reduced First Amendment protection for no reason other than its

---

patient relationship), the fiduciary nature of that relationship and the transaction costs involved in the recipient of the information obtaining alternative opinions significantly alter the constitutional calculus concerning First Amendment protection. But such exceptions are relatively few, and should not apply to generally distributed communications. Note also that in the narrow context of defamation, negligent falsehoods uttered about individuals who are not public figures or somehow in the public eye may, consistent with the First Amendment, be punished. But that exception is largely unique to the defamation context. My analysis here assumes that the false commercial speech in question is distributed to a relatively large audience and concerns a product that could reasonably be expected to be purchased by a similarly large audience.

[206] See discussion *supra* at 42–45.
[207] *United States v. Alvarez*, 132 S. Ct. 2537, 2545 (2012) (plurality opinion).
[208] See id.

lesser value to the interests of the First Amendment.[209] To suggest that the exact same fully protected speech conveyed to the exact same audience is somehow of less value simply because the speaker is motivated by commercial profit is either wholly illogical or nothing more than ideologically driven discrimination against the capitalistic system of which such speech is a central element.[210] It does not necessarily follow, however, that all false commercial speech must receive the same level of First Amendment protection extended to noncommercial speech. It simply means that to the extent the two categories of speech are to be treated differently, it must be for some principled reason other than gradation in First Amendment value.

To the extent that commercial speech may be extended a reduced level of protection consistent with the dictates of the equivalency principle, it can be due to one of two possible reasons: (1) protected commercial speech is not negatively impacted in the same manner and to the same degree that noncommercial speech would be impacted by the same manner of regulation;[211] or (2) commercial speech gives rise to a unique level of harm to which noncommercial speech does not.[212] The prior section demonstrated the speciousness of the former basis of distinction.[213] The second basis of distinction, however, is more complex and actually may in fact justify reduced constitutional protection for false commercial speech in certain, relatively narrow contexts.

As to the first ground for distinction, it has already been shown that every basis used to justify providing a lower level of protection for false commercial speech than false noncommercial speech ultimately fails.[214] Thus, under the equivalency principle, to the extent that false commercial and noncommercial speech are to be distinguished for purposes of constitutional protection, it must be on the second ground – in other words, that false commercial speech gives rise to a uniquely significant danger of harm. This insight leads to the recognition of the need for a framing of a taxonomy of categorical harms to which false speech can give rise, and then a determination of whether false commercial speech gives rise to harms society deems of sufficient gravity to justify suppression.

It is appropriate to discern five categorical harms to which false speech may conceivably give rise: (1) financial; (2) political; (3) reputational; (4) health and

---

[209] See discussion *supra* at 34–41.
[210] For a detailed exploration of this theory see generally Redish, *supra* note 125, at 75–121.
[211] See discussion *supra* at 47–49.
[212] See discussion *supra* at 34–39.
[213] See discussion *supra* at 47–49.
[214] See id.

safety; and (5) interpersonal. "Financial" refers to the listeners' loss of money as a direct result of reasonable reliance on the false speech of the speaker. This basically describes the classic situation of commercial fraud. "Political" refers to the harm that flows in the form of governmental choices not consistent with the true desires or interests of the listeners, caused by the listener's reliance on false representations about the speaker's qualifications for office or past accomplishments. "Reputational" refers to the harm caused by false statements about a person that cause his/her reputation to be undermined or damaged among the listeners or readers. "Health and safety" is defined as harm to the well-being of the listeners caused by the listeners' reasonable reliance on the speaker's false statements concerning the impact of a particular product or practice on the listeners' health (for example, "drink this product once a day and it will make you feel great" when in reality doing so will cause serious internal harm).[215] By "interpersonal," I mean personal decisions that the listener may make because of the listeners' reliance on the speaker's false statements (for example, inducing the listener to engage in sexual relations on the basis of the false assertion that the speaker is an astronaut, or that the speaker is free of sexually transmitted diseases). To the extent that false speech gives rise to harm, that harm will fall within one of these five categories. It should be noted, however, that the categories are not necessarily mutually exclusive. For example, false speech could simultaneously undermine health and safety as well as cause damage to listeners' financial interests. A false claim that a product will improve health when in reality it will undermine health simultaneously threatens health and safety and gives rise to financial harm.

To assert that false commercial speech receive the same level of First Amendment protection afforded to false noncommercial speech of course does not necessarily imply that false commercial speech receives anything approaching absolute protection. If one examines the noncommercial speech doctrinal landscape, one quickly sees that it is by no means the case that all false noncommercial speech receives full First Amendment protection. In numerous situations, knowingly false noncommercial speech that causes one or more of these harms is excluded from the scope of First Amendment protection. For example, this is clearly the case for reputational harm, *even when the speech concerns core elements of the political process*.[216] If one candidate or her supporter in the midst of the campaign defames her opponent with knowledge of the statement's falsity, that speech

---

[215] Consider, for example, President Trump's suggestion to the nation that injecting or otherwise consuming Clorox Bleach could prevent and/or cure Covid-19.

[216] See discussion *supra* at 42–47.

is unprotected by the First Amendment, even though it is properly characterized as pure political speech.[217]

Similarly, noncommercial speech that intentionally defrauds listeners or readers out of money is no more protected than fraud in the purely commercial context. If one needs proof of this fact, one need only consider the examples of journalists Stephen Glass and Jayson Blair, both of whom intentionally falsified stories for their publications (the *New Republic* and the *New York Times*, respectively).[218] No one could reasonably doubt that both were potentially subject to liability for fraud, and no one even suggested that their actions were protected by the First Amendment merely because their articles appeared in fully protected publications or concerned matters of public importance.[219] And this result makes perfect sense, as both practical and constitutional matters. Similarly, if a candidate for office knowingly misrepresents his qualifications in an effort to convince potential contributors to make contributions to his campaign that speech should be as punishable as any commercial fraud-behavior that neither should be nor is ever protected by the First Amendment.

Similarly, speech promoting the health and safety benefits of a product uttered with knowledge of the falsity of that speech should never receive First Amendment protection. This is true, regardless of whether or not the speech comes in the form of commercial or noncommercial speech. By way of illustration, consider the following hypothetical situation, used at other points in this book. The manufacturer of bee pollen takes out an advertisement claiming health effects of the product, with knowledge that such a claim is false. Presumably no one would dispute that such expression falls outside the protective reach of the First Amendment. Now assume that instead of including the speech in the form of an advertisement, the manufacturer writes a book that makes the very same knowingly false claims. Assuming the book reaches roughly the same audience that is reached by the advertisement, by what logic could we deny First Amendment protection to the former but grant it to the latter? The two forms of expression are, in this hypothetical, assumed to give rise to the exact same nature and degree of harm; the two forms of expression are both assumed to have been made with full knowledge of falsity. The only

---

[217] See id.
[218] See *New York Times: Reporter Routinely Faked Articles*, CNN (May 11, 2003, 4:30 PM), www.cnn.com/2003/US/Northeast/05/10/ny.times.reporter/ [https://perma.cc/5YSZ-XDUL]; Hanna Rosin, *Hello, My Name Is Stephen Glass, and I'm Sorry*, New Republic (November 10, 2014), https://newrepublic.com/article/120145/stephen-glass-new-republic-scandal-still-haunts-his-law-career [https://perma.cc/7JSB-DJPJ].
[219] See *New York Times: Reporter Routinely Faked Articles*, supra note 218.

distinction is that the former comes in the form of traditional commercial speech while the latter comes in the form of traditionally protected noncommercial speech. Having anything turn on this distinction for First Amendment purposes does nothing more than place form over substance.

Consider also a different hypothetical: Assume that the speaker stands to make no commercial profit out of convincing the listeners of health benefits or lack of health risks of a particular product. Instead, the speaker makes the claims with full knowledge of their falsity, simply as a prank or purely out of vindictiveness. Should the fact that the speech is not uttered for purposes of commercial profit lead to the conclusion that it is deserving of First Amendment protection? Such a conclusion, would, of course, be pure nonsense. The speech gives rise to the exact same level of serious harm, whether it is uttered for purposes of commercial profit or for purposes of vindictiveness or misguided playfulness. Such knowingly false speech no more serves First Amendment values than does commercially motivated knowingly false speech.

Note, however, that under the constitutional model proposed here, in the case of unknowingly, widely communicated false speech,[220] even in the presence of these significant harms, the noncommercial expression would likely receive First Amendment protection.[221] Therefore, under the equivalency principle, unknowingly false, widely communicated commercial speech should be protected, even when it gives rise to similarly unique harms. In contrast, knowingly false but non-defamatory speech uttered in the course of political debate is, as a categorical matter, usually assumed not to give rise to sufficient harm to exclude that speech from the scope of First Amendment protection.[222] This is so, even though the voters might be deceived and as a result cast their votes in ways in which they would not have done had they known the truth.[223] Such generic "political" harm is apparently deemed to be so diffuse and its individual harm so diluted that it is deemed not to rise to the level required to exclude even knowingly false speech from the scope of First Amendment protection.

---

[220] Recall, however, that in the case of one-on-one communication between a professional and an individual in the course of a professional fiduciary relationship, common sense dictates that the First Amendment's role must be far more limited.

[221] This is certainly true of unknowingly false defamatory speech of public figures, pursuant to the *New York Times Co.* actual malice test.

[222] See State *ex rel. Pub. Disclosure Comm'n* v. *119 Vote No! Comm.*, 957 P.2d 691, 697–99 (Wash. 1998).

[223] id.

One might well debate the wisdom of this view. Stealing a citizen's vote could arguably be deemed as harmful as stealing a citizen's money. But at this point I am willing to assume its correctness, if only for purposes of argument. As for knowingly false expression causing interpersonal harm, it is likely that the level of protection turns on the nature of that harm. Speech tricking another into having sexual relations on the basis of knowingly false representations, it is safe to assume, would not receive protection, even though the speech is of course not motivated by the desire for commercial profit. The Court in *Alvarez*, on the other hand, seemed to assume that at least some knowingly false speech causes no harm at all.[224] While the accuracy of this conclusion is debatable,[225] it can be accepted at least for purposes of this taxonomy.

In the context of noncommercial speech, then, protection for knowingly or recklessly false expression turns entirely on the categorical nature of the harm caused. Under the equivalency principle, protection for knowingly or recklessly false commercial speech should turn on the exact same criteria. It would not follow, however, that the end result would be that knowingly false commercial speech is protected as often as knowingly false noncommercial speech is protected. This is simply because the harm caused by knowingly false commercial speech will generally fall under the heading of financial harm, harm to health or safety, or both. And those harms are categorically (and reasonably) considered more serious than the far more diffuse "political" harm caused by the protected category of knowingly false noncommercial speech.

I should emphasize, once again, that I am not urging that false commercial speech receive identical treatment to that received by false noncommercial speech. At this point, however, we should be able to understand what that would mean in terms of doctrinal reality. With the background of the taxonomy of harms I have shaped, I am arguing merely that under the persuasive logic of the harm-based analysis – the guiding directive the Court seems to have adopted and applied in the case of truthful commercial speech – false commercial speech should be evaluated under the same standard that knowingly false noncommercial speech is measured: Protection turns on the nature and degree of the harm to which the speech gives rise. But because most knowingly false commercial speech will usually give rise to either direct financial, safety, or health harms, it is highly likely that even under the equivalency principle, more knowingly false commercial speech will be suppressed than knowingly false noncommercial speech.

---

[224] See discussion *supra* at 45–56.
[225] See discussion *supra* at 46.

THE PROBLEM OF MISLEADING SPEECH

To this point, the analysis has focused on the question of how knowingly false commercial speech is to be treated for First Amendment purposes. The conclusion here is that it is generally to be denied constitutional protection, even though at least some knowingly false noncommercial speech is protected, not because it is less valuable for First Amendment purposes, but solely because of the categorically more severe nature of the harm generally caused by knowingly false commercial speech.[226] I have purposely chosen not to consider the issue of how falsity is defined, because the equivalency principle demands only "most favored nation status" for commercial speech. In other words, when, and only when, noncommercial speech would be characterized as "false" may commercial speech be characterized as false. For present purposes, then, the analysis is therefore agnostic to the definition of falsity. To this point, however, my analysis has omitted a particularly thorny problem: the issue of First Amendment protection for commercial speech that is not technically false, but can be properly characterized as misleading. In many ways, technically true but misleading speech can be thought to cause financial or health/safety harms equivalent to those caused by directly false statements (though, as the Supreme Court has demonstrated, the harms caused by misleading speech are more easily curable than are those caused by directly false statements, by the use of required disclaimers).[227]

At first blush, it may appear that adherence to the equivalency principle places one in a dilemma: Either we abandon the equivalency principle and allow misleading commercial speech to be regulated, we adhere to the equivalency principle and protect truthful but misleading commercial speech resulting in significant societal harm, or my analysis brings about the very dilution whose existence we have denied[228] by imposing sweeping restrictions on the manner in which public debate is normally conducted. More careful analysis, however, reveals that no such dilemma exists. Once we recall the harm-centric approach to the regulation of false speech,[229] it is relatively easy to distinguish the regulation of misleading commercial speech from that of most forms of misleading noncommercial speech. Recall that most false or misleading noncommercial speech will not give rise to either direct financial

---

[226] See discussion *supra* at 48.
[227] *Zauderer v. Office of Disciplinary Counsel of the Supreme Court of Ohio*, 471 U.S. 626, 651 (1985). See the detailed discussion of *Zauderer* in Chapter 4, *infra*.
[228] See discussion *supra* at 39–41.
[229] See Chapter 1, *supra*.

or safety/health harms.[230] To the extent such speech does in fact give rise to such harms, there is no constitutional basis for denying government power to regulate misleading speech through required use of disclaimers, just as is done in the case of commercial speech.

There is one conceivable role the First Amendment should potentially play in the context of the regulation of misleading speech. The mere fact that speech – commercial or noncommercial – gives only one side of a debate should not permit government to deem that speech misleading and therefore regulable by means of either suppression or required use of disclaimers. The First Amendment protects advocacy,[231] and commercial advertisers, like speakers generally, are permitted to advocate on behalf of their views and beliefs. To be sure, when an advertised product is found to give rise to potentially significant health risks that may well influence a reasonable person's decision whether to use the product, under the taxonomy of categorical harms I propose that government should be permitted to require those disclosures, even if the speech absent those disclosures cannot properly be characterized as misleading. But once again, this is not because the speech is commercial, but because it gives rise to the proximate danger of significant threats to health and safety. Even noncommercial speech found likely to be viewed by roughly the same group of listeners as commercial speech making the identical claims on behalf of the product in question should logically be subjected to an identical level of regulation as the commercial speech is.[232] I deem this not to be a form of dilution, but rather simply tempering the First Amendment inquiry with principled analysis and common sense.

CONCLUSION

The idea that false commercial speech is deserving of any level of First Amendment protection will no doubt shock scholars and jurists alike. Mere intuition, if nothing else, should tell us that false commercial speech automatically falls outside the First Amendment's scope. This is so, even if truthful commercial speech does not. Indeed, the Supreme Court has proceeded on

---

[230] See discussion *supra* at 54–55.
[231] See generally Redish, *supra* note 125, at 89–90.
[232] I qualify this First Amendment standard, for both commercial and noncommercial speech, by emphasizing that I refer to required disclaimers only for undisputed dangers. When the speaker – again, commercial or noncommercial – reasonably disputes the existence of such dangers, the required disclaimers become a form of forced expression inconsistent with the First Amendment.

just this notion since the beginning of its commercial speech doctrine.[233] But as I have previously argued, intuition is not always the best way to shape First Amendment doctrine.[234] The irony of reliance on right-brained intuitionism to categorically reject First Amendment protection for false commercial speech resembles the kind of knee-jerk, summary dismissal of protection for truthful commercial speech many years ago.[235] It is reasonable to think that First Amendment thought has come a long way since those days. Hopefully, this analysis of false commercial speech and the equivalency principle will at some point in the near future similarly be able to overcome the kind of emotive shock that scholars will no doubt have in response to our proposal.

---

[233] See discussion *supra* at 30.
[234] See generally Martin H. Redish, *Commercial Speech, First Amendment Intuitionism and the Twilight Zone of Viewpoint Discrimination*, 41 Loy. L.A. L. Rev. 67 (2007).
[235] See, e.g., Thomas H. Jackson & John Calvin Jeffries, Jr., *Commercial Speech: Economic Due Process and the First Amendment*, 65 Va. L. Rev. 1, 14 (1979) (arguing that "[w]hatever else it may mean, the concept of a first amendment right of personal autonomy in matters of belief and expression stops short of a seller hawking his wares").

3

The Right of Publicity, Commercial Speech, and the Equivalency Principle

INTRODUCTION

Celebrity images pervade our modern, media-consumed culture. From red carpet award shows to celebrity gossip website to social media networks, American consumers crave glimpses of their icons – and both celebrities and profit-making corporations know it.[1] But when profit-making corporations seek to draw on the obvious and evoke celebrity images for direct commercial benefit, they run up against a decrepit free speech shackle known as the right of publicity.[2] In both its statutory and common law formulations, the right of publicity operates as a means for people to control and profit from the commercial use of their identities.[3] Plaintiffs' assertions of this right, however, can directly impede both speakers' rights to free expression and listeners' and readers' rights to be informed. It may seem that our most fundamental constitutional guarantee would safeguard speech interests in a contest with what are principally pecuniary interests in control of one's own publicity. The

---

[1] See, e.g., James Franco, Selfies: The Attention Grabber, N.Y. Times, December 29, 2013, at AR20 ("In this age of too much information at a click of a button, the power to attract viewers amid the sea of things to read and watch is power indeed. It's what the movie studios want for their products, it's what professional writers want for their work, it's what newspapers want-hell, it's what everyone wants: attention."); Alex Ben Block, Why New Award Shows Are Crowding TV's Calendar, Hollywood Reporter (January 9, 2014, 5:00 AM), www.hollywoodreporter.com/news/golden-globes-why-new-award-668767 [http://perma.cc/SNF4-L85K] (describing demand for award shows); Scott Goodson, The 30 Most Popular Celebrity Gossip Sites and Why Big Brands Love Them, Forbes (May 24, 2013, 2:20 PM), www.forbes.com/sites/marketshare/2013/05/24/the-30-most-popular-celebrity-gossip-sites-and-why-big-brands-love-them [http://perma.cc/R3EK-VUGU] ("Celebrity drives viewership. No doubt. They are eyeball magnets. Celebrity content pulls tons of views. And nothing, it seems, attracts more eyeballs than celebrity gossip websites."); see also Julie Creswell, Nothing Sells Like Celebrity, N.Y. Times, June 22, 2008, at BUN1 ("[C]orporate brands have increasingly turned to Hollywood celebrities and musicians to sell their products.").

[2] See discussion infra at 64–72.

[3] See discussion infra at id.

unconventional doctrinal development of publicity rights, substantially detached from the modern theory and doctrine of the First Amendment, is producing troubling, even bizarre results. Today, courts routinely prioritize the pecuniary interest in publicity rights over the First Amendment right of free expression. In so doing, courts and defendants are failing to capitalize on over forty years of evolution in the law of commercial speech. Moreover, they are ignoring the compelling logical implications of the equivalency principle, which lies at the heart of this book's thesis.

Modern cases involving celebrity avatars in video games illustrate the erroneous First Amendment applications at work. Not all that long ago, the Supreme Court brought video games within the ambit of constitutionally protected expression.[4] Both the Third and Ninth Circuits have blinked, however, narrowing that protection in response to publicity rights claims.[5] The nature of the courts' contractions on free expression in video games has hinged on the purpose for which video game makers included celebrity identities and the courts' perceived value of those uses. In *Hart v. Electronic Arts, Inc.*, the Third Circuit highlighted the centrality of realistic football player depictions to both "the core of the game experience" and to its marketability.[6] In *In re NCAA Student-Athlete Name and Likeness Licensing Litigation*, the Ninth Circuit underscored how the interactive game featuring avatars of real athletes was just that – "a game, not a reference source" capable of providing informational value.[7] The video games in *In re NCAA* thus had less First Amendment worth, according to the Third and Ninth Circuits, because they were made by profit-making corporations to entertain, not to inform. The courts addressing right of publicity claims thus discriminated on both the bases of the speakers and the content of the speech at issue.

Such reasoning is flawed for several reasons. First, it is all but impossible to distinguish the "informational" from the "entertaining." Second, even if one somehow could draw such a distinction, the two are by no means mutually exclusive, as the Ninth Circuit implies. Finally, and perhaps most importantly, the courts' analyses completely ignore two key Supreme Court precepts: its caution against distinguishing between discourse on public matters and

---

[4] See *Brown v. Entm't Merchs. Ass'n*, 131 S. Ct. 2729, 2733 (2011) ("Like the protected books, plays, and movies that preceded them, video games communicate ideas – and even social messages – through many familiar literary devices ... and through features distinctive to the medium (such as the player's interaction with the virtual world).").
[5] See *In re NCAA Student-Athlete Name & Likeness Licensing Litig.*, 724 F.3d 1268, 1271 (9th Cir. 2013); *Hart v. Elec. Arts, Inc.*, 717 F.3d 141, 170 (3d Cir. 2013).
[6] *Hart*, 717 F.3d at 168.
[7] *In re NCAA*, 724 F.3d at 1283.

entertainment,[8] and its oft-cited reminder that commercial motivation does not render speech unworthy of First Amendment protection.[9] These critical missteps on the part of the Third and Ninth Circuits, although problematic, are unfortunately not aberrational in the law of publicity rights. When it comes to adjudicating publicity rights claims against free speech interests, courts are stupefied.[10] They apply absurd distinctions, and they routinely discriminate against speech solely on the basis of speakers' profit motivation.[11]

How could the law possibly arrive at this point? My analysis finds the culprit of this jurisprudence to be a surprisingly backwards right of publicity law, which has failed to keep pace with modern commercial speech development, in either doctrinal or theoretical terms, since 1976. Although jurists and scholars have bemoaned the confusing state of publicity rights doctrine and have conjured up many solutions for bringing order to the morass,[12] they continue to ignore a simple, basic principle that rings even truer today: "Commercial speech is no longer the stepchild of the First Amendment."[13] In fact, unless the commercial speech in question is deemed false or misleading, the level of constitutional protection courts extend to commercial speech differs very little, if at all, from the degree of protection extended to traditionally protected noncommercial speech.[14] Equally troubling, if not more so, is the judiciary's failure to recognize the compelling logic of the commercial

---

[8] See, e.g., *Brown*, 131 S. Ct. at 2733 ("The Free Speech Clause exists principally to protect discourse on public matters, but we have long recognized that it is difficult to distinguish politics from entertainment, and dangerous to try. 'Everyone is familiar with instances of propaganda through fiction. What is one man's amusement, teaches another's doctrine.'" (quoting *Winters v. New York*, 333 U.S. 507, 510 (1948))).

[9] See, e.g., *Time, Inc. v. Hill*, 385 U.S. 374, 397 (1967) ("That books, newspapers, and magazines are published and sold for profit does not prevent them from being a form of expression whose liberty is safeguarded by the First Amendment." (quoting *Joseph Burstyn, Inc. v. Wilson*, 343 U.S. 495, 501–02 (1952))).

[10] See, e.g., *Jordan v. Jewel Food Stores, Inc.*, 743 F.3d 509, 514 (7th Cir. 2014) ("[T]here is no judicial consensus on how to resolve conflicts between intellectual-property rights and free speech rights.").

[11] See, discussion *infra* at 84–91.

[12] See, e.g., *ETW Corp. v. Jireh Publ'g, Inc.*, 332 F.3d 915, 954 (6th Cir. 2003) (Clay, J., dissenting) ("[T]he point of confusion most associated with the right of publicity law is its interplay with the First Amendment."); Mark S. Lee, *Agents of Chaos: Judicial Confusion in Defining the Right of Publicity-Free Speech Interface*, 23 Loyola L.A. Ent. L. Rev. 471 (2003) ("[T]he current legal landscape is a confusing morass of inconsistent, sometimes non-existent, or mutually exclusive approaches, tests, standards, and guidelines, with the confusion only increased by several recent rulings.").

[13] See Martin H. Redish, *Commercial Speech, First Amendment Intuitionism and the Twilight Zone of Viewpoint Discrimination*, 41 Loyola L.A. L.J. 67 (2007).

[14] See Chapter 2, *supra*.

speech equivalency principle. This failure results in a logically undefinable distinction among the free speech rights of profit-making corporations.

This conclusion should lead to a simple insight: both as a doctrinal and as a theoretical manner, commercially motivated expression is appropriately extended the same level of First Amendment protection against right of publicity claims as traditionally protected expression receives.[15] Note that the argument fashioned here is not that commercial speech will necessarily prevail over the competing right of publicity in all instances. Rather, the argument is only that commercial speech appropriately deserves the doctrinal equivalent of "most favored nation" status when measured against fully protected noncommercial speech. It is this form of protection that logically follows from the dictates of the equivalency principle fashioned and applied throughout this book.

This chapter contains three main sections. The first section focuses on the development of the right of publicity, charting its origin and studying its leading philosophical justifications. It shows how the right operates as an instrument for pursuing and protecting financial gain, in much the same manner as commercial speech does.[16] The next section explores the adversarial relationship between the right of publicity and the First Amendment, discussing areas of completely protected speech, the evolving balancing tests that now orient publicity rights and lesser protected "expressive" speech, and the complete absence of any commercial speech-based defenses. The final section challenges courts' reflexive dismissal of commercial speech interests on a variety of levels. It shows that the primary defect in the current status of the First Amendment limitation on publicity rights is the wholly unjustified assumption that speech contained in commercial advertisements is somehow less valuable – and therefore less protected – than traditionally protected categories of expression. Further, the section invokes current commercial speech doctrine to show that even if our efforts to attack the courts' reduced protection for commercial expression fail in the publicity rights context, the modern approach for evaluating commercially motivated speech is considerably more protective than recent publicity rights cases apparently assume. Ultimately, the chapter concludes that courts' dismissive approaches to commercially motivated expression relative to publicity rights derive from flawed assumptions concerning outdated thinking and doctrine. Modernizing courts' approaches to the law of commercial speech protection leads to the rejection of publicity rights claims in favor of First Amendment interests.

---

[15] See discussion *infra* at 92–98.
[16] See discussion *infra* at 71–72.

FOUNDATIONS OF THE RIGHT OF PUBLICITY

Since the right of privacy doctrine's curious beginnings, scholars and courts have sought to make sense of the so-called right of publicity, questioning everything from its name to its relationship with constitutionally protected speech. This section describes the foundations and growth of the right of publicity, beginning with its origin as a concept imbedded in the right to privacy.

The right of publicity finds its origins in the statutory and common law right of privacy. When Samuel Warren and Louis Brandeis authored their famous article on the right to privacy in 1890, their conception of "the right to be let alone" contemplated an individual's power to decide what expression of herself, if any, she would make available for public consumption.[17] Although the focus of the Warren and Brandeis article concerned press intrusion into personal life, rather than the commercial use of a person's likeness for proprietary gain, their argument in defense of privacy provided fertile ground from which courts could glean a variety of protections.[18]

The very first court to consider remedying an allegedly infringed right to privacy in the manner Warren and Brandeis proposed, however, balked at the opportunity to do so. The Court of Appeals of New York in *Roberson v. Rochester Folding Box Co.* held that a young woman asserting a cause of action in equity for the unauthorized publication of her photograph had no valid legal claim.[19] According to the court, the defendant's use of Abigail Roberson's likeness as part of an advertisement for Franklin Mills Flour did not libel her.[20] Further, because no precedent recognized a common law action for an invasion of a right to privacy, and the court believed that doing so would give rise to waves of litigation, it rejected her claim.[21] Enraged by the court's rejection, the New York State Legislature responded in short order. On September 1, 1903, a statutory right to privacy took effect, recognizing the unauthorized use of one's likeness "for the purposes of trade" to constitute

---

[17] Samuel D. Warren & Louis D. Brandeis, *The Right to Privacy*, 4 Harv. L. Rev. 193, 193, 198–99 (1890) ("The common law secures to each individual the right of determining, ordinarily, to what extent his thoughts, sentiments, and emotions shall be communicated to others.... It is immaterial whether it be by word or by signs, in painting, by sculpture, or in music. In every such case the individual is entitled to decide whether that which is his shall be given to the public." (footnotes omitted)).

[18] See Neil M. Richards & Daniel J. Solove, *Prosser's Privacy Law: A Mixed Legacy*, 98 Calif. L. Rev. 1887, 1893 (2010) ("Although courts developed these early torts in response to Warren and Brandeis's article, the torts involved a different context from the one that Warren and Brandeis had envisioned.").

[19] 64 N.E. 442, 448 (N.Y. 1902).

[20] id. at 447–48.

[21] id. at 443.

both a misdemeanor and a tort.[22] Soon thereafter, the Supreme Court of Georgia rejected *Roberson* in a case with nearly identical facts, thereby becoming the first jurisdiction to recognize a common law right to privacy.[23] Strangely, both the New York State Legislature and the Supreme Court of Georgia found the label of "privacy" sufficient also to encompass a wholly pecuniary interest in controlling the commercial use of one's likeness.[24]

Despite these swift advancements, the right to privacy and its supposedly imbedded right of publicity held an uncertain place in tort law in the decades that followed. Treatises and casebooks treated privacy as a residual category of torts, protecting against intentional torts that were not otherwise covered.[25] The Restatement (First) of Torts in 1939 recognized a cause of action for "unreasonabl[e] and serious" invasions of privacy.[26] But by 1940, only fourteen states recognized a righty to privacy – twelve by common law and two by statute.[27] Early versions of Prosser's treatise on torts similarly expressed uncertainty about the nature of the right to privacy. Prosser raised the possibility that the right would be swallowed up by the tort of intentional infliction of emotional distress,[28] and doctrinally, he placed privacy among other "miscellaneous" topics at the end of his book.[29] Prosser's earliest iteration on privacy nevertheless identified the discrete causes of action that the right of privacy encompassed, including: (1) intrusions on a plaintiff's solitude; (2) publicity given to his name or likeness, or to private information about him; and (3) the commercial appropriation of elements of his personality.[30] In 1953,

---

[22] N.Y. Civ. Rights Law §§ 50-51 (McKinney 1903) (amended 1921).
[23] *Pavesich v. New England Life Ins. Co.*, 50 S.E. 68, 70 (Ga. 1905) ("The right of one to exhibit himself to the public at all proper times, in all proper places, and in a proper manner is embraced within the right of personal liberty. The right to withdraw from the public gaze at such times as a person may see fit, when his presence in public is not demanded by any rule of law, is also embraced within the right of personal liberty. Publicity in one instance, and privacy in the other, are each guaranteed. If personal liberty embraces the right of publicity, it no less embraces the correlative right of privacy, and this is no new idea in Georgia law.").
[24] Like many others today, I reject a characterization of the right of publicity as anything other than a property right exercised by plaintiffs to make profits. Early suggestions that publicity rights are cut from the cloth of privacy rights misunderstand how plaintiffs might use privacy/publicity rights to seek profit, not shelter, from the limelight. In addition, they fail to comprehend the expansive reach of other tort protections, such as claims for defamation and false light.
[25] Richards & Solove, *supra* note 18, at 1894 nn.34–36 (collecting treatises and casebooks published between 1916 and 1933).
[26] Restatement (First) of Torts § 867 (1939).
[27] Louis Nizer, *The Right to Privacy: A Half-Century's Developments*, 39 Mich. L. Rev. 526, 529–30 (1941).
[28] William L. Prosser, *Handbook of the Law of Torts* (1st ed. 1941), pp. 1053–54.
[29] id. at 1051.
[30] id. at 1054–56.

Prosser added the category of false light,[31] bringing the total to four causes of action for infringing a right of privacy, as it stands today.[32]

The same year that Prosser solidified his four-part understanding of privacy, Judge Jerome Frank wrote the Second Circuit's decision in *Haelan Laboratories v. Topps Chewing Gum*.[33] *Haelan* involved a contract dispute in which a baseball player gave the plaintiff chewing gum company the exclusive rights to use his photograph, but the defendant rival chewing gum manufacturer induced the player to authorize that manufacturer also to use his photograph.[34] The court rejected the defendant's contention that the plaintiff's contract with the baseball player "created [no] more than a release of liability, because a ... legal interest in the publication of his picture" did not exist outside of the right to privacy.[35] In so doing, Judge Frank articulated for the first time a "right of publicity."[36] He wrote:

> We think that, in addition to and independent of that right of privacy (which in New York derives from statute), a man has a right in the publicity value of his photograph, i.e., the right to grant the exclusive privilege of publishing his picture This right might be called a "right of publicity." For it is common knowledge that many prominent persons (especially actors and ball-players), far from having their feelings bruised through public exposure of their likeness, would feel sorely deprived if they no longer received money for authorizing advertisements, popularizing their countenances, displayed in newspapers, magazines, buses, trains and subways.[37]

Judge Frank dismissed as "immaterial" whether the right of publicity should be labeled as a property right or some other type of right, and he spent little time justifying its philosophical footing.[38] But a bevy of commentators over the ensuing six decades have sought to fill that void.

---

[31] William Lloyd Prosser, *Selected Topics on the Law of Torts* (1954), pp. 119–20 (publishing five lectures from 1953). In 1960, Prosser lamented how Warren's and Brandeis's article had developed "four loosely related torts," recognizing that "it is high time that we realize what we are doing, and give some consideration to the question of where, if anywhere, we are to call a halt." William L. Prosser, *Privacy*, 48 Calif. L. Rev. 383, 422, 423 (1960).

[32] See W. Page Keeton et al., Prosser & Keeton on the Law of Torts § 117 (5th ed. 1984).

[33] 202 F.2d 866 (2d Cir. 1953).

[34] id. at 867.

[35] id. at 868.

[36] id.

[37] id.

[38] id. He noted that "the tag 'property' simply symbolizes the fact that courts enforce a claim which has pecuniary worth." id. But whereas Judge Frank preferred to create a new label and context for this right, Prosser continued to recognize "appropriation privacy," a term he believed already encompassed the proprietary nature of the use of a plaintiff's name and likeness as an aspect of her identity. See Prosser, *supra* note 31, at 389.

PHILOSOPHICAL JUSTIFICATIONS FOR THE RIGHT OF PUBLICITY

Courts and scholars offering justifications for the right of publicity – or "misappropriation", as it is sometimes called – have defined its protection both narrowly (such as commodified celebrity goodwill)[39] and broadly (such as encompassing both dignitary and economic interests).[40] Borrowing the framework that Professor Michael Madow first espoused,[41] this section divides justifications recognizing publicity rights into both moral and economic categories. The "moral" category tracks the right's substance as protecting something more than property, encompassing arguments relating to celebrities' intrinsic personhood. Publicity rights thus are said to: (1) reward labor, and relatedly, prevent unjust enrichment; (2) protect individual autonomy and personal dignity; and (3) prevent value misrepresentation. The "economic" category concerns itself more with property rationales for justifying the right, including: (1) incentivizing socially useful activity; (2) promoting efficiency and avoiding rent dissipation; and (3) protecting against consumer confusion.

Although scholars and courts largely agree about the contours of these arguments, Professor Madow suggests that their subtext involves something greater: "control over the production and circulation of meaning in our society."[42] Some see exercising control through publicity rights as

---

[39] Robert C. Post, *Rereading Warren and Brandeis: Privacy, Property, and Appropriation*, 41 Case W. Res. L. Rev. 647, 666 (1991) (defining the right as "a property right that would safeguard the goodwill created by celebrities in their public persona"). Although Professor Post defines the right narrowly at the outset, he later addresses how "[t]he right of publicity ... divides a person in to two ... the objectified image ... which has become a thing of value capable of being owned and transferred," and what he says Oliver Wendell Holmes would call "the 'natural personality.'" id. at 678 (citations omitted).

[40] Jennifer E. Rothman, *The Inalienable Right of Publicity*, 101 Geo. L.J. 185, 227 (2012) ("The right of publicity encompasses rights far beyond the mere collection of income and entitlement to the economic value that flows from uses of a person's identity. The right of publicity provides control over the use of a person's identity and, therefore, ultimately over the person herself.").

[41] Michael Madow, *Private Ownership of Public Image: Popular Cultural and Publicity Rights*, 81 Calif. L. Rev. 125, 178 (1993). Professor Madow divided the main justifications for publicity rights into three categories: (1) moral arguments (reaping only what you have sown); (2) economic arguments (such as incentivizing creative effort and promoting allocative efficiency); and (3) consumer protection. id. He argued that "the rationales most commonly advanced in support of the right of publicity nowadays are no more compelling than those put forward by Judge Frank and Melville Nimmer in the early 1950s." id.

[42] id. at 142. Earlier in his article, Professor Madow distinguishes "'cultural pessimists' ... who [view] ... popular culture as a field in which dominant, repressive (in other words, consumerist, patriarchal, etc.) meanings are systematically reproduced and reinforced" from "'cultural

redistributing wealth and facilitating censorship of popular culture,[43] whereas others view control as properly returning to those whom associative value attaches, rather than transferring it to those merely seeking to profit.[44]

Rewarding Labor and Preventing Unjust Enrichment

Just one year after Judge Frank authored the opinion in *Haelan Laboratories*, Melville Nimmer took up the cause of the right of publicity. Nimmer, at the time an attorney for Paramount Pictures, lauded *Haelan* as "a major step in the inexorable process of reconciling law and contemporary problems."[45] Quite aware of efforts in Hollywood to persuade the American public that film stars owed their fame to old-fashioned hard work,[46] Nimmer carefully justified the right of publicity as the product of a person's creation:

> [I]n most instances a person achieves publicity values of substantial pecuniary worth only after he has expended considerable time, effort, skill, and even money. It would seem to be a first principle of Anglo-American jurisprudence, an axiom of the most fundamental nature, that every person is entitled to the fruit of his labors unless there are important countervailing public policy considerations.[47]

Without specifically citing John Locke, Nimmer invoked the Lockean labor theory of property[48] to gift wrap the right of publicity for courts and legislatures.[49] Just as Locke once touted the labor of a person's body and the

---

> populists ... [who] view popular culture as contested terrain in which individuals and groups ... [seek] to make and establish their own meanings and identities." id. at 138–39. Siding with cultural populists, he challenges the right of publicity by arguing that the "[l]aw can accelerate the already powerful trend toward centralized, top-down management of popular culture, or it can fight a rearguard (and perhaps futile) action on the side of a more decentralized, open, democratic cultural practice." id. at 142.

[43] See, e.g., id. at 136, 138.
[44] See, e.g., Sheldon W. Halpern, *The Right of Publicity: Maturation of an Independent Right of Personality*, 46 Hastings L.J. 853, 871–72 (1995). Professor Halpern dismisses Professor Madow's "strong words" about wealth distribution and meaning control, writing that "the reliance on conjectural extrapolation rather than on examination of the right's core paradigm leaves the burden still on those who would undo the work of the past forty years." id. at 872–73.
[45] Melville Nimmer, *The Right of Publicity*, 19 Law & Contemp. Probs. 203, 223 (1954).
[46] See Madow, *supra* note 41, at 176.
[47] See Nimmer, *supra* note 45, at 216 (emphasis added).
[48] See John Locke, *The Second Treatise of Government* 17 (Thomas P. Peardon ed., Liberal Arts Press 1952) (1690).
[49] More than forty years later, Professor Roberta Kwall described celebrity "construction" in a similar way, noting that "the effort in constructing the celebrity persona represents an intellectual, emotional, and physical effort on the part of the celebrity that requires protection." Roberta Rosenthal Kwall, *Fame*, 73 Ind. L.J. 1, 41 (1997).

work of his hands as "his," many others similarly began to characterize a person's celebrity as "his."[50] According to the argument, a person invests his time, energy, and resources to amass his celebrity likeness, and therefore, the benefit derived from its appropriation rightly belongs to him.[51]

If the value resulting from a person's celebrity is the fruit of his labor, as these jurists and scholars suggested, then collecting and failing to return his profits constitutes unjust enrichment. The unjust enrichment argument, part and parcel of the labor theory, posits that no social purpose is served by allowing the defendant to freely take what the plaintiff could sell.[52] Rather, a third party who unjustly benefits under such a scenario, according to one court, is no better than an "average thief."[53] That third party has even committed "a form of commercial immorality [in reaping] where another has sown."[54]

This labor justification, however, has been rendered less compelling in the modern media age. Achieving celebrity today can be as much about serendipity as it is about labor. Modern fame can reflect a person's timing and asininity, as much as his talent and intelligence.[55] Considering these developments, one might predict that the unraveling of the labor theory would present grave

[50] See, e.g., Alice Haemmerli, *Whose Who? The Case for a Kantian Right of Publicity*, 49 Duke L.J. 383, 388 (1999) ("Both proponents and critics of the right of publicity generally perceive it as a property claim grounded in Lockean labor theory. Although other rationales are occasionally propounded, no serious attempt has been made to elaborate an alternative philosophical justification for the right.").
[51] id.
[52] See Harry Kalven, Jr., *Privacy in Tort Law – Were Warren and Brandeis Wrong?*, 31 Law & Contemp. Probs. 326, 331 (1966); see also *Carson v. Here's Johnny Portable Toilets, Inc.*, 698 F.2d 831, 837 (6th Cir. 1983) ("Vindication of the right will also tend to prevent unjust enrichment by persons ... who seek commercially to exploit the identity of celebrities without their consent."); *Bi-Rite Enters., Inc. v. Button Master*, 555 F. Supp. 1188, 1198 (S.D.N.Y. 1983) (noting that the right "prevents unjust enrichment by providing a remedy against exploitation of the goodwill and reputation that a person develops in his name or likeness through the investment of time, effort, and money").
[53] *Midler v. Ford Motor Co.*, 849 F.2d 460, 462 (9th Cir. 1988) (quoting the district court judge in a case in which Bette Midler's voice was mimicked for an automobile advertisement with a "sound alike").
[54] *Hirsch v. S. C. Johnson & Son, Inc.*, 280 N.W.2d 129, 134-35 (Wis. 1979) (internal quotation marks omitted) (ruling in favor of Elroy "Crazy Legs" Hirsch for the unauthorized use of his nickname on women's shaving gel because Hirsch had "assiduously cultivated a reputation not only for skill as an athlete, but as an exemplary person").
[55] As examples, one needs look no further than Paris Hilton, or Perez Hilton, or any number of stars who are, as Daniel Boorstin put it, famous for being famous. See Daniel J. Boorstin, The Image: A Guide to Pseudo-Events in America 57 (1961); see also Neal Gabler, Daniel Boorstin Got It Right in "The Image," L.A. Times (April 15, 2012), http://articles.latimes.com/2012/apr/15/entertainment/la-ca-neal-gabler-20120415 [http://perma.cc/YRB8-U93J].

problems for publicity rights. Their statutory iterations nevertheless endure. At least two courts have recognized the diminishing importance of the labor theory while simultaneously protecting plaintiffs' abilities to exploit their fortuitous worth. In *White v. Samsung Electronics America*, the Ninth Circuit took up television personality Vanna White's right of publicity claim against an electronics company which had used a wig and jewelry clad robot in an advertisement.[56] Ruling for White, the court first recognized that sometimes celebrities expend "[c]onsiderable energy and ingenuity" to achieve and sell their value.[57] Even if that is not the case, and the celebrity has achieved her fame as a result of dumb luck, "[t]he law protects the celebrity's sole right to exploit this value."[58] In *Fraley v. Facebook*, the District Court for the Northern District of California similarly noted that California's right of publicity statute did not require that a plaintiff's "commercially exploitable value" be the result of the fruits of his talents or labor.[59] Rather, "[i]n a society dominated by reality television shows, YouTube, Twitter, and online social networking sites, the distinction between a 'celebrity' and a 'non-celebrity' seems to be an increasingly arbitrary one."[60]

Protecting Individual Autonomy and Personal Dignity

Another less prominent moral justification for the right of publicity is grounded in its ability to protect an individual's personal conception of the "self." One scholar has argued that the right of publicity implicates a person's interest in autonomous self-definition, which prevents others from interfering with the meanings and values that the public associates with her.[61] That argument posits that the value of celebrity stems not necessarily from the time and labor a person expends, but from "the messages conveyed by her associational decisions."[62] If a third party takes some control of the meaning

---

[56] 971 F.2d 1395, 1396 (9th Cir. 1992).
[57] id. at 1399.
[58] id.
[59] 830 F. Supp. 2d 785, 808 (N.D. Cal. 2011) (involving a class action lawsuit against Facebook for its advertising practice of "Sponsored Stories," which used members' names, profile pictures, and assertions that the people "liked" certain advertisers, along with the advertisers' logos, as part of other members' Facebook pages).
[60] id. For an argument that granting non-celebrities publicity rights is a "problematic expansion of the tort," see Alicia M. Hunt, Comment, *Everyone Wants to Be a Star: Extensive Publicity Rights for Noncelebrities Unduly Restrict Commercial Speech*, 95 Nw. U. L. Rev. 1605 (2001).
[61] See Mark P. McKenna, *The Right of Publicity and Autonomous Self-Definition*, 67 U. Pitt. L. Rev. 225, 282 (2005).
[62] See id.

associated with a celebrity, then the celebrity has to "live with that meaning and with what it says about her."[63]

Critics have given little credence to arguments justifying publicity rights that rely on autonomy and dignity.[64] It is arguable, however, that these justifications are premised upon a level of control over one's identity that is simply not realistic in a free and open society. Third parties routinely take some control over the meaning associated with celebrities. Magazines choose which photographs to publish; bloggers and journalists frame their articles around dominant narratives. Stepping into the public eye has long been associated with relinquishing some aspect of self-definition in this regard.

WHAT ACTUALLY JUSTIFIES THE RIGHT OF PUBLICITY?

While numerous moral rationales for the right of publicity have been asserted, careful analysis of those arguments demonstrates the serious flaws of those arguments. Ultimately it is fair to say that it is the naked economic interest in reserving the economic value of an individual's name and likeness as a property right for the individual that serves as the primary justification for the right. Because others are denied free use of a celebrity's name or likeness, the celebrity is in a position to sell either or both as a valuable asset.

In the abstract, nothing is inherently wrong or improper with such a rationale. When an individual is able to assert the property right in her name and likeness and disrupt the free flow of information and opinion, however, problems arise because the First Amendment right of free expression, for the most part, supersedes all but the most compelling competing interests. Courts have made some modifications to the right of publicity to take into account the public's interest in the free flow of information and opinion.[65] There can be little doubt that ultimately, these modifications, purportedly made "in the public interest," ultimately derive from the First Amendment right of free expression. In other words, but for creation of this sub-constitutional exception to the right of publicity for matters of public interest, the right would have to be held unconstitutional in such contexts. But when speakers disseminate the exact same information and opinion to the exact same audience in the form of commercial advertisements, First Amendment

---

[63] id. at 283. J. Thomas McCarthy articulates a similar argument by equating a person's identity to property, saying that "[p]erhaps nothing is so strongly intuited as the notion that my identity is mine – it is my property to control as I see fit." J. Thomas McCarthy, 1 The Rights of Publicity and Privacy § 2.1 (2d ed. 2009).
[64] See discussion *infra* at 68–69.
[65] See discussion *infra* at 68–69.

protections seem to quickly melt away, for no reason other than the speaker's commercial motivation. While historically such discrimination against commercially motivated expression regularly characterized First Amendment doctrine, there is a unique constitutional irony in the context of the right of publicity, in two ways. The first irony is that the competing interest being protected against commercially motivated speech – i.e., the right of publicity – has at its roots the same form of commercially motivated property interest. The second irony is that the speakers who usually benefit by the subconstitutional exception to the right of publicity for matters in the public interest – members of the press – are themselves motivated by commercial interests. On two grounds, then, refusal to recognize the superior First Amendment interest of commercial advertisers is inherently illogical and inconsistent with core First Amendment precepts.

The section that follows explores the ways in which the rights of publicity and free expression have intersected. This discussion will demonstrate how the judiciary's categorical rejection of First Amendment protections for commercial speech in the face of assertions of the right of publicity is justified by neither doctrine, theory, nor logic.

THE RIGHT OF PUBLICITY AND THE FIRST AMENDMENT COLLIDE

The right of publicity and the First Amendment are obvious adversaries. The former protects a listener's right to control what a speaker says, which inevitably tends to invade the latter's constitutionally protected right to communicate truthful information and opinion. The Supreme Court has failed to directly define the rules governing this clash,[66] leaving lower courts to rely upon incomplete, often confusing direction and to employ numerous convoluted tests in attempts to reconcile the two rights.[67] Through these efforts, however, a familiar dichotomy emerges. Speech deemed "newsworthy," or in some cases "expressive," is generally afforded (either directly or indirectly) broad constitutional protection in the face of right of publicity claims, whereas

---

[66] In the Supreme Court's only case addressing the right of publicity, it ruled narrowly on the facts of the case. The Court's language provides little guidance to subsequent courts addressing the conflict. See *Zacchini v. Scripps-Howard Broad. Co.*, 433 U.S. 562, 574–75 (1977) ("Wherever the line in particular situations is to be drawn between media reports that are protected and those that are not, we are quite sure that the First and Fourteenth Amendments do not immunize the media when they broadcast a performer's entire act without his consent.").

[67] See discussion *infra* at 73–82.

expression characterized as "commercial speech" has received much shorter shrift.[68] As this section shows, defendants are generally, and not surprisingly, eager to characterize their speech as a contribution to the debate over matters of public concern or as a communication having expressive value. However, they are much less willing to emphasize their economic motivations. The analysis proceeds to address how courts treat each of these types of speech in kind.

Even though right of publicity statutes across the country "present a crazy quilt of different responses at different times to different demands on the legislatures,"[69] a unifying commonality may be found in how their provisions automatically distinguish speech that is newsworthy or in the public interest from speech for commercial or trade purposes. California and New York, states with high volumes of cases on this subject, provide illustrative publicity rights schemes.

California

California recognizes a newsworthiness exemption and a public interest defense to claims asserting violations of common law publicity rights and statutory misappropriation, respectively. The California public interest defense under common law is similar to the defense applicable to a statutory claim.[70] California Civil Code section 3344(d) provides that "a use of a name, voice, signature, photograph, or likeness in connection with any news, public affairs, or sports broadcast or account, or any political campaign, shall not constitute a use for which consent is required."[71] Courts have construed this defense broadly,[72] in part because it exempts matters of both "news" and "public affairs." As the California Court of Appeals explained, limiting the defense only to topics that might be covered in "news" would "jeopardize society's right to know," because the court may impose liability for using a person's name or likeness in expressions about subjects that "do not relate to politics or public policy, and may not even be important, but are of

---

[68] See discussion *infra* at 82–83.
[69] See discussion *infra* at 78–79.
[70] McKinney v. Morris, No. B240830, 2013 WL 5617125, at *19 (Cal. Ct. App. Oct. 15, 2013) (dismissing plaintiff's cause of action for common law and statutory misappropriation for using her in a documentary that concerned a subject of widespread public interest); see also Stewart v. Rolling Stone LLC, 105 Cal. Rptr. 3d 98, 111 (Ct. App. 2010); Dora v. Frontline Video, Inc., 18 Cal. Rptr. 2d 790, 794 (Ct. App. 1993).
[71] Cal. Civ. Code § 3344(d) (West 2010) (emphasis added).
[72] McKinney, 2013 WL 5617125, at *19.

interest."[73] Thus, speech involving "public affairs" is protected in California, even when its content involves "something less important than news."[74]

In contrast, commercial use of the exact same information, such as in an advertisement, automatically removes the use from the scope of the statutory exception. For example, in *Abdul-Jabbar v. General Motors Corp.*, General Motors used NBA superstar Kareem Abdul-Jabbar's statistics and former name, Lew Alcindor, in a television commercial without his consent.[75] The Ninth Circuit held that "[w]hile Lew Alcindor's basketball record may be said to be 'newsworthy,' its use is not automatically privileged. [General Motors] used the information in the context of an automobile advertisement, not in a news or sports account."[76] Similarly, in *Fraley v. Facebook, Inc.*, Facebook's repackaging of members' activity in clicking to "like" certain content as sponsored stories with a commercial purpose removed the underlying actions from the newsworthiness privilege, even if they had newsworthy value.[77] The court noted that newsworthy material can still subject speakers to liability "when published for commercial rather than journalistic purposes."[78] Thus, the exact same information conveyed to the exact same audience automatically loses its "newsworthiness" protection for no reason other than the speaker's motivation to promote sales.

In addition to excluding categorically commercial advertisements from the "newsworthiness" protection, courts may now also choose to focus on whether the speech at issue constitutes a traditionally protected "broadcast or account." Although California courts had previously focused little attention on such a distinction, the Ninth Circuit in *In re NCAA* rejected both common law and

---

[73] See Dora, 18 Cal. Rptr. 2d at 794; see also *Eastwood v. Superior Court*, 198 Cal. Rptr. 342, 350 (Ct. App. 1983) ("The scope of the privilege extends to almost all reporting of recent events even though it involves the publication of a purely private person's name or likeness.").

[74] Dora, 18 Cal. Rptr. 2d at 794; see also *Doe v. Gangland Prod., Inc.*, 730 F.3d 946, 961 (9th Cir. 2013) (concluding that even if a documentary on gang activities was not "news" for the purpose of the statute, it fell within the public affairs exception).

[75] 85 F.3d 407, 409 (9th Cir. 1996); cf. *Jordan v. Jewel Food Stores, Inc.*, 743 F. 3d 509 (7th Cir. 2014) (reversing a district court's finding that a grocery store's page in a commemorative magazine issue, which used Michael Jordan's image without his consent, constituted non-commercial speech).

[76] Abdul-Jabbar, 85 F.3d at 416. The U.S. District Court for the Northern District of Ohio favorably cited this proposition in a case concerning Ohio's public affairs exception. See *Bosley v. Wildwett.com*, 310 F. Supp. 2d 914, 924 (N.D. Ohio 2004).

[77] 830 F. Supp. 2d 785, 805 (N.D. Cal. 2011); see also *Estate of Fuller v. Maxfield & Oberton Holdings, LLC*, 906 F. Supp. 2d 997, 1010-11 (N.D. Cal. 2012) (finding the use of a name "for purposes of selling and advertising" and "increasing sales" to constitute a commercial use beyond the scope of the newsworthiness exception).

[78] Fraley, 830 F. Supp. 2d at 805.

statutory defenses for using celebrity depictions in video games, stating that those defenses protected only "the act of publishing or reporting."[79] The Ninth Circuit reasoned that the defendant's video game did not "publish" or "report factual data" as a reference source, and was simply "a means by which users can play their own virtual football games."[80]

New York

In New York, the state's highest court long ago rejected the existence of any common law rights of privacy;[81] instead, only a statutory right of publicity exists. Sections 50 and 51 of New York's Civil Rights Law make it a misdemeanor to use a person's name or portrait without consent "for advertising purposes, or for the purposes of trade,"[82] and allow for any person whose name, portrait, picture, or voice is used without consent for these purposes to sue.[83] The New York Court of Appeals has repeatedly observed that these provisions are strictly limited to nonconsensual commercial appropriations – "'for advertising purposes or for the purposes of trade' only, and nothing more."[84] As a result, two exceptions have evolved: a newsworthiness exception and an "incidental use" exception for works of art and advertising produced in connection with a protected use.[85]

The newsworthiness exception applies liberally, not only to reports of political events but also to consumer interest stories.[86] For example, in

---

[79] *In re NCAA Student-Athlete Name & Likeness Licensing Litig.*, 724 F.3d 1268, 1282 (9th Cir. 2013).
[80] See id. at 1283. The court's preference for traditional reportage over entertaining speech illustrates its bias against profit-motivated, nontraditional speech. See infra Part III.B.1.
[81] See *Roberson v. Rochester Folding Box Co.*, 64 N.E. 442, 447–48 (N.Y. 1902).
[82] N.Y. Civ. Rights Law § 50 (McKinney 2012). The Restatement (Third) of Unfair Competition similarly characterizes the right of publicity tort in section 46 as appropriating the commercial value of a person's identity without permission by using the person's name, likeness, or other indicia of identity "for purposes of trade." Restatement (Third) of Unfair Competition § 46 (1995). The statement "[f]or purposes of trade" does not encompass using the person's identity in news reporting, commentary, entertainment, or works of fiction or nonfiction, or in advertising that is incidental to such uses. id. § 47. These exemptions reflect the fact that "[t]he use of a person's identity primarily for the purpose of communicating information or expressing ideas is not generally actionable as a violation of the person's right of publicity." id. § 47 cmt. c.
[83] N.Y. Civ. Rights Law § 51 (McKinney 2012).
[84] *Finger v. Omni Publ'ns Int'l, Ltd.*, 77 N.E.2d 141, 143 (N.Y. 1990) (citations and quotations omitted).
[85] See *Hoepker v. Kruger*, 200 F. Supp. 2d 340, 350 & n.16, 353 (S.D.N.Y. 2002) (calling this exception the "ancillary use" or "incidental use" exception).
[86] See *Finger*, 77 N.E.2d at 144.

Stephano v. News Group Publications, Inc., the court protected a defendant's use of a plaintiff's photograph in a column about clothing deals without the plaintiff's consent.[87] Even though the plaintiff agreed to model for one article only and the defendant might have had a commercial motivation, "the availability of the clothing displayed" was an "event or matter of public interest."[88] The court found the content of the column newsworthy; therefore, it was not subject to liability as a trade usage. The court held that a contrary rule "would unreasonably and unrealistically limit the exception to nonprofit or purely altruistic organizations which are not the only, or even the primary, source of information concerning newsworthy events and matters of public interest."[89] Moreover, the Court of Appeals did not want judges resolving questions of "newsworthiness," which are best left "to reasonable editorial judgment and discretion."[90]

The First Amendment similarly drives the "incidental use" exception to allow speakers to publicize their own protected communications.[91] As a result, courts protect the use of a plaintiff's photograph in promotional materials for a documentary about him as incidental,[92] but do not protect the use of a plaintiff's picture on the cover of an unrelated fictional book cover.[93] Thus, neither New York exception protects speech when courts find that the primary purpose for using the celebrity image is commercial in nature, regardless of the level of public interest involved. As the Court of Appeals stated, commercial entities "may not unilaterally neutralize or override the long-standing and significant statutory privacy protection by wrapping its advertising message in the cloak of public interest, however commendable the educational and informational value."[94]

---

[87] See 474 N.E.2d 580, 586 (N.Y. 1984).
[88] id. at 585. Notably, the defendant was not making a profit from what it chose to feature in the column. See id.
[89] id.
[90] *Finger*, 77 N.E.2d at 144. Simply because speech is presumably created and distributed for the purpose of making a profit does not confer upon it the title of "advertising" or "purposes of trade." See, e.g., *Time, Inc. v. Hill*, 385 U.S. 374, 397 (1967) (interpreting New York law and finding that because "books, newspapers, and magazines are published and sold for profit does not prevent them from being a form of expression whose liberty is safeguarded by the First Amendment" (quoting *Joseph Burstyn, Inc. v. Wilson*, 343 U.S. 495, 501–02 (1952))).
[91] See *Groden v. Random House, Inc.*, 61 F.3d 1045, 1050–51 (2d Cir. 1995) (internal quotation marks omitted).
[92] See, e.g., *Alfano v. NGHT, Inc.*, 623 F. Supp. 2d 355, 360 (E.D.N.Y. 2009).
[93] See, e.g., *Yasin v. Q-Boro Holdings, LLC*, No. 13259109, 2010 WL 1704889, at *2 (N.Y. Sup. Ct. Apr. 23, 2010) ("[T]he use of Yasin's image on the front cover of defendant's book is purely for marketing and trade purposes; solely as a means to attract customers and generate sales.").
[94] *Beverly v. Choices Women's Med. Ctr., Inc.*, 587 N.E.2d 275, 279 (N.Y. 1991).

Like California and New York, other states' statutory and common law publicity rights schemes exempt only so-called noncommercial uses from liability, such as uses related to news, public affairs, or sports broadcasts or accounts.[95] In this way, these statutory and doctrinal regimes reflect enmity toward commercial speech and, specifically, toward advertising.[96]

"Expressive" Speech Subjected to a Balancing Test

Moving down the hierarchy of protection, one finds "expressive" speech, which is subject to various balancing tests to determine its First Amendment worth relative to publicity rights. The evolution of courts' sloppy and often inconsistent tests for weighing the right of publicity against First Amendment rights can be traced back to the United States Supreme Court decision in *Zacchini v. Scripps-Howard Broadcasting Co.*[97] In a unique set of facts, petitioner, Hugo Zacchini, sought damages from a television station which broadcasted his human cannonball act, a fifteen-second performance in which he was shot from a cannon into a net roughly two-hundred feet away.[98] The Ohio Supreme Court held that the First Amendment privileged the broadcast as a matter of public interest.[99] The United States Supreme Court, however, rejected this view:

> Wherever the line in particular situations is to be drawn between media reports that are protected and those that are not, we are quite sure that the First and Fourteenth Amendments do not immunize the media when they broadcast a performer's entire act without his consent. The broadcast of a film of petitioner's entire act poses a substantial threat to the economic value of that performance.[100]

In other words, the Court recognized that the television station, without compensating Zacchini, reproduced the entire narrative giving value to his performance – beginning, middle, and end – thereby removing it from the

---

[95] See, e.g., Fla. Stat. Ann. § 540.08(4) (West 2007); 765 Ill. Comp. Stat. Ann. 1075/35(b)(2) (West 2014); Ind. Code Ann. § 32-36-1-1(c)(1)(B) (West 2009); Ohio Rev. Code Ann. § 2741.02 (D)(1) (West 2014).
[96] See, e.g., 765 Ill. Comp. Stat 1075/30; 42 Pa. Cons. Stat. Ann. § 8316(a) (West 2014); Tenn. Code Ann. § 47-25-1105(a) (West 2010). In Illinois, for example, a "commercial purpose" means holding out a person's identity in connection with selling a product or service, advertising, or fundraising. 765 Ill. Comp. Stat. 1075/5 (West 2014).
[97] 433 U.S. 562 (1977).
[98] id. at 563–64.
[99] *Zacchini v. Scripps-Howard Broad. Co.*, 351 N.E.2d 454, 461-62 (Ohio 1976), rev'd, 433 U.S. 562 (1977).
[100] *Zacchini*, 433 U.S. at 574–75.

scope of First Amendment protection. But the Supreme Court did not clearly articulate the limitation of the public interest exception in this case, nor did the Court clearly explicate a test for measuring future conflicts between publicity rights and the First Amendment. Instead, the Court decided *Zacchini* narrowly on the "entire act" conception and suggested that relevant interests should be weighed, providing more confusion than clarity for lower courts.[101] After *Zacchini*, several analytical frameworks have taken shape across federal and state courts to perform the balancing inquiry Zacchini seemingly demanded, including (1) the Transformative Use Test, (2) the Predominant Use Test, and (3) the *Rogers* Test.

Transformative Use Test

The Transformative Use Test, formulated by the California Supreme Court, weighs publicity rights and First Amendment interests by asking whether the use "adds significant creative elements so as to be transformed into something more than a mere celebrity likeness or imitation."[102] Only a transformative use can outweigh the interests of a person asserting his publicity rights, the court noted.[103] "[W]hen a work contains significant transformative elements, it is not only especially worthy of First Amendment protection, but it is also less likely to interfere with the economic interests protected by the right of publicity."[104] In devising the defense, the court emulated copyright law.[105] According to the court, copyright law was an apt body from which to draw because "both the First Amendment and copyright law have a common goal of encouragement of free expression and creativity, the former by protecting such expression from government interference, the latter by protecting the creative fruits of intellectual and artistic labor."[106]

Courts subsequently applying the California Supreme Court's Transformative Use Test have relied on at least five factors in determining whether a use is sufficiently transformative to obtain First Amendment protection.[107] They have

---

[101] See, e.g., *Hart v. Elec. Arts, Inc.*, 717 F.3d 141, 152 (3d Cir. 2013) (noting that Zacchini "sets the stage for our analysis of three systematized analytical frameworks that have emerged as courts struggle with finding a standardized way for performing this balancing inquiry").
[102] See *Comedy III Prods., Inc. v. Gary Saderup, Inc.*, 21 P.3d 797, 799 (Cal. 2001).
[103] id. at 806–08.
[104] id. at 808.
[105] id. at 807.
[106] id. at 808. The Transformative Use Test in this way gives preference to the labor theory of justification for the right of publicity.
[107] *In re NCAA Student-Athlete Name & Likeness Licensing Litig.*, 724 F.3d 1268, 1274 (9th Cir. 2013).

looked to whether: (1) the celebrity likeness "is the very sum and substance of the work," (2) the work is the artist's creative expression, (3) the imitative elements predominate in the work, (4) the economic value is derived primarily from the celebrity's fame, and (5) the overall goal is to exploit a celebrity's fame.[108] On this basis, they have rejected as not sufficiently transformative t-shirts bearing a likeness of The Three Stooges,[109] video game avatars closely based on real singers,[110] college football players,[111] and a birthday card that mimicked a celebrity.[112] Yet, they have deemed as transformative comic book caricatures of celebrities[113] and video game avatars only apparently loosely based on real people.[114]

The exact relationship between this Transformative Use Test and a more general First Amendment defense is confusing, to say the least, because courts still reference the profit motivation inherent in the speech when they determine its worth. For example, when the Ninth Circuit in *Hoffman v. Capital Cities/ABC, Inc.* afforded full First Amendment protection, it conducted a traditional speech analysis and found that the speech at issue was "entitled to the full First Amendment protection awarded [to] noncommercial speech."[115] Although *Hoffman* addressed the Transformative Use Test in a footnote, it suggested that the test was inapplicable because the speaker in *Hoffman* was a magazine, not an artist.[116]

When the Los Angeles Superior Court afforded full First Amendment protection to the Call of Duty video game's use of an avatar resembling

---

[108] See id.
[109] Comedy III Prods., 106 P.3d at 811 ("[The artist's] undeniable skill is manifestly subordinated to the overall goal of creating literal, conventional depictions of The Three Stooges so as to exploit their fame. Indeed, were we to decide that [the] depictions were protected by the First Amendment, we cannot perceive how the right of publicity would remain a viable right other than in cases of falsified celebrity endorsements.").
[110] No Doubt v. Activision Publ'g, Inc., 122 Cal. Rptr. 3d 397, 411 (Ct. App. 2011) ("[T]he avatars perform rock songs, the same activity by which the band achieved and maintains its fame. Moreover, the avatars perform those songs as literal recreations of the band members.").
[111] In re NCAA, 724 F.3d at 1276; Hart v. Elec. Arts, Inc., 717 F.3d 141, 170 (3d Cir. 2013).
[112] Hilton v. Hallmark Cards, 599 F.3d 894, 911 (9th Cir. 2009).
[113] Winter v. DC Comics, 134 Cal. Rptr. 2d 634, 641 (Cal. 2003); see also ETW Corp. v. Jireh Publ'g, Inc., 332 F.3d 915, 938 (6th Cir. 2003) (finding that an artist's work combined images of a celebrity to describe a significant event in sports history and to convey a message about that event).
[114] Kirby v. Sega of Am., Inc., 50 Cal. Rptr. 3d 607, 616 (Ct. App. 2006) ("[The avatar] is more than a mere likeness or literal depiction of [the singer]."); Noriega v. Activision/Blizzard, Inc., No. BC551746, slip op. at 5 (Cal. Super. Ct. Oct. 27, 2014) ("The complex and multi-faceted [video] game is a product of defendant's own expression, with de minimis use of [the former Panama military dictator's] likeness.").
[115] 255 F.3d 1180, 1189 (9th Cir. 2001).
[116] See id. at 1184 n.2.

Manuel Noriega, it downplayed the video game company's economic interest on its way to finding the speech protected over the publicity right at issue.[117] In this way, the transformative use analytical framework operates as yet another means for elbowing out speech that is primarily commercially motivated in the traditional sense. The test offers a means for elevating only that profit motivated speech that has been creatively altered to the court's liking.[118]

Predominant Use Test

The Predominant Use Test is less subtle as to its intent to exclude protection for commercial speech. First articulated by the Missouri Supreme Court, the Predominant Use Test balances the rights at issue by distinguishing uses that predominantly exploit the commercial value of a celebrity's fame from uses that make expressive comments.[119] The court drew the language of the test from intellectual property litigator Mark Lee's law review article, in which he defended such an approach as "do[ing] justice to both the expressive and property interests" by protecting the "intellectual property that is being exploited by others" and permitting creative expression that makes meaningful comments.[120] The Missouri Supreme Court, sitting en banc, applied this test to find that the makers of a comic book used a hockey player's name predominantly in "a ploy to sell comic books and related products rather than an artistic or literary expression."[121] Under these circumstances, according to the court, "free speech must give way to the right of publicity."[122] The Missouri test constitutes an extremely problematic application of the public interest exception because its singular focus is profit motivation. If the predominant purpose of the speech is something other than conveying a judicially accepted expression, it receives no First Amendment protection.

Perhaps that is why a number of courts have rejected opportunities to employ the Predominant Use Test, even levying sharp criticism in its direction.[123] The Third Circuit described the test as "subjective at best, arbitrary at worst, and in either case calls upon judges to act as both impartial

---

[117] See *Noriega*, No. BC551746, slip op. at 5 n.3 ("Because the video game is transformative, economic considerations are not relevant.").
[118] See id. at 2 & n.2.
[119] *Doe v. TCI Cablevision*, 110 S.W.3d 363, 374 (Mo. 2003) (en banc).
[120] Lee, *supra* note 12, at 500.
[121] *Doe*, 110 S.W.3d at 374.
[122] id.
[123] See, e.g., *Hart v. Elec. Arts, Inc.*, 717 F.3d 141, 154 (3d Cir. 2013).

jurists and discerning art critics."[124] The Eastern District of Missouri managed to sidestep the test entirely in a subsequent case applying Missouri law.[125]

The Rogers Test

In contrast to the predominant use test, the *Rogers* test looks to the relationship between the celebrity image and the use of the celebrity's identity as a whole.[126] Also called the relatedness test or the restatement test,[127] the test's namesake case involved dancer-actress Ginger Rogers's suit against the producers and distributors of a film called Ginger and Fred for infringing her right of publicity and for violating the Lanham Act.[128] In *Rogers v. Grimaldi*, the Second Circuit dismissed Rogers's right of publicity claim because the title of the film was "clearly related to the content of the movie and [was] not a disguised advertisement for the sale of goods and services or a collateral commercial product."[129] The Sixth Circuit, in applying the *Rogers* test in a subsequent decision, linked the thrust of its relatedness inquiry to the Restatement (Third) of Unfair Competition.[130] Like the *Rogers* test, the Restatement frowns upon exploitative uses of celebrity identity. Under the Restatement, "use of a person's identity in news reporting, commentary, entertainment, works of fiction or nonfiction, or in advertising that is incidental to such uses" does not amount to a prohibited use,[131] but using a celebrity's identity "solely to attract attention" to something unrelated to that person can subject the user to liability.[132]

Modern evaluations of the *Rogers* test, including the Third and Ninth Circuits' evaluations, have opted not to apply it in the context of publicity rights claims because of its perceived misplaced goal: protecting the

---

[124] id.
[125] See *C.B.C. Distrib. & Mktg., Inc. v. Major League Baseball Advanced Media, L.P.*, 443 F. Supp. 2d 1077, 1096 n.26 (E.D. Mo. 2006).
[126] *Rogers v. Grimaldi*, 875 F.2d 994, 1004–05 (2d Cir. 1989); see *Hart*, 717 F.3d at 154.
[127] See *Hart*, 717 F.3d at 154 n.17.
[128] *Rogers*, 875 F.2d at 996–97.
[129] id. at 1004–05.
[130] *Parks v. LaFace Records*, 329 F.3d 437, 461 (6th Cir. 2003). Despite the Sixth Circuit's seeming adoption of the Rogers test in Parks, the court opted to apply the Transformative Use Test within the same year. *ETW Corp. v. Jireh Publ'g, Inc.*, 332 F.3d 915, 936 (6th Cir. 2003) (noting that the transformative elements test adopted by the Supreme Court of California "will assist us in determining where the proper balance lies between the First Amendment" and Tiger Woods's intellectual property rights).
[131] Restatement (Third) of Unfair Competition §§ 46–47 (1995).
[132] id. § 47 cmt. c.

consumer from confusion, rather than protecting the celebrity.[133] Although these recent cases are trending more towards the Transformative Use Test, the lack of clarity regarding the nature in which constitutional First Amendment rights are balanced against celebrities' pecuniary interests in publicity rights remains troubling.

COMMERCIAL SPEECH AS A FIRST AMENDMENT DEFENSE

Up to this point, the chapter's analysis has examined the most common First Amendment or First Amendment-like defenses for escaping liability when speakers are accused of infringing on publicity rights.[134] Yet, one defense is clearly absent from the discussion. Whether resulting from defendants' uneasiness in confronting statutory and common law animosity toward commercial speech, or resulting from their sheer ignorance of the modern version of the commercial speech doctrine, defendants are not seeking to raise commercial speech arguments to protect their free expression rights.[135] To the contrary, defendants usually tout their speech's expressive value and ask courts to characterize it as noncommercial.[136] And courts are often willing to find

---

[133] See *In re NCAA Student-Athlete Name & Likeness Licensing Litig.*, 724 F.3d 1268, 1280 (9th Cir. 2003); *Hart v. Elec. Arts, Inc.*, 717 F.3d 154, 158 (3d Cir. 013).

[134] See discussion *supra* at 72–73.

[135] Despite the 1677 cases Westlaw returned in winter 2014 with the search term, "right of publicity," a subsequent search using both the terms "commercial speech" and "right of publicity" yielded only ninety-eight cases (5.8 percent of right of publicity cases). Of those cases, roughly twenty affirmatively found the speech in question to be commercial in nature, but only one case found the speech at issue to be protected by the First Amendment. Even that case did not couch its holding in commercial speech reasoning. See *Hebrew Univ. of Jerusalem v. Gen. Motors*, 903 F. Supp. 2d 932, 942 (C.D. Cal. 2012). In *Hebrew Univ. of Jerusalem*, the U.S. District Court for the Central District of California considered a university's claim of exclusive control over Albert Einstein's name and likeness as a beneficiary under his will. id. at 932–33. Noting in a footnote that General Motors's speech was commercial speech protected "to some extent," the court proceeded to find that the university had no right of publicity claim. id. at 941 n.7. But the court did not anchor its holding in commercial speech reasoning. Instead, it prohibited the action by capping the maximum duration for claiming infringement of one's right of publicity at fifty years. id. at 942.

[136] Compare *Yeager v. Cingular Wireless LLC*, 673 F. Supp. 2d 1089, 1099 (E.D. Cal. 2009), with *Joe Dickerson & Assocs. v. Dittmar*, 34 P.3d 995, 1003 (Colo. 2001) (en banc). In *Dickerson*, a convicted felon plaintiff had no publicity claim against a detective agency that touted its role in her investigation and prosecution. *Dickerson*, 34 P.3d at 1004. The agency's use of her name in its advertising newsletter "related to a matter of public concern" and was "primarily noncommercial" in nature. id. In *Yeager*, however, an emergency preparedness pamphlet that used the name of the plaintiff, a legendary test pilot, was "not purely informational in nature" and was "properly characterized as commercial speech." *Yeager*, 673 F. Supp. 2d at 1097, 1099.

speech to be noncommercial, usually with seemingly little analysis. In fact, the paucity of judicial decisions applying the Supreme Court's famed four-part *Central Hudson* test to determine the appropriate protection for speech relative to publicity rights claims is astounding.[137] Until very recently, courts in near universality avoided analyzing the juncture of commercial speech and publicity rights altogether.[138] Chief Judge Alex Kozinski poignantly characterized courts' circumvention of binding Supreme Court precedent in his dissent in *White v. Samsung Electronics*, the case brought by television game show personality Vanna White.[139] "The Supreme Court didn't set out the *Central Hudson* test for its health," he wrote.[140] Furthermore, he stated:

> Maybe applying the test would have convinced the majority to change its mind; maybe going through the factors would have shown that its rule was too broad, or the reasons for protecting White's "identity" too tenuous. But we should not thumb our nose at the Supreme Court by simply refusing to apply its test.[141]

As the following section will demonstrate, modern First Amendment jurisprudence not only demands that courts apply *Central Hudson*; it also prescribes a number of normative and doctrinal ways in which commercial speech-based arguments should invalidate publicity rights claims.

---

[137] In a search of cases during winter 2014 citing *Central Hudson Gas & Electric Corp. v. Public Service Commission*, 447 U.S. 557 (1980), only thirty-six cases contained the terms "right of publicity" or "publicity rights." In publicity rights cases, when courts did find the speech at issue to be "commercial," it was unprotected. See, e.g., *Bosley v. Wildwett.com*, 310 F. Supp. 2d 914, 928–29 (N.D. Ohio 2004); see also *White v. Samsung Elecs. Am., Inc.*, 971 F.2d 1395, 1399 (9th Cir. 1992); *Yeager*, 673 F. Supp. 2d at 1097; *Herman Miller, Inc. v. A. Studio S.L.R.*, No. 1:04-CV-781, 2006 WL 13079404, at *9–10 (W.D. Mich. May 9, 2006). Most of the speech was deemed to be noncommercial, largely without thorough analysis. See, e.g., *ETW Corp. v. Jireh Publ'g, Inc.*, 332 F.3d 915, 925 (6th Cir. 2003) (protecting expressive speech); *Cardtoons, L.C. v. Major League Baseball Players Ass'n*, 95 F.3d 959, 970 (10th Cir. 1996) (protecting expressive speech); *Lane v. Random House, Inc.*, 985 F. Supp. 141, 152 (D.D.C. 1995) (protecting incidental speech); *Rogers v. Grimaldi*, 695 F. Supp. 112, 120–21 (S.D.N.Y. 1988) (protecting expressive speech); *Taylor v. Nat'l Broad. Co.*, No. BC110922, 1994 WL 762226 (Cal. Super. Ct. Sept. 29, 1994) (protecting expressive speech).

[138] See *Jordan v. Jewel Food Stores, Inc.*, 743 F.3d 509 (7th Cir. 2014); *Dryer v. Nat'l Football League*, No. 09-2182 (PAM/ FLN), slip op. (D. Minn. Oct. 10, 2014).

[139] *White v. Samsung Elecs. Am., Inc.*, 989 F.2d 1512 (Kozinski, J., dissenting).

[140] id. at 1520.

[141] id. Judge Kozinski's disdain for his court's reverence of publicity rights is further evident in *Wendt v. Host Int'l*, 197 F.3d 1284, 1288–89 (9th Cir. 1999) (Kozinski, J., dissenting) ("[W]e again let the right of publicity snuff out creativity. We pass up yet another opportunity to root out this weed. Instead, we feed it Miracle-Gro.").

ADDING A COMMERCIAL SPEECH PERSPECTIVE: WHAT THE MODERN LAW OF COMMERCIAL SPEECH TELLS US ABOUT THE RIGHT OF PUBLICITY, AND VICE VERSA

At the outset of the First Amendment analysis, it should be emphasized what is *not* being argued here. No one is claiming that the First Amendment protection of commercial speech categorically and absolutely supersedes the right of publicity. In situations such as the one involved in *Zacchini*, for example,[142] it is at least plausible to believe that the competing free speech interest, whether in the form of commercial or noncommercial speech, should give way. Determining exactly when the commercial speech right does or does not take precedence over the right of publicity is beyond the scope of this analysis. All this chapter is claiming is that for a variety of reasons, at least when truthful commercial speech is involved, the commercial speech interest should receive the same level of First Amendment protection afforded to traditionally protected noncommercial speech.

The results in modern publicity rights cases do not always reflect this conclusion. If there is one recurring theme in publicity rights law, it is that courts accommodate First Amendment interests for so-called newsworthy uses of names or likenesses, but routinely and summarily penalize purely commercial uses as violations of the victims' common law or statutory rights. Such summarily negative treatment of commercial speech, however, appears more suited to the constitutional law of over forty years ago than it does to today's First Amendment world. In the period since the Supreme Court first provided a significant level of constitutional protection to commercial speech,[143] the degree of commercial speech protection has grown exponentially. Indeed, the government has failed to win a single case involving a challenge to governmental suppression of truthful commercial speech at the Supreme Court in over twenty-five years. And in that time, the Court has imposed substantial limitations on governmental power to control commercial expression.[144] One would think that at the very least, courts acting in the third decade of the twenty-first century would be far less negatively cavalier in their treatment of

---

[142] *Zacchini v. Scripps-Howard Broad. Co.*, 433 U.S. 562 (1977).
[143] *Va. State Bd. of Pharmacy v. Va. Citizens Consumer Council, Inc.*, 425 U.S. 748, 763 (1976).
[144] See, e.g., *Thompson v. W. States Med. Ctr.*, 535 U.S. 357, 371–72 (2002) (rejecting regulations under *Central Hudson's* final prong, finding that alternative, less restrictive regulations on commercial speech were available); *Greater New Orleans Broad. Ass'n, Inc. v. United States*, 527 U.S. 173, 188–89 (1999); *44 Liquormart, Inc. v. Rhode Island*, 517 U.S. 484, 507 (1996) (plurality opinion); *Rubin v. Coors Brewing Co.*, 514 U.S. 476, 490–91 (1995).

commercial speech than they have consistently been in expounding the law of the right of publicity.[145] As the following analysis will show, simply applying well-established commercial speech doctrine would present enormous problems for such summary exclusion, and as a result, would necessarily alter existing law.

Even more importantly, applying current commercial speech theory to the current law of the right of publicity underscores important defects in the entire basis of that theory. As has been made clear in earlier chapters, despite the fact that commercial speech today receives significant First Amendment protection, in certain areas the level of that protection is undoubtedly distinctly lower than the level of protection extended to noncommercial speech.[146] Yet application of the foundational theory of modern commercial speech doctrine to the right of publicity underscores the starkly irrational nature of the rationale for such reduced protection. Simply put, commercial speech receives reduced protection for no reason other than the profit motivation behind it.[147] As established publicity right doctrine demonstrates, however, equally profit-motivated speech – that of commercially driven media, which does not directly promote purchase of a particular commercial product or service – receives full First Amendment protection. Thus, the intersection of publicity rights with modern commercial speech law reveals a great deal about both the right of publicity and the current state of commercial speech protection. On the one hand, this intersection reveals that commercial speech protection – even in its current doctrinal form – presents a far greater problem for the right of publicity than courts enforcing that right currently understand. Commercially motivated right of publicity claims cannot so easily overcome commercial First Amendment protection.[148] On the other hand, by applying commercial speech doctrine to the right of publicity, the fundamental flaws underlying reduced protection for commercial speech in the first place can be highlighted.

In developing these theoretical arguments, I in no way claim to resolve all conceivable conflicts between the right of publicity and the First Amendment. As *Zacchini* illustrates, not even the traditional media are constitutionally

---

[145] See discussion *supra* at 71–82.
[146] Compare *United States v. Alvarez*, 132 S. Ct. 2537, 2445–47 (2012) (holding as unconstitutional the Stolen Valor Act, which criminalized false claims of receiving military decorations), with *Cent. Hudson Gas & Elec. Corp. v. Pub. Serv. Comm'n*, 447 U.S. 557, 563 (1980) ("The government may ban forms of communication more likely to deceive the public than to inform it.").
[147] See discussion *infra* at 87–91.
[148] See discussion *supra* at 71–82.

insulated from all liability under the right of publicity,[149] and I take no position on the correctness of those decisions. The goal here, rather, is to justify a type of "most favored nation" status for commercial invasions of the right of publicity: whatever level of First Amendment protection that traditionally protected media would receive for infringing the right of publicity, commercial advertisers should be deemed equally protected.

To explain the approach I advocate, I employ as my hypothetical baseline a very limited form of a publicity rights violation: a commercial advertiser's use – without permission from the individual in question – of an individual's name and/or likeness to truthfully inform the public that the individual uses the advertiser's product. To be sure, under current doctrine such a commercial advertisement would constitute a constitutionally unprotected violation of either common law or statutory rights of publicity. But my goal here is to distinguish it, for First Amendment purposes, from a variety of other hypothetical violations of publicity rights: appropriation of another's commercial work product as in *Zacchini*,[150] a knowingly or recklessly false assertion about an individual, and any violation of an individual's physically defined privacy (for example, photos secretly taken in traditionally private areas). The analysis here makes no claims for First Amendment protection in any of these contexts. Rather, the point to be made here is that, as a matter of both normative First Amendment theory and accepted First Amendment doctrine, the constitutional guarantee of free expression should trump any assertion of a right of publicity in our baseline situation.

I first consider the fundamental theoretical flaws in the commercial speech doctrine's definitional divide between commercial and noncommercial expression, and then apply that critique to the right of publicity context. I then consider how the right of publicity fares under existing commercial speech doctrine. My analysis concludes that to the extent that commercial speech doctrine supports a reduced level of First Amendment protection for truthful commercial advertising, the existing doctrine is grounded in categorically insupportable rationales and must be rejected in favor of a more principled basis of constitutional analysis. I further conclude that even if we are to suspend disbelief and assume the validity of the current constitutional framework, the way in which publicity rights doctrine summarily rejects First Amendment protection for commercial speech is constitutionally improper, purely as a doctrinal matter.

---

[149] See *Zacchini v. Scripps-Howard Broad. Co.*, 433 U.S. 562, 575 (1977).
[150] *Zacchini*, 433 U.S. at 575.

PROFIT MOTIVATION AND THE FIRST AMENDMENT: THE FLAWED THEORETICAL FOUNDATION OF EXISTING COMMERCIAL SPEECH DOCTRINE

Evaluating Rationales for Stratifying Speech

As already demonstrated, under well-established publicity rights doctrine, a sharp line divides *prima facie* violations by commercial advertisers from *prima facie* violations by traditionally recognized media.[151] It is black letter law that *prima facie* violations by traditional media are protected in most cases, if not directly by the First Amendment, then by a First Amendment-inspired common law or statutory "newsworthiness" privilege.[152] Commercial advertisements, by comparison, are automatically vulnerable to liability, receiving neither First Amendment nor common law protection.[153] Although this stark division ignores the substantial level of First Amendment protection currently afforded to classic commercial speech,[154] in the generic sense this stratification in protection levels accurately reflects a dichotomy firmly established in the Supreme Court's First Amendment jurisprudence.

After the Supreme Court first extended First Amendment protection to commercial advertising in 1976,[155] it made clear that commercial speech is deserving of only "a limited measure of protection, commensurate with its subordinate position in the scale of First Amendment values."[156] Under the four-part *Central Hudson* test,[157] at least in the early years of its application,[158] the Court was able to condone numerous restrictions on commercial speech that would almost certainly have been deemed impermissible in the world of noncommercial speech protection.[159] Thus, even

---

[151] See, e.g., discussion *supra* at 60–63.
[152] See discussion *supra* at 72–74.
[153] See, e.g., discussion *supra* at 60–63.
[154] See discussion *supra* at 84.
[155] *Va. State Bd. of Pharmacy v. Va. Citizens Consumer Council, Inc.*, 425 U.S. 748, 763 (1976). Note that the following description of the development of modern commercial speech doctrine appears, in a variety of forms, at various points in this book. I repeat it here, however, for purposes of the completeness of the analysis.
[156] *Ohralik v. Ohio State Bar Ass'n*, 436 U.S. 447, 456 (1978).
[157] *Cent. Hudson Gas & Elec. Corp. v. Pub. Serv. Comm'n*, 447 U.S. 557, 566 (1980).
[158] In more recent years, this very same test has received a far more protective application.
[159] See, e.g., *Metromedia, Inc. v. San Diego*, 453 U.S. 490, 507–11 (1981) (deferring to the city's judgment in holding that an ordinance prohibiting billboards met *Central Hudson* requirements). In the years between *Virginia State Board of Pharmacy* and *Central Hudson*, the level of protection that the Court extended to commercial speech was also quite limited. See, e.g., *Friedman v. Rogers*, 440 U.S. 1, 12–14 (1979); *Ohralik*, 436 U.S. at 447.

though publicity rights doctrine pervades an almost cavalier dismissal of commercial speech that strangely and incorrectly understates even its most modest level of First Amendment protection in the post-*Virginia State Board* era,[160] courts enforcing publicity rights are surely accurate in their stratification of First Amendment concern on the basis of context. This stratification occurs when courts consider whether the alleged violation appears in a commercial advertisement promoting sale or in a more traditional medium of expression, such as a book, newspaper, or television or radio program. What makes no sense purely as a matter of First Amendment theory, however, is the stratification itself. In this sense, applying the commercial speech doctrine to the right of publicity tells us considerably more about problems with the commercial speech doctrine than it tells us about problems with the right of publicity.

In light of the Supreme Court's established definition of commercial speech as speech that "does no more than propose a commercial transaction,"[161] understanding the logic implicit in the Court's commercial/noncommercial distinction requires employing a process of reverse engineering. It is necessary to glean from the distinction some principled basis, grounded in acceptable premises of free speech theory, which justifies the protective dichotomy the Court has drawn between commercial and noncommercial expression. Such an analysis requires us to ask, in short, why, as a matter of the theory of free expression, commercial speech is less deserving of First Amendment protection than noncommercial expression.

In answering this query, it is important at the outset to note that the Court's distinction does not turn on the subject or content of the expression in question.[162] The expression's impact on the safety or effectiveness of a commercial service or product – as does much commercial advertising – is irrelevant to the distinction.[163] As long as the speaker is not motivated to promote commercial sale, under the Court's definition, the speech is not

---

[160] See discussion *supra* at 86–87.
[161] *Va. State Bd. of Pharmacy v. Va. Citizens Consumer Council, Inc.*, 425 U.S. 748, 776 (1976) (Stewart, J., concurring). In reality, the inquiry is somewhat more complex. But ultimately, it comes down to some sort of focus on commercial motivation. See *Bolger v. Youngs Drug Prods. Corp.*, 463 U.S. 60, 66–67 (1983) (setting up a three-factor test to determine whether speech is to be deemed commercial). For an example of how complex the inquiry can become, see *Kasky v. Nike, Inc.*, 45 P.3d 243 (Cal. 2002). For a detailed discussion of *Bolger*, see Martin H. Redish, *Product Health Claims and the First Amendment: Scientific Expression and the Twilight Zone of Commercial Speech*, 43 Vand. L. Rev. 1433 (1990).
[162] See generally *Va. State Bd. of Pharmacy*, 425 U.S. at 776.
[163] See id.

"commercial" and therefore does not deserve the reduced level of constitutional protection afforded to that expressive category.[164] This is so, regardless of the subject or content of the expression involved. For example, as noted in earlier chapters, Ralph Nader's attacks on the Chevrolet Corvair's safety are not considered to be commercial speech,[165] even though they concern the merits of a commercially sold product. But General Motors' defenses of its product in response are considered to be commercial speech because they are part and parcel of a promotion of sale.[166] Nothing matters but the speaker's motivation, as the court so determines it.[167]

What is the logic behind such an entirely motivationally based distinction? Surely it cannot turn on the value of the expression because the speech of both Nader and General Motors concerns the exact same issue. Nor can it be grounded in some *ex ante* presumption that those attacking a commercial product or service tell the truth while those advocating purchases lie, because no factual basis supports either position. Is it, as Robert Post has suggested, that commercial speech cannot be deemed protected "public discourse" because it "should be understood as an effort ... simply to sell products" and not an effort "to engage public opinion"?[168] For several reasons, this line of thought is sorely misguided. Initially, it ignores the basis of the listener-centric perspective described in

---

[164] See id.
[165] See Ralph Nader, *Unsafe at Any Speed: The Designed-In Dangers of the American Automobile* (1965).
[166] Cf. *Kasky*, 45 P.3d at 258–60. The California Supreme Court reasoned that Nike's statements were commercial speech "[b]ecause in the statements at issue here Nike was acting as a commercial speaker, because its intended audience was primarily the buyers of its products, and because the statements consisted of factual representations about its own business operations." id. at 259.
[167] See also Ronald J. Krotoszynski, Jr., *Into the Woods: Broadcasters, Bureaucrats, and Children's Television Programming*, 45 Duke L.J. 1193, 1217–18 (1996) (discussing Andy Warhol's Campbell's soup cans and arriving at the conclusion that "it is impossible to maintain a viable theory of commercial speech without substantial reliance on an intent-based test").
[168] Robert C. Post, *The Constitutional Status of Commercial Speech*, 48 UCLA L. Rev. 1, 18 (2000). At another point in his analysis, Post asserts that his proposed dichotomy "is not ultimately a judgment about the motivations of particular persons, but instead about the social significance of a certain kind of speech." id. at 12. However, the reason he believes that commercial speech lacks sufficient "social significance" is "because we most naturally understand persons who are advertising products for sale as seeking to advance their commercial interests rather than as participating in the public life of the nation." id. Hence, we have come full circle because Post defines "social significance" in terms of speaker motivation. id. For a more detailed critique of Post's theory, see Martin H. Redish, *The Adversary First Amendment: Free Expression and the Foundations of American Democracy* 43–74 (Standford, CA: Stanford University Press, 2013).

Chapter 1. The participants *receiving* the information, opinion, and advocacy enrich that public discourse as much as those who contribute to the process.[169] This should hardly be a controversial assertion.[170] Thus, if only from the listener-centric perspective, reducing or excluding First Amendment protection for profit-motivated commercial speech contravenes key premises of First Amendment theory.[171] If value lies in information receipt, then what possible difference can the speaker's motivation make? Whether the speaker is Mother Theresa, Standard Oil, or Darth Vader, the information and opinion conveyed can play an equally legitimate role in shaping the citizenry's views, thoughts, and positions and, in so doing, further the democratic system's operation and the individual citizens' intellectual growth. Thus, once one recognizes the importance and value of an expression's receipt,[172] any distinction premised on the speaker's motivation is rendered completely incoherent.

Although that point alone should sufficiently demonstrate the wholly vacuous and misguided nature of Post's theory, other equally dispositive reasons support categorically rejecting his arguments. Even if we suspend disbelief on the speaker-recipient dichotomy and accept a theory favoring speech expressed for the purpose of contributing to public discourse, Post's theory remains flawed because it disregards speech's potential to reflect multiple motives. He denies that a speaker may speak for the purpose of advocating the sale of a product *and* for the purpose of affecting public opinion, when absolutely no basis to support such an assumption exists.[173] The commercial viability of books, movies, and even now video games

---

[169] See Alexander Meiklejohn, *Political Freedom: The Constitutional Powers of the People* 42 (1965).

[170] Indeed, some respected scholars have grounded their theories of the First Amendment on the assumption that the only relevant consideration for purposes of First Amendment protection is the listener, not the speaker. See id. at 56–57. Although this theory seriously understates the First Amendment benefit to the speaker, it surely is correct in recognizing the constitutional value to the recipient of expression. At a later point in his scholarship, Post recognized the First Amendment value of commercial speech in its conveyance of information about commercial products and services. See Post, *supra* note 168, at 28. The level of protection he extends such expression, however, is still reduced because of its failure to contribute directly to public discourse. See id. at 27.

[171] See Chapter 1, *supra*.

[172] See, e.g., *Va. State Bd. of Pharmacy v. Va. Citizens Consumer Council, Inc.*, 425 U.S. 748, 763 (1976) ("[A] particular consumer's interest in the free flow of commercial information ... may be as keen, if not keener by far, than his interest in the day's most urgent political debate."); see also *Edenfield v. Fane*, 507 U.S. 761, 767 (1993) ("The commercial marketplace, like other spheres of our social and cultural life, provides a forum where ideas and information flourish.").

[173] See Post, *supra* note 168, at 27.

proves quite the opposite. Consider *Jordan v. Jewel Food Stores, Inc.*, a right of publicity district court case in which a grocery store designed a page for a Sports Illustrated commemorative issue devoted to celebrating Michael Jordan.[174] The grocery store's congratulatory page included both its logo and a play on words with its slogan.[175] Even though one could affirmatively distinguish the page's purpose from other traditional means of advocating product sales,[176] United States District Judge Gary Feinerman wrote that to ascribe an "economic motivation" to a for-profit corporation like Jewel "is to state a truism."[177] The Seventh Circuit, although it reversed Judge Feinerman's commercial speech determination, likewise "recognize[d] the obvious: that Jewel had something to gain by conspicuously joining the chorus of congratulations on the much-anticipated occasion of Jordan's induction into the Basketball Hall of Fame."[178] Post, in comparison, somehow manages to ignore this truth. Finally, even if we ignore the fatal problem of ascribing to a speaker a single motivation for purposes of evaluating Post's argument, the fact remains that no obvious evidentiary basis exists on which to determine a speaker's dominant motive.[179]

As a result of all of these flaws, Post's theory dangerously invites judges to abuse the process, allowing them to punish speakers whom they dislike by concluding that the dominant motive underlying their speech is something other than an effort to contribute to public discourse. Any one of these flaws, standing alone, should sufficiently dispose of Post's theory. But when the dust settles, Post's theory is fatally flawed because it turns exclusively on the speaker's motivation in speaking – an inquiry made in no other area of free speech law. Yet, speaker motivation inherently and unavoidably lies at the core of the Court's doctrinally embodied definition of commercial speech.[180] The conclusion is inescapable, then, that the Court's speaker-motivation basis for reducing commercial speech protection is fatally misguided.

---

[174] 851 F. Supp. 2d 1102, 1104 (N.D. Ill. 2012), rev'd, 743 F.3d 509 (7th Cir. 2014).
[175] id.
[176] id. at 1109.
[177] id. at 1111.
[178] *Jordan v. Jewel Food Stores, Inc.*, 743 F.3d 509, 520 (7th Cir. 2014).
[179] In *Jewel*, Judge Feinerman identified this point when he noted how the conclusion regarding whether speech is commercial "rests in part on judgments regarding how reasonable readers would view the page." *Jewel*, 851 F. Supp. 2d at 1111. When critical data are consumer surveys and psychological analyses, however, such determinations quickly regress toward battles of the experts.
[180] See discussion *infra* at 93–99.

SORRELL AND THE RIGHT OF PUBLICITY

As demonstrated in prior chapters, *Sorrell v. IMS Health, Inc.* adds a surreal quality to the Court's commercial speech jurisprudence.[181] In that case, the Court subjected a law penalizing commercial speech, but not noncommercial speech, to strict scrutiny because the law discriminated among speakers, favoring non-manufacturer expression regarding doctors' prescribing practices over drug manufacturer expression concerning identical subjects.[182] The Court wrote that "[t]he law on its face burdens disfavored speech by disfavored speakers."[183] Because the law censored only drug manufacturers' speech, it went "beyond mere content discrimination, to actual viewpoint discrimination."[184] But in so holding, the Court completely ignored the fact that its own commercial speech doctrine commits the identical act of invidious discrimination: the exact same expression receives different levels of protection, solely on the basis of the speaker's commercial motivation. In effect, the Court (to be sure, without knowing it) appears to have rendered its own preexisting doctrine unconstitutional. The consequence of the Court's protective dichotomy between commercial and noncommercial speech is unavoidable: the very same information or opinion, conveyed to the exact same audience, receives more or less protection, solely because of the speaker's motivation.[185]

Applying *Sorrell*'s holding to publicity rights further demonstrates the invidious discrimination inherent in some aspects of modern commercial speech doctrine. As a preliminary matter, publicity rights offer perhaps the primary area of law in which one can argue that the level of constitutional protection indeed turns entirely on the speaker's economic purpose.[186] To the extent that one can rationalize publicity rights as a form of unjust enrichment, providing an economic advantage to the speaker-violator that rightfully belongs to the victim,[187] the doctrine arguably makes sense only when financial gain is the speaker's purpose for using the victim's name or likeness. But even in this context, competing unjust enrichment concerns should not automatically outbalance free speech interests. *Sorrell* proceeds on the implicit premise that a speaker's commercial motivation for expression does not negatively impact the level of First Amendment protection that the Court

---

[181] 131 S. Ct. 2653, 2656 (2011). For a more detailed discussion of *Sorrell*, see Chapter 1, *supra*.
[182] See *Sorrell*, 131 S. Ct. at 2667.
[183] id. at 2663.
[184] id. (internal quotation marks omitted).
[185] Compare *Yeager v. Cingular Wireless LLC*, 673 F. Supp. 2d 1089, 1099 (E.D. Cal. 2008), with *Joe Dickerson & Assocs. v. Dittmar*, 34 P.3d 995, 1004 (Colo. 2001) (en banc).
[186] See discussion *supra* at 73–77.
[187] See discussion *supra* at 68–70.

extends to that speech.[188] Because the value of speech may be significant regardless of the speaker's motive, and fully protected expression can be restricted only to further a compelling interest, it is by no means clear that the economic interest in preventing unjust enrichment for a victim of infringed publicity rights trumps the speaker's First Amendment interests.

Society can suppress fully protected expressions only when doing so would prevent a threat of imminent violence or other form of extreme harm.[189] If we proceed on the premise that commercial advertising deserves full First Amendment protection because no principled basis can distinguish it from fully protected categories of expression, then a compelling interest must support any burden on commercial expression. And it is difficult to imagine that the interest in avoiding unjust enrichment constitutes such an interest. For example, the concern in avoiding unjust enrichment pales in comparison to a concern in protecting the public's health. It is nothing more than an individual's economic concern, and in that sense, it does not differ from economically motivated commercial speech. At the very least, under the analysis advocated here, a court enforcing the right of publicity – certainly in the context of the posited baseline hypothetical[190] – would struggle to reconcile competing interests within the framework of a compelling interest structure. If there is one thing we can be sure that courts enforcing the right of publicity have never done, it is expending any effort to perform such a difficult weighing function. To the contrary, when commercial speech interests are involved, courts have universally failed to consider any possible competing First Amendment interests.

As the following section demonstrates, however, there are more persuasive reasons to invalidate right of publicity claims, even when pure commercial speech is involved. The simple fact is this: Excluding commercial speech from full First Amendment protection constitutes unconstitutionally underinclusive discrimination among constitutionally similar categories of expression.

THE IRRATIONAL DISTINCTION BETWEEN FORMS OF PROFIT MOTIVATION

Although right of publicity cases categorically exclude protection for commercial speech, they do not draw a strict dichotomy, for purposes of First Amendment (or at least First Amendment-like) protection, between those

---

[188] See *Sorrell*, 131 S. Ct. at 2665.
[189] See, e.g., *Brandenburg v. Ohio*, 385 U.S. 444, 447 (1969) (per curiam).
[190] Recall that my baseline hypothetical includes only a commercial advertiser's use of a person's name and/or likeness, without consent, to convey truthful information about that person's use of the advertiser's product.

motivated by financial gain and those who act out of purely altruistic purposes. Nor do these cases formally distinguish between those speakers concerned with profits and those concerned with promoting noncommercial types of self-interest. Rather, courts enforcing publicity rights draw speaker distinctions between those who use names or likenesses as part of commercial advertisements and those who use names or likenesses in more traditional profit-motivated communicative media.[191] In both situations, communicators seek to make a profit. Furthermore, we can even assume, for purposes of argument, that the exact same information is communicated to the exact same audience. For example, if one says that Tom Cruise drives a BMW, the informational impact is the same, regardless of which of the two profit-making expressive forms conveys the communication. Yet, under long-accepted commercial speech doctrine, when this information is conveyed in an advertisement promoting sales of BMW, it receives less constitutional protection, and in publicity rights cases, none at all.[192] In the context of publicity rights, then, use of a name or likeness in commercial advertisements receive absolutely no protection, whereas use of a name or likeness in profit-making traditional media receives virtually absolute protection.[193] Thus, the attempt to justify this distinction fails the requirements of the rationalist-centric model, described in Chapter 1.[194]

The basis for constitutionally distinguishing between the two categories of expression for publicity rights is even weaker than the basis for differentiating between profit-motivated and non-profit-motivated expression, despite the fact that even that distinction is itself illogical and unjustified on the basis of any principled application of free expression theory.[195] Here, *both* expressive categories are motivated by profit. As Justice Brennan once perceptively noted, the fact that information comes in the form of an advertisement is no different, for First Amendment purposes, from "the fact that newspapers and books are sold."[196] But this insight, brilliant in its simplicity and obviousness, has somehow been lost in the shuffle of time and the shifting sands of constitutional doctrine.[197]

---

[191] Compare *White v. Samsung Elecs. Am., Inc.*, 971 F.2d 1395, 1396 (9th Cir. 1992), with *Joe Dickerson & Assocs. v. Dittmar*, 34 P.3d 995, 1004 (Colo. 2001) (en banc).
[192] See discussion *supra* at 82–83.
[193] See discussion *supra* at 77–81.
[194] See Chapter 1, *supra*.
[195] See discussion *supra* at 183–84.
[196] N.Y. Times Co. v. Sullivan, 376 U.S. 254, 266 (1964).
[197] In fairness, Justice Brennan was speaking of an advertisement concerning a matter of political concern. See id. at 256. However, given that commercial speech today is not defined by the subject of the expression, but rather by the commercial motivation of the speaker, that factor should play no role in determining the relevance of Justice Brennan's statement to other contexts.

Sorrell highlights the need for the Court to revisit that insight.[198] Recall that the *Sorrell* Court subjected a commercial/noncommercial distinction to strict scrutiny because the law imposed a speaker-based distinction. In *Sorrell*, the law at issue differentiated between academic researchers, who were permitted to use data-mined prescriber information, and drug manufacturers, who were prohibited from doing so.[199] Thus, the state sought to distinguish profit-motivated speakers from non-profit-making academics.[200] Yet, the Court held that the distinction should be subjected to the strict scrutiny test, which is of course extremely difficult to satisfy.[201] Importing this baseline from *Sorrell* into publicity rights cases further demonstrates the absurdity of the speaker-based distinction. In contrast to *Sorrell*'s commercial/noncommercial distinction, publicity rights doctrine differentiates between sub-forms of profit-motivated speech.[202] This distinction is even more dubious under the First Amendment than the distinction rejected in *Sorrell*. When the speaker in both cases – a commercial advertiser and a more traditional profit-making communications medium – acts out of a profit motivation to convey the exact same information to roughly the same audience, drawing a dichotomy for purposes of First Amendment protection, as Justice Brennan recognized in *New York Times Co. v. Sullivan*, is wholly illogical.[203]

Is there any even arguably principled basis on which to distinguish, for purposes of the level of First Amendment protection, between profit-motivated speech that comes in the form of a commercial advertisement promoting sale on the one hand and profit-motivated speech that comes in the form of a traditional medium of communication on the other, even though both communications' substance and the audience are identical? The answer is no. However, it is possible to conceive of three conceivable arguments that scholars might fashion to justify such a distinction. The following discussion illustrates the flaws in each argument.

REJECTING ATTEMPTS TO JUSTIFY THE DISTINCTION BETWEEN FORMS OF PROFIT-MOTIVATED EXPRESSION

Three conceivable arguments could support the distinction between commercial advertisements and the communications media for both First Amendment

---

[198] See discussion *supra* at 94.
[199] See *Sorrell v. IMS Health, Inc.*, 131 S. Ct. 2653, 2663 (2011).
[200] id.
[201] id. at 2664.
[202] See Chapter 1, *supra*.
[203] *N.Y. Times Co. v. Sullivan*, 376 U.S. 254, 266 (1969).

and right of publicity purposes, even if both convey the exact same information to roughly the same audience. First, one could suggest that a commercial advertiser's speech is designed to persuade the listener to purchase a product or service, while the commercial success of the speech of the traditionally protected communicator generally does not turn on persuading a reader or viewer to do anything. Second, one could argue that, purely as a matter of constitutional tradition, commercial advertisements have received no or at least reduced protection, while expression conveyed in books, newspapers, and magazines, and on television and radio have received the highest level of First Amendment protection. Finally, one might argue that expression in news media receives the special protection that the First Amendment extends to the press, while commercial advertisements receive only the level of protection afforded to free speech. Even a casual examination of each of these arguments, however, reveals fatal flaws in their logic or accuracy.

The Persuasive Goal of Expression Does Not Reduce the Level of Expression

As to the first suggested distinction, the expression of commercial advertisers, it can safely be assumed, always advocate purchase, while more traditional communications media are generally not so motivated. Of course, even if one conceded the logic of this distinction solely for purpose of this argument, the theory fails to explain the *ex ante* categorical distinction between the two communicators in situations in which the traditionally protected medium in fact strives to persuade the listener to purchase. But even putting that fatal flaw aside, it remains unclear why this difference in motivation, in and of itself, justifies stratification in the level of First Amendment protection. No logical bases exist to suggest that the First Amendment applies any less to speech used to persuade rather than merely to inform. Indeed, one of the classic justifications for free speech protection is that it facilitates self-governing choices.[204] There is no basis for categorically assuming, *ex ante*, that the commercial advertiser's expression is more likely to be false or misleading than the traditional communications medium's expression. Such a conclusion would, of course, necessarily depend on an examination of the specific facts in each case. After all, purely political expression, which often appears in traditional communications media, is often self-promotional. Purely political expression often

---

[204] See Meiklejohn, *supra* note 169, at 19–21.

seeks to persuade the listener to take actions that will benefit the speaker,[205] but surely such speech does not lose protection as a result.

In the right of publicity context, the rationale makes even less sense because my working hypothesis assumes that the expression is identical in both cases (for example, Tom Cruise drives a BMW). Speech, therefore, is no more likely to be false or misleading in one instance than in the other. Moreover, to the extent that courts assume publicity rights are grounded in unjust enrichment concerns, the danger of unjustly usurping profit is just as great when the speaker-violator is a profit-making communications entity as when it is a commercial advertiser.[206] Because courts afford the First Amendment privilege to traditional profit-motivated media in right of publicity cases, celebrities are denied the opportunity to benefit financially from the traditional media's use of their names or likenesses, even though those media outlets profit from that use.[207]

Noncommercial Speech Does Not Deserve Special Treatment Because of "Tradition"

The second asserted distinction, grounded in traditionally accepted notions of what modes of expression receive protection, is even more dubious. When the exact same expression is disseminated to the exact same audience, it does not make even the slightest bit of sense to rely on some mindless notion of historical practice. By this very reasoning, it is unclear why expressions disseminated on television, radio, or through the Internet receive full First Amendment protection when all of these can be considered relatively new media. Indeed, the Supreme Court's recognition that commercially motivated, violent video games deserve full First Amendment protection[208] renders any appeal to notions of tradition a hollow – or disingenuous – exercise.

The Press Clause Does Not Provide Greater Protection to Media Speech

Finally, it might be argued that the "newsworthy" privilege can be justified under the First Amendment clause that protects the freedom of the

---

[205] In fact, political advertising has been borrowing strategies from commercial advertising since the 1950s. Andrew Rosenthal, *For the Idyllic Political Ad, A Fadeout*, N.Y. Times, June 21, 1987, at 22; see also Arthur Sandburg, Creating Effective Political Ads, in *Lights, Camera, Campaign! Media, Politics, and Political Advertising* 1-2 (David A. Schultz ed., 2004) (comparing successful product ads and political ads).
[206] See discussion *supra* at 96.
[207] id.
[208] Brown v. Entm't Merchs. Ass'n, 131 S. Ct. 2729, 2742 (2011).

press – a clause that does not apply to commercial advertisers. But the suggested distinction based on the added First Amendment protection afforded to the press makes no more sense as a justification of the right of publicity than the other two asserted rationales. Purely as a doctrinal matter, the Court has never held that the press freedom provides greater protection than the speech clause.[209] Nor would it be reasonable for it to do so, especially in today's media climate. Expression that comes in the form of pure speech has never been deemed to take a back seat for protective purposes to printed expression.[210] Moreover, if one proceeded on the accuracy of this assumption, it is by no means clear that press protection should extend to new media, such as radio and television, both of which involve far more "speech" than they do printed word. Finally, efforts to distinguish expressive forms of communication and other forms of "press" would certainly be frustrated were a commercial advertiser to choose to publish a monthly magazine or sponsor a blog.

Once courts enforcing publicity rights reject the unprincipled distinction between different forms of profit-motivated expression, they arguably have an option. In order to establish logical consistency, they can either subject the publicity right to First Amendment protection for profit-motivated speech or enforce the right against all profit-motivated speech, despite the presence of the First Amendment. The latter route is clearly untenable, however, both as a practical matter and as a matter of First Amendment analysis. Therefore, the conclusion that the First Amendment protects commercial advertisers against liability for violating a right of publicity – at least in contexts in which it would also protect the expression of traditional media[211] – is logically inescapable.

---

[209] See, e.g., *Branzburg v. Hayes*, 408 U.S. 665, 681–83 (1968). In *Branzburg*, the Court rejected a reporter's argument that he should be immune from the obligation to reveal the criminal conduct of his confidential sources after a grand jury subpoena. id. at 692. The Court reasoned that "[i]t has generally been held that the First Amendment does not guarantee the press a constitutional right of special access to information not available to the public generally." id. at 684; see also *First Nat'l Bank v. Belloti*, 435 U.S. 765, 782–83 (1978) ("[T]he press does not have a monopoly on either the First Amendment or the ability to enlighten. Similarly, the Court's decisions involving corporations in the business of communication or entertainment are based not only on the role of the First Amendment in fostering individual self-expression but also on its role in affording the public access to discussion, debate, and dissemination of information and ideas." (citations omitted)).

[210] See *First Nat'l Bank*, 435 U.S. at 783.

[211] See Chapter 1, *supra*.

APPLYING MODERN COMMERCIAL SPEECH DOCTRINE TO THE RIGHT OF PUBLICITY

Let us assume, for present purposes, that the existing doctrinal universe of First Amendment protection remains unchanged. Although much of this chapter has been designed to explain the serious flaws in that framework, it is important to recognize that even under the doctrinal status quo courts should hold that the current structure of the right of publicity violates the First Amendment. The problem is, simply, that the judiciary's current practice is that once a court enforcing the right of publicity finds commercial speech involved, it automatically dismisses possible First Amendment concerns.[212] Although the Supreme Court currently provides a slightly lesser standard of constitutional protection to commercial speech than it does to noncommercial expression, it would be a gross mistake to assume that the level of protection given to commercial speech is meager or nonexistent, as courts enforcing the right of publicity universally do today. To the contrary, although the Supreme Court arguably continues to adhere to the four-pronged *Central Hudson* test,[213] that test as currently applied offers far more constitutional protection to commercial speech than it did in its early years.[214] Yet, in the context of publicity rights, courts somehow have not received the message. Once the modern version of the *Central Hudson* test is applied to right of publicity claims, the dichotomy in the existing doctrinal framework between commercial advertisers and other forms of profit-motivated communication proves even more questionable.

As noted at various points in this book, in *Central Hudson* the Court adopted a four-part test.[215] The first inquiry is whether the speech in question promotes the sale of an unlawful product or service, or is found to be false or misleading.[216] If the answer to either of these questions is in the affirmative, the court automatically excludes the expression from the First Amendment's protective reach.[217] If the answer to both questions is in the negative, the reviewing court proceeds to examine the remaining three

---

[212] See discussion *supra* at 95.
[213] *Cent. Hudson Gas & Elec. Corp. v. Pub. Serv. Comm'n*, 447 U.S. 557, 564 (1980). But see Chapter 1, *supra*.
[214] Compare *Thompson v. W. States Med. Ctr.*, 535 U.S. 357, 358 (2002), with *Posadas de P.R. Assocs. v. Tourism Co. of P.R.*, 478 U.S. 328, 329 (1986). See the discussions in Chapters 1 and 2, *supra*.
[215] *Cent. Hudson*, 447 U.S. at 566.
[216] id.
[217] id. Note that while this is unambiguously established doctrine, the position is challenged in Chapter 2, *supra*.

factors.[218] Under the test's second prong, the government must demonstrate that its regulation of commercial speech serves a "substantial" governmental interest.[219] Once that inquiry has been satisfied, the court "must determine whether the regulation directly advances the governmental interest asserted."[220] The court should invalidate the regulation if it "only indirectly advance[s] the state interest involved."[221] The regulation must *materially* advance the state's interest.[222] The government has the burden of establishing, beyond mere speculation, that the regulation actually does so.[223] Even if the government satisfies this requirement, however, the court must then proceed to the test's fourth prong: whether the regulation is "[no] more extensive than is necessary to serve [the substantial governmental] interest."[224] The third and fourth prongs have often been grouped together under the heading of a "reasonable fit" requirement.[225] In applying the *Central Hudson* test since the mid-1990s, the Supreme Court has regularly invalidated regulations suppressing commercial speech.[226]

The constitutional problem here for the right of publicity – what can appropriately be called the flaw of "under-inclusion" – derives from the "reasonable fit" requirement. Although the Court in one of its earlier decisions stated that the government need not remove all causes of a problem to suppress commercial speech giving rise to that problem,[227] later decisions appear to have largely undermined this sweeping assertion. Under controlling commercial speech case law, the government cannot justify commercial speech suppression when a significant danger of the exact same harm would continue to exist.[228] For example, in *City of Cincinnati v. Discovery Network, Inc.*,[229] the Court invalidated the city's prohibition of news-racks that distributed

---

[218] id.
[219] id.
[220] id. Despite the seeming weaknesses of the moral and economic government interests advanced by publicity rights, this prong has not shown to be easily surmountable for commercial speech proponents.
[221] Cent. Hudson, 447 U.S. at 564.
[222] id. at 566.
[223] Edenfield v. Fane, 507 U.S. 761, 770–71 (1993).
[224] Cent. Hudson, 447 U.S. at 566.
[225] See Lorillard Tobacco Co. v. Reilly, 533 U.S. 525, 528 (2001).
[226] See, e.g., Thompson v. W. States Med. Ctr., 535 U.S. 357 (2002); Lorillard, 533 U.S. at 525–26; Greater New Orleans Broad. Ass'n v. United States, 527 U.S. 173 (1999); 44 Liquormart, Inc. v. Rhode Island, 517 U.S. 484 (1996); Rubin v. Coors Brewing Co., 514 U.S. 476 (1995); City of Cincinnati v. Discovery Network, Inc., 507 U.S. 410 (1993).
[227] Bd. of Trustees v. Fox, 492 U.S. 469, 479 (1989).
[228] See Greater New Orleans Broad. Ass'n, 527 U.S. at 174; Discovery Network, Inc., 507 U.S. at 411.
[229] 507 U.S. at 410.

commercial advertising newspapers in the name of improving aesthetics because the commercial news-racks "are no greater an eyesore than the news racks permitted to remain on Cincinnati's sidewalks."[230] Similarly, in *Greater New Orleans Broadcasting Association, Inc. v. United States*,[231] the Court rejected the government's argument that a prohibition on casino gambling advertising would deter gambling, in part on the basis of its conclusion that "any measure of the effectiveness of the Government's attempt to minimize the social costs of gambling cannot ignore Congress's simultaneous encouragement of tribal casino gambling, which may well be growing at a rate exceeding any increase in gambling or compulsive gambling that private casino advertising could produce."[232]

These decisions are important because they demonstrate that government may not discriminate against commercial speech by suppressing it when significant amounts of noncommercial expression giving rise to the exact same problem remain unregulated. In a certain sense, these decisions anticipated the Court's subsequent holding in *Sorrell* that subjected expressive discrimination against commercial speakers to strict scrutiny.[233] Likewise, the decisions give rise to substantial difficulty for current doctrine concerning the right of publicity because existing doctrine imposes a stark and unjustified discrimination against commercial expression. Although courts have summarily denied First Amendment protection to profit-motivated commercial expression that uses a person's name or likeness, profit-motivated expression conveyed in a communications medium that invades the victim's exact same interest receives full protection.

Whatever rationale one employs to justify the right of publicity, the harm caused by the expression is identical in both situations. Both moral and economic arguments underscoring publicity rights illustrate victims' primary concern for attaining and protecting financial gain.[234] These pecuniary concerns place people seeking to exercise publicity rights on the same level as traditional media speakers. If there were some basis for believing that the impact of a commercial advertiser's expression is more harmful to or invasive of individuals' publicity rights than that caused by traditional media and that

---

[230] id. at 425.
[231] 527 U.S. at 173.
[232] id. at 189; see also *Rubin v. Coors Brewing Co.*, 514 U.S. 476, 488 (1995) (holding a prohibition on beer labels from displaying alcohol content unconstitutional "because of the overall irrationality of the Government's regulatory scheme" in light of the law's permission for the printing of alcoholic content on labels on distilled spirits).
[233] *Sorrell v. IMS Health, Inc.*, 131 S. Ct. 2653, 2656 (2011).
[234] See discussion *supra* at 71–72.

the dichotomy reflects privacy concerns rather than economic considerations, however, the distinction could be justified. But when motivations are financial, as they universally appear to be, publicity rights' constitutional flaw is identical to the one that led the *Discovery Network* Court to hold the city's selective exclusion of commercial newspaper boxes on its streets for aesthetic reasons, when traditional newspaper boxes give rise to the exact same harm, as unconstitutional.[235]

CONCLUSION

The right of publicity has a long and, some would say, venerable history in the jurisprudence of American tort law. For years, however, it has been widely understood that the right potentially gives rise to First Amendment problems because of its obviously suppressive impact on the communication of information and opinion. Nevertheless, courts universally assume that the First Amendment interest is fully satisfied by recognizing a "newsworthiness" privilege, which categorically excludes any expression included in a commercial advertisement from its protective scope. This jurisprudence has proceeded, however, with mystifying ignorance of the last forty years of evolution and expansion in the level of First Amendment protection afforded to such speech.

The cavalier rejection of protection for commercial advertising ignores well-established doctrine and sound precepts of First Amendment theory. It is now time for the right of publicity to be introduced to the twenty-first century of First Amendment law.

---

[235] *City of Cincinnati v. Discovery Network, Inc.*, 507 U.S. 410, 425 (1993).

4

Compelled Commercial Speech and the First Amendment

INTRODUCTION: COMPELLED EXPRESSION AS A VIOLATION OF THE FIRST AMENDMENT

For the most part, the First Amendment is viewed as a means of restricting government's authority to suppress expression. Both speakers and listeners are assumed to benefit from speech, and therefore the more communication of opinion and information, the better it is for both society and the democratic system. However, for a variety of important reasons, the courts have extended First Amendment protection to limit government's power to *compel* expression by private individuals and entities. The Supreme Court has wisely recognized that governmental compulsion to speak can often bring about many of the very same constitutional and democratic pathologies brought on by suppression.[1]

Despite their similarities, suppression and compulsion of speech have by no means been viewed as identical for First Amendment purposes by the Court.[2] On occasion, the Court has recognized that governmentally compelled speech may actually advance First Amendment interests more than undermine them.[3] As noted throughout this book, beginning with the work of famed free speech theorist Alexander Meiklejohn,[4] it has been widely recognized – even by the Court[5] – that the First Amendment right belongs at least as much to the listener as it does to the speaker.[6] After all, one can evolve morally,

---

[1] See discussion *infra* at 109–111.
[2] See discussion *infra* at 109–10.
[3] *Red Lion Broadcasting Co.* v. *FCC*, 395 U.S. 367, 390 (1969).
[4] See generally Alexander Meiklejohn, *Political Freedom: The Constitutional Powers of the People* (1965), p. 55.
[5] *Red Lion Broadcasting Co.* v. *FCC*, 395 U.S. 367 (1969).
[6] Meiklejohn actually believed the right to be exclusively that of the listener; the speaker, he argued, should be deemed to have no independent First Amendment right. See generally Alexander Meiklejohn, *Free Speech and its Relation to Self-Government* (1948). However, one

intellectually, or personally as much by reading great works of literature, science, or political theory as by expressing one's own views on the subject. Moreover, as Meiklejohn argued, if the First Amendment "springs from the necessities of self-government,"[7] the voters – whom Meiklejohn called the true "governors" in a democratic society[8] – need to receive and absorb as much information and opinion as possible in order for the process of self-government to operate effectively. While Meiklejohn made the mistake of wishing to confine the First Amendment to this listener perspective, he was surely correct in recognizing the value of expression to the listener. This, in short, describes the listener-centric model set out in Chapter 1.

As a general matter, governmental suppression of all but the most consciously false communication undermines *both* listener- *and* speaker-centric values of free expression: the speaker is harmed by not being able to speak, and the listener is harmed by not being allowed to listen, see, or hear the intended communication. The constitutional analysis of governmentally compelled speech, however, is considerably more complicated, and unfortunately, the Court has failed to provide a coherent theoretical explanation of its decisions on the subject. Even if speakers are compelled to communicate against their will, thereby triggering the constitutional pathologies normally associated with compelled speech,[9] it is at least conceivable that such forced speech could benefit the recipients of the expression by providing them with valuable information that could potentially aid them in making self-governing decisions, whether of the political or private varieties.[10] In this sense, compelled speech may actually *further* First Amendment values, by providing potentially valuable information to the listeners that will aid them in performance of their self-governing function. In so doing, compelled speech enhances the intersection of democracy and free expression.

Traditionally, compelled speech by individuals in the noncommercial context has, for the most part, been held to be constitutionally prohibited.[11] But this is not so in all cases. For example, individuals who contribute to

---

not need accept so extreme and questionable a position in order to conclude that an important element of the First Amendment right belongs to the listener.

[7] Meiklejohn, *supra* note 6, at 26.
[8] Meiklejohn, *supra* note 4, at 9 ("If men are to be governed, we say, then that governing must be done, not by others, but by themselves.").
[9] See discussion *infra* at 111–114.
[10] For a discussion of the differences and similarities between political and private forms of self-government, see Martin H. Redish, *Money Talks: Speech, Economic Power, and the Values of Democracy* (2001), pp. 22–29.
[11] *Wooley v. Maynard*, 430 U.S. 705 (1977); *W. Va. State Bd. of Educ. v. Barnette*, 319 U.S. 624 (1943).

political candidates' campaigns are legislatively required to publicly reveal their names, and the Supreme Court has found these legislative directives to be constitutional.[12] This is at least in part designed to deter and expose possible corruption. But the requirement also provides valuable information to the electorate by informing them of who has contributed to the various candidates for office. Thus, while there exists a strong constitutional presumption against compelled speech in traditional expressive contexts, the protection is not absolute.

To this point, the Supreme Court has generally (though not always) been less than receptive to pleas for First Amendment protection against compelled commercial speech.[13] This is so, despite its long established protection against compelled noncommercial speech. But a sharp dichotomy, for First Amendment purposes, between compelled commercial and noncommercial speech would represent the same misguided, superficial reasoning that for many years led to an equally sharp dichotomy between limitations on the *suppression* of commercial and noncommercial speech. For many years, the Supreme Court summarily dismissed the notion that commercial speech was deserving of First Amendment protection against governmental suppression.[14] As explained throughout this book, however, the Court has long since recognized its error, now providing substantial protection to truthful commercial speech in a manner largely equivalent to the level of protection extended to noncommercial speech.[15] The thesis of this chapter is that it is time for the Court to recognize that the issue of *compelled* commercial speech is similarly far more complex, both doctrinally and theoretically, than it has previously thought. Moreover, I argue that recognition of these analytical complexities should logically lead to a substantial increase in First Amendment protection against compelled commercial speech.

Does this mean that compelled commercial speech should be deemed as constitutionally unacceptable as compelled noncommercial speech is widely recognized to be? The answer is not immediately clear. But if not, it is important to understand three points: (1) To a large extent, the difference, when properly understood, flows not from the fact that commercial speech is less valuable than its noncommercial counterpart, as a matter of First Amendment theory, but rather from the generally distinct harms that are

---

[12] *Buckley v. Valeo*, 421 U.S. 1 (1976).
[13] See, e.g., *Glickman v. Wileman Bros. & Elliott*, 521 U.S. 457 (1997); *United States v. United Foods*, 533 U.S. 405 (2001); *Johanns v. Livestock Marketing*, 544 U.S. 550 (2005).
[14] *Valentine v. Chrestensen*, 316 U.S. 54 (1942).
[15] E.g., *City of Cincinnati v. Discovery Network*, 507 U.S. 410 (1993); *Rubin v. Coors Brewing Co.*, 514 U.S. 476 (1995); *44 Liqouormart v. Rhode Island*, 517 U.S. 484 (1996).

risked by commercial speech and which may be avoided or at least diluted by compelled speech; (2) to the extent noncommercial speech gives rise to the very same dangers of harm, it is at least arguable that compelled speech designed to avoid these very same harms in the context of noncommercial speech should be deemed just as constitutionally permissible in that context; and (3) even if one were to assume, solely for purposes of argument, that compelled commercial speech is more constitutionally permissible in that context than compelled noncommercial speech, such a conclusion has absolutely no relevance, logically or practically, to the constitutional analysis of *suppression* of commercial speech. The fact that compelled speech may be deemed more constitutionally appropriate in the context of commercial speech than it is in the context of noncommercial speech (a conclusion, I should emphasize, which I categorically reject) in no way justifies greater suppression of commercial speech than noncommercial speech, absent a showing that the commercial speech in question gives rise to more serious dangers of harm than comparable noncommercial speech.[16]

In determining the constitutionality of compelled commercial speech, it is appropriate to make use of the same analytical models that one employs, or at least should employ, in judging the constitutionality of compelled noncommercial speech. And those analytical models are parallel to the analytical models one should employ in measuring the constitutionality of the *suppression* of any form of expression. As described at the outset of this book,[17] there are, broadly speaking, four such models – (1) speaker-centric, (2) listener-centric, (3) regulatory-centric, and (4) rationalist-centric. The speaker-centric model, as the name suggests, views the suppression of speech through the lens of the speaker: in what ways is the would-be speaker harmed by not being allowed to speak? Where a restriction on expression causes constitutionally pathological harm to the speaker, the restriction must – at least as a *prima facie* matter – be deemed a violation of the First Amendment. The listener-centric model similarly views the pathologies of expressive suppression through the lens of the listener: how is the listener harmed by being deprived of the opportunity to learn the information and opinion that the would-be speaker wishes to convey? Where a restriction on expression undermines the democratic values fostered by

---

[16] See discussion *infra* at 125–31.
[17] See Chapter 1, *supra*. See also Martin H. Redish & Peter B. Siegel, *Constitutional Adjudication, Free Expression, and the Fashionable Art of Corporation Bashing*, 91 Tex. L. Rev. 1425, 1469 (2013). While Chapter 1 provides a full description of the models, for purposes of completeness of the chapter, I include a detailed description of them here as well.

listener receipt of information and ideas, here, too, the restriction must be deemed a *prima facie* violation of the First Amendment.[18]

Somewhat more complex in its operation is the regulatory-centric model. Under this model, the constitutional concern is with the need to preserve the implicit social contract between government and citizen in a liberal democratic society, and the extent to which the suppression of expression undermines that contractual relationship. Therefore in applying this model one asks, to what extent does the government's suppression of expression reflect disrespect for the individual citizens as an integral whole, worthy of respect on the part of the government that represents them. A clear example of such pathological behavior by government is the selective suppression of truthful information on the basis of the paternalistic fear that the citizenry will make the wrong lawful choices on the basis of that information. Instead of trusting the citizens to make lawful choices on the basis of free and open debate, selective governmental suppression of one side of that debate represents a violation of the regulatory-centric model: government is exercising its regulatory authority in a democratically pathological manner.

Inherently intertwined with all three of these models is the rationalist-centric model. This model requires that governmental interference with expression must be grounded in principled, nondiscriminatory rationales.

One key to understanding how these four models function is to grasp that each model operates as a necessary, but not a sufficient, condition for satisfying the First Amendment. In other words, as a matter of First Amendment theory, it is not enough that a regulation satisfies any one of these four models. A violation of any one of them constitutes a significant disruption of the role performed by the First Amendment. Rather, to be held constitutional in the absence of the showing of a compelling interest, a restriction on expression must satisfy the dictates of all four of these models. Thus, the fact that the constitutional interests fostered by free and open speaker communication are not undermined by an expressive restriction is irrelevant, if the listener's democratically protected interests are undermined by the same restriction. Similarly, if the restriction undermines the liberal-democratic social contract by paternalistically reflecting governmental disdain for the citizens, the restriction sufficiently undermines First Amendment interests to be deemed unconstitutional. This is so, even if one were to assume, if only for purposes of argument, that, because of its uniquely profit-motivated expression,

---

[18] By inserting the phrase *prima facie* I am allowing for the possibility that in the relatively rare instance in which a compelling governmental interest justifying the suppression is established, the First Amendment interest may be forced to give way.

a commercial speaker is not fostering First Amendment values in the same manner as a noncommercial speaker.[19] The fact that listeners are deprived of the potentially valuable information or opinion the would-be commercial speaker seeks to convey sufficiently undermines First Amendment values to render that regulation unconstitutional. Indeed, Meiklejohn long ago argued that the *only* relevant First Amendment interest is that of the recipient of the expression, because the essence of free expression is the extent to which it facilitates performance of the self-governing function by informing the voters of all relevant information and opinion.[20] While such an extreme position clearly goes too far in its categorical rejection of the speaker-centric model, it is certainly perceptive in recognizing that First Amendment values of individual development and the facilitation of life-governing decisions is significantly fostered by the receipt, as well as the expression of information and opinion.

Admittedly, application of the analytical framework for judging the constitutionality of governmental *suppression* of expression operates in a more complicated manner when it is employed to determine the constitutionality of *compelled* speech. I have argued throughout this book that suppression of commercial speech should be deemed as constitutionally suspect as suppression of noncommercial speech, and for the most part,[21] the Supreme Court in recent years has approached acceptance of this position, even if it has not formally adopted it.[22] But for reasons already mentioned,[23] compelled speech gives rise to complications not present when the issue concerns the constitutionality of suppression. In order to understand those differences, especially for purposes of understanding how the four-pronged analytical model operates in this context, it is necessary to understand why compelled expression has traditionally been deemed pathological to First Amendment values. After explaining how that rationale is established as a constitutional baseline and reference point, we will be able to apply it to measure the constitutionality of compelled commercial speech. Once one understands the extent to which

---

[19] But see Chapter 1, *supra* and Chapter 2, *supra* (rejecting the commercial/noncommercial dichotomy).

[20] Meiklejohn, *supra* note 6, at 26.

[21] The one glaring exception is suppression of false speech, where the Supreme Court categorically rejects First Amendment protection for false commercial speech but is far more protective of false noncommercial speech. See, e.g., *Central Hudson*. This is a view that I have in large part rejected, though here, too, the issue is far more complex than many believe. See generally Chapter 2, *supra*.

[22] Coleen Klasmeier & Martin H. Redish, *Off-Label Prescription Advertising, the FDA, and the First Amendment: A Study in the Values of Commercial Speech Protection*, 37 Am. J. of L. & Med. 315, 339 (2011).

[23] See discussion *supra* at 105–06.

compelled commercial speech is appropriately deemed to violate at least one of the four prongs of the analytical model I have posited,[24] it will be possible to determine what sorts of compelling interests will nevertheless justify governmental compulsion.

WHY COMPELLED SPEECH IS UNCONSTITUTIONAL: ESTABLISHING THE FIRST AMENDMENT BASELINE

The Supreme Court and Compelled Speech

When one examines the Supreme Court's First Amendment doctrine of compelled speech, one naturally thinks of two cases: *Barnette* and *Wooley*. These are the names of the two famous Supreme Court decisions that set out the Court's explication of the serious dangers to First Amendment values to which compelled speech gives rise. In *West Virginia State Board of Education v. Barnette*,[25] the Court held unconstitutional West Virginia's enforcement of a regulation requiring children in public schools to salute the American flag. The child in question was a Jehovah's Witness, a religion that construes the Second Commandment's prohibition on worshiping graven images to prohibit them from saluting the flag.[26]

In holding the regulation unconstitutional, Justice Jackson's opinion for the Court noted that the protection claimed by the student and her parents "stand on a right of self-determination in matters that touch individual opinion and personal attitude."[27] Viewing the flag salute as "a form of utterance,"[28] the Court found that "the State employs a flag as a symbol of adherence to government as presently organized. It requires the individual to communicate by word and sign his acceptance of the political ideas it thus bespeaks."[29] The Court found no compelling justification for requiring students to salute the flag, and therefore held the compelled expression of allegiance to the state unconstitutional.[30] In his opinion for the Court, Justice Jackson wrote what has come to be known as among the most important statements of American constitutional democracy: "If there is one fixed star in our constitutional

---

[24] See discussion *supra* at 106–08.
[25] 319 U.S. 624 (1943).
[26] id. at 329.
[27] id. at 631.
[28] id. at 632.
[29] id. at 633.
[30] id. 633–34 ("here the power of compulsion is invoked without any allegation that remaining passive during a flag salute ritual creates a clear and present danger that would justify an effort even to muffle expression.").

constellation, it is that no official, high or petty, can prescribe what shall be orthodox in politics, nationalism, religion, or other matters of opinion, or force citizens to confess by word or act their faith therein."[31]

Some 34 years later, in Wooley v. Maynard,[32] the Court applied its reasoning in Barnette to invalidate invocation of a New Hampshire criminal statute making it a misdemeanor to cover up lettering on a license plate to an effort by a Jehovah's Witness couple to cover up the state's license plate slogan, "Live Free or Die." The Court noted that "the right of freedom of thought protected by the First Amendment against state action includes both the right to speak freely and the right to refrain from speaking at all."[33] The Court held application of the statute to the couple's behavior unconstitutional, because "[t]he First Amendment protects the right of individuals to hold a point of view different from the majority and to refuse to foster, in the way New Hampshire commands, an idea they find morally objectionable."[34]

Both Barnette and Wooley can be viewed as applications of the Court's general prohibition on viewpoint regulation – selective governmental regulation of expression grounded in either distaste for or disagreement with the viewpoint expressed – in the compelled speech context.[35] In this context viewpoint regulation is translated into governmental penalization of a private individual for refusal to express governmentally dictated orthodoxy. Such expressive regulation contravenes all four of the elements of my analytical model: It undermines the speaker's expressive interest in communicating; it undermines the listeners' interest in receiving information and opinion; it undermines the regulatory-centric model's preservation of the implicit liberal democratic social contract by interfering with the individual's control of her own expression; and it undermines the rationalist-centric model by imposing expressive discrimination not grounded in neutral, principled analysis. Though of course compelled speech does not directly involve suppression, the expressive pathology found to be present in both decisions was the government's attempt to use compelled speech as a means of either promoting acceptance of government as presently constituted or forcing private citizens to express viewpoints held by the government. The fact that in neither case did the state prohibit private individuals from expressing views counter to state-

---

[31] id. at 642.
[32] 430 U.S. 705 (1977).
[33] id. at 714.
[34] id. at 715.
[35] See, e.g., Matal v. Tam, 137 S. Ct. 1744 (2017); Rosenberg v. Rector & Visitors of the Univ. of Va., 515 U.S. 819 (1995); Texas v. Johnson, 491 U.S. 397, 414 (1989).

held orthodoxy did not deter the Court from finding the required utterance of or publicly displayed adherence to governmentally held positions sufficiently disruptive of First Amendment interests as to make them unconstitutional.

Compelled Speech and First Amendment Theory

In neither *Barnette* nor *Wooley* did government put forth a serious or even arguably compelling interest to justify the forced speech. Indeed, for the most part, government's defense in both was simply that the state possesses the authority to require its citizens to spout normative political orthodoxy – the antithesis of a truly compelling interest, and a direct contradiction of core premise of the First Amendment.[36] Thus, at least on the basis of these two famous decisions, we cannot be sure how the Court would have ruled on a claim of First Amendment protection against compelled speech in situations in which the government presents even an arguably compelling interest.

In order to make this determination, it is first necessary to reverse-engineer the conclusion that, at least as a *prima facie* matter, the First Amendment prohibits compelled speech. To be sure, the opinions in both *Barnette* and *Wooley* waxed eloquent about the foundational precept that government cannot force-feed political orthodoxy to its citizens. But what if it is not political orthodoxy but potentially important factual information that the government wants a speaker – even a noncommercial speaker – to convey to readers or listeners? Without the benefit of some form of analysis of why, as a matter of the deep structure of American constitutional and political theory, the First Amendment is construed to prohibit compelled speech, it will be difficult to determine whether there are situations of compelled speech that fail to trigger the theoretical concerns underlying the holdings in *Barnette* and *Wooley*. Moreover, it will be impossible to determine whether, even in cases where the First Amendment interest is triggered, there will ever be any competing governmental concerns so strong as to overcome the First Amendment interest in preventing forced speech. It is therefore appropriate to take the issue of compelled speech beyond the obviously egregious fact situations of these two decisions, and decide how the prohibition would operate under more nuanced circumstances.

In answering these questions, the appropriate place to begin is with discussion of the issues surrounding compelled speech in general in my earlier

---

[36] For an examination of the underlying theoretical framework of the decision in *Barnette*, see generally Leora Harpaz, *Justice Jackson's Flag Salute Legacy: The Supreme Court Struggles to Protect Intellectual Individualism*, 64 Tex. L. Rev. 817 (1986).

writing. There I argued that "[c]ompelled speech undermines the interests fostered by protection of free expression by giving rise to four distinct but related harms ... ."[37] These harms may best be described as confusion, dilution, humiliation, and psychological manipulation.[38] Compelled speech undermines the values of free expression by (1) potentially confusing the populace as to the actual strength and popularity of substantive positions advocated by the government; (2) diluting the force of the speaker's persuasiveness in support of his own views in the eyes of his readers or listeners; (3) publicly humiliating speakers by forcing them to utter positions with which they disagree, thereby possibly demoralizing them and undermining their resolve to maintain their own positions; and (4) psychologically manipulating speakers by continually forcing them to express views contrary to their own and eventually rationalizing such forced expression by subconsciously adopting the positions they have been forced to express. Each of these four pathologies undermines the relationship between private citizen and government in a liberal democracy and threatens core constitutionally protected values of democratic discourse. Citizens' ability to perform the self-governing function is substantially undermined by any one of these harms.

It is helpful to view these pathologies through the lens of the four-pronged analytical model I have proposed. The confusion pathology is best viewed as undermining the values fostered by the listener-centric model: intentional confusion of the populace by the government effectively renders the democratic process little more than a sham, for voters will be performing their electoral function on the basis of governmentally manipulated false information and an intentional misrepresentation of the popularity of governmental policies. Moreover, there is no principled or rational basis for such selective expressive compulsion. Dilution of a speaker's persuasiveness, on the other hand, can appropriately be viewed as pathological from the perspectives of both the speaker and listener-centric models. Like the confusion pathology, the dilution danger undermines the populace's ability to perform its governing function by artificially altering its perception of a speaker's attempts to persuade them. A speaker who wishes to convince the populace to adopt position "X" can hardly be deemed an effective advocate for her position if she is simultaneously forced by government to advocate for position "Y," or even position "Not X." And this is likely to be true, if only on a subconscious level,

---

[37] Redish, *supra* note 10 at 175.
[38] Note that this categorization represents a slight modification of my previous scholarship. See id. at 158.

even if listeners are made aware of the fact that the government is forcing the speaker to advocate on behalf of "not X" or "Y." Imagine, for example, that while Martin Luther King was permitted to advocate integration and equal rights, he was required by government at the outset of his speech to extoll the supposed values of segregation. No matter what he were to say at that point, the impact of his message would have been severely diluted by the proximately forced utterance of the diametrically opposed position. In addition to undermining the listener-centric model by distorting communication central to citizens' performance of the self-governing function, such forced expression would severely disrupt a speaker's desire to influence that process, thereby simultaneously undermining the speaker-centric value of free expression.

The harms to the values of both free expression and the democratic process that likely follow from the humiliation pathology should also be clear. The personal demoralization that flows from a speaker being forced to utter supposedly factual or normative statements with which he disagrees might detract from his desire to continue to communicate, thereby undermining the speaker-centric model. The psychological manipulation that may result from continual and required repetition of statements with which the speaker disagrees is closely related to the demoralization and humiliation just discussed. At some point, the possibility arises that the speaker will subconsciously rationalize his forced statements by coming to believe them.

Will any of these psychological dangers *necessarily* arise in all instances? It is unlikely. Some speakers who possess the intellectual, moral, and personal strength to resist such governmental manipulation may even become more committed to their original positions. But surely we must recognize at least the possibility that many speakers will in fact be negatively impacted, both intellectually and personally, by forced repetition.[39]

All of the pathologies just described can, in one way or another, be deemed to undermine the liberal democratic social contract between government and citizen, and therefore fail the test of the regulatory-centric model. For all of the reasons just explained, governmentally compelled speech undermines the notion of the individual citizen as an integral whole, worthy of respect. Instead, the separation between government and citizen is dangerously undermined by government's ability to disrupt communication between private speaker and private listener. It is thus not surprising that the courts have

---

[39] This is especially true of governmentally forced expression by school children. For a detailed description of these dangers, see Martin H. Redish, *The Logic of Persecution: Free Expression and the McCarthy Era* (Stanford, CA: Stanford University Press, 2005), pp. 187–90 (describing totalitarian use of forced expression as a means of gaining acceptance among school children).

extended full First Amendment protection not only to governmental *suppression* of expression but also to protection against *compulsion* of expression. Both forms of governmental manipulation of private expression lead to similar pathologies sought to be prevented by the First Amendment guarantee.

COMPELLED COMMERCIAL SPEECH

Compelled Commercial Speech in the Supreme Court

In the context of the suppression of commercial speech, the Supreme Court historically proceeded on the assumption that such speech restrictions could be justified more easily than could restrictions on more traditionally protected categories of expression.[40] Instead of testing the constitutionality of such restrictions on the basis of strict scrutiny, the Court traditionally employed the "intermediate scrutiny" of the so-called *Central Hudson* test.[41] As explained in earlier chapters, however, more recently the Court's approach has evolved to provide a far more protective level of protection to truthful commercial speech advocating purchase of a lawful product or service. This level of protection approaches, if not equals, that given to traditional forms of expression.[42]

While the Court has on occasion dealt with First Amendment questions surrounding compelled commercial speech, it has never fully explored the question of whether such compulsion is to be measured by the same standards as suppression of commercial speech. The one thing that does seem to be clear by this point is that the Court considers the First Amendment to extend at least some level of constitutional protection against such compulsion. But the contours of this protection are clouded in mystery.

The Court's decisions break down into two categories: (1) governmentally compelled payments to support generic advertising campaigns with which individual contributors may disagree and (2) required disclaimers included in advertising to dispel potentially misleading claims. Three decisions fall into the first category: *Glickman v. Wileman Brothers & Elliott, Inc.*,[43] *United States v. United Foods, Inc.*,[44] and *Johanns v. Livestock Marketing*

---

[40] See, e.g., *Virginia State Bd. of Pharmacy v. Virginia Citizens Consumer Council*, 425 U.S. 748 (1976). See the discussion in Martin H. Redish, *Freedom of Expression: A Critical Analysis* (1984), pp. 60–68.
[41] *Central Hudson Gas & Elec. Corp. v. Public Serv. Comm'n*, 447 U.S. 557 (1980).
[42] See, e.g., *Sorrell v. IMS Health, Inc.*, 544 U.S. 512 (2011). See the discussion in Chapter 1, *supra*.
[43] 521 U.S. 457 (1997).
[44] 533 U.S. 405 (2001).

Association.[45] Each decision involved a compelled assessment imposed on commercial food growers or producers to support a governmentally sanctioned or organized generic advertising campaign.

The first of the three cases to be decided was *Glickman*. The Court there held that a statute compelling certain California fruit growers to contribute to generic advertising for their produce was constitutional, because "[b]usiness entities are compelled to fund generic advertising as part of a broader collective enterprise in which the regulatory scheme already constrains their freedom to act independently."[46] Furthermore, because the statute's provisions that allegedly compelled speech were part of a broader scheme of economic regulation, the "First Amendment does not provide a basis for reviewing such economic regulation, which enjoys the same strong presumption of validity that this Court accords to other policy judgments made by Congress."[47] In other words, First Amendment scrutiny would be inappropriate, because when viewed in a holistic manner subject to review was nothing more than a form of economic regulation.

In *United Foods*, a similar statute compelling funds from private businesses was at issue, but this time, the Court was dealing with a different business – mushroom growers. Here the Court held that such compelled contributions for purposes of expression were unconstitutional.[48] The Court sought to distinguish the case from *Glickman*: "The program sustained in *Glickman* differs from the one at issue here in a fundamental respect: The mandated assessments for speech in that case were ancillary to a more comprehensive program restricting marketing autonomy."[49] The statute regulating the mushroom growers was more limited in scope, primarily focused on compelling funds for generic advertising.

In *Johanns*, the regulated businesses challenged the constitutionality of a system involving the collection of taxes from the sale of their cattle, using the funding to generate generic advertising for the beef industry.[50] While acknowledging the similarities to the situation in *United Foods*, the Court nevertheless ruled that the system was constitutional, because it characterized the expression not as compelled private speech, but rather as "government speech."[51]

[45] 544 U.S. 550 (2005).
[46] 521 U.S. at 458.
[47] id. at 459.
[48] 533 U.S. at 405.
[49] id.
[50] 544 U.S. at 550.
[51] id. at 551.

Thus, while in *United Foods* the Court held that the program violated the First Amendment, in the other two decisions the Court upheld the compelled assessments. But in both of those cases, the Court relied on factors that, while highly questionable as a matter of either logic or practicality, at the very least leave open the possibility that as a general matter such compelled assessments are constitutionally problematic.

In one sense, these decisions arguably differ from more traditional forms of compelled speech, because they involve compelled assessments to support speech, rather than direct compulsion of speech by a private party.[52] More representative of this traditional form of compelled expression are disclaimers required by government designed to dispel potentially misleading commercial claims. The Court dealt with this issue primarily in *Zauderer v. Office of Disciplinary Counsel*.[53] There the Court authorized use of a required disclaimer in an attorney's advertisement in order to prevent it from potentially misleading readers.[54] But while it is true that the Court upheld the compulsion of expression by a private speaker, it is important to note the context in which the Court's ruling was made. The Court viewed such compulsion as a less invasive alternative to outright suppression of the advertisement. While indicating that *inherently* misleading advertisements could be constitutionally suppressed,[55] the Court found governmental suppression of advertisements that are merely *potentially* misleading to violate the First Amendment.[56] Pointing to "material differences between disclosure requirements and outright prohibitions on speech,"[57] the Court noted that in insisting upon such disclosures the state "has not attempted to prevent attorneys from conveying information to the public; it has only required them to provide somewhat more information than they might otherwise be inclined to present."[58]

While in upholding such required disclaimers the Court, consistent with the established doctrinal view of the time (but no longer), indicated that commercial speech received reduced protection.[59] The Court nevertheless recognized that the First Amendment imposed meaningful limits on the state's power. The Court noted that in requiring the disclaimer the state

---

[52] But see *Abood v. Detroit Bd. of Educ.*, 431 U.S. 209 (1977), overruled on other grounds, *Janus v. AFSCME*, 585 U.S.___ (2018) (forced contributions for political expression constitute unconstitutional forced political speech).
[53] 471 U.S. 626 (1985).
[54] id. at 650–51.
[55] id. at 641 [citing *In re RMJ*, 455 U.S. 191, 203 (1982)].
[56] id.
[57] id. at 650.
[58] id.
[59] id. at 651.

would be requiring the expression of "purely factual and uncontroversial information" about the services being offered.[60] "We do not suggest," the Court was careful to add, "that disclosure requirements do not implicate the advertiser's First Amendment rights at all. We recognize that *unjustified* or *unduly burdensome* disclosure requirements might offend the First Amendment by chilling protected commercial speech."[61]

It is true that the Court went on to state that "an advertiser's rights are adequately protected as long as disclosure requirements are *reasonably related* to the State's interest in preventing deception of consumers."[62] Thus, the Court could be construed to have applied only a highly deferential "reasonableness" test to determine whether the forced disclosure will be upheld. But even assuming this to be a correct reading of the Court's intent, it is misleadingly incomplete today to rely on *Zauderer* as controlling doctrine, without acknowledging the dramatic expansion of commercial speech protection in cases stretching from the mid-1990s to the present – all decided long after *Zauderer*.[63] To do so would place us in a doctrinal time warp. Instead, *Zauderer* must today be read with the gloss of the far more protective subsequent line of commercial speech cases. Under that considerably more protective approach, the state bears "a heavy burden" to show that its restriction on commercial speech truly advances a state interest.[64] In any event, the key takeaway from *Zauderer*, for present purposes, is that while the Court expressed its willingness to uphold compelled disclosures involving commercial speech, it did so (1) to prevent deceiving consumers in a manner that could result in economic harm and (2) only as a less invasive alternative to outright suppression.

Does Compelled Commercial Speech Trigger the Expressive Pathologies of Compelled Expression?

As described earlier, the four expressive pathologies to which compelled speech gives rise are (1) confusion, (2) dilution, (3) humiliation/demoralization, and (4) psychological manipulation. It is on the basis of these concerns that compelled speech has properly been held unconstitutional. Does compelled commercial speech trigger these same pathologies? It may not trigger *all* of them. But it is

[60] id.
[61] id. (emphasis added).
[62] id. (emphasis added).
[63] See, e.g., *Sorrell v. IMS Health*, 564 U.S. 552 (2011); *Greater New Orleans Broadcasting Ass'n v. United States*, 527 U.S. 173, 176 (1999); *44 Liquormart v. Rhode Island*, 517 U.S. 484 (1996).
[64] See cases cited in note 63, *supra*. See generally Chapter 1, *supra*.

not difficult to see how compelled commercial speech could trigger one or more of them, and from the perspective of First Amendment theory, the pathologies should be deemed sufficient, rather than necessary conditions. Giving rise to any one of them should be deemed to render compelled commercial speech unconstitutional, because any one of these pathologies causes a significant harm to First Amendment interests and values.

The first situation in which presumably all four pathologies could be triggered is when the commercial advertiser is an individual or group of individuals, rather than a corporation. If, for example, an individual honey seller sincerely believes that honey cures certain ills, the government's requiring him to include in his advertisements the statement that any claim that honey cures any illness is false will undoubtedly confuse the populace, dilute the force of his message, bring about both humiliation and demoralization, and potentially result in psychological manipulation of the speaker. This is just as true when the honey seller is forced to include this information as when the writer of a magazine or blog article extolling the medicinal virtues of honey is required by the government to state that honey has no medicinal value. To be sure, it does not necessarily follow that such a governmentally imposed requirement should be held unconstitutional; it may be that such a requirement could serve a compelling interest that would satisfy even fully protected exercises of First Amendment rights – an issue to which my analysis will return subsequently.[65] But at least as a *prima facie* matter, it is difficult to see how the honey seller's situation would be different from a traditional noncommercial compelled speech case. True, the honey seller is seeking to gain financially from acceptance of his speech, and as a result he can hardly be deemed an objective observer. But surely we do not automatically disqualify self-interested speakers, or even those hoping for financial gain as a result of the acceptance of their expression, from substantial First Amendment protection.[66] Other than stark ideological opposition to the capitalism of which the honey seller's speech is one small part – hardly a principled ground for exclusion from the First Amendment's scope and a clear violation of the rationalist-centric model's dictates – there exists no logical basis to give protection against compulsion of his speech any less protection than one gives to the compelled expression of any speaker.

More difficult problems arise when, as is usually the case, the commercial speaker takes the form of a profit-making corporation. Application of the "four pathologies" analysis of compelled speech – confusion, dilution, humiliation,

---

[65] See discussion *infra* at 120–25.
[66] For a more detailed exposition of this point, see Redish, *supra* note 10, at 6–27.

and psychological manipulation[67] – to a corporate speaker produces mixed and complicated results. For example, the idea that corporations can be demoralized by being forced to communicate must presume that a corporation has some sort of emotional framework similar to that of a human. Most will deem this a stretch, even for those who believe in the First Amendment rights of corporate speakers, though it is important to recall that behind every corporation are the humans who formed and benefit from it.[68] But just because one of the four pathologies is not triggered, it does not necessarily follow that *all* of them are similarly unaffected. And as long as any one of the four separate interests has been undermined, the First Amendment right itself has been undermined. For example, even if a speaker has not been demoralized, foundational interests of free expression and democratic theory are seriously threatened if those receiving the information have been confused either about the level of private acceptance of the government's position or about the strength of the speaker's convictions. There is no reason that governmental satisfaction of one of the four pathologies should be deemed sufficient to support a finding of constitutionality. For the right of free expression to thrive, the triggering of *any* of the pathologies should, at least as a *prima facie* matter, be deemed to constitute a First Amendment violation because if a governmental compulsion to speak undermines any one of them, a serious harm has resulted that is sufficient to constitute a violation of the First Amendment, problems for the furtherance of the values and interests of free expression result.

In any event, the issues surrounding a corporate speaker are not confined to the commercial speech context. Commercial newspapers, books, and magazines are published by profit-making corporations. Governmentally compelled speech by these speakers no more gives rise to speaker demoralization than compelled commercial speech by profit-making corporations. Of course, there are those who continue to argue that in *either* context – suppression or compulsion – commercial speech is deserving of either no protection or, at the very least, a level of protection far lower than that extended to noncommercial speech.

Under the approach I have proposed to measure the extent of First Amendment protection that particular expression should receive,[69] one could argue that there exists no speaker-centric interest being fostered by commercial speech, at least when the speaker is a corporation, because

---

[67] See Chapter 1, *supra*.
[68] See generally Martin H. Redish & Howard M. Wasserman, *What's Good for General Motors: Corporate Speech and the Theory of Free Expression*, 66 Geo. Wash. U. L. Rev. 235 (1998).
[69] See Chapter 1, *supra*.

corporations cannot develop or evolve the way individuals can.[70] The point is open to debate; it should never be forgotten that corporations are formed by humans to assist them in realizing their goals and potential, and thus can plausibly be characterized as a form of catalytic self-realization. In any event, because satisfaction of any one of the three perspectives is a necessary rather than a sufficient condition to satisfy the First Amendment, this fact should in no way alter constitutional protection against governmental suppression of commercial speech.

It is true that in the case of the compulsion of commercial speech, the listener-centric model could conceivably be *advanced* by compelled speech, because such speech could often result in enrichment of the listeners in the performance of their private self-governing function. But the same could often be said of compelled noncommercial speech. In any event, in certain contexts compulsion of commercial speech would seriously undermine both the confusion and dilution pathologies of compelled speech, thereby actually undermining the values of the listener-centric model.

In short, in deciding whether compelled commercial speech violates the First Amendment, the devil is in the details. From the perspective of free speech theory, then, there are occasions where compelled speech will not only fail to trigger the compulsion pathologies, it will actually foster free speech values. In other contexts, however, compelled speech will be very harmful to the interests of free expression. In the section that follows, I attempt to fashion a roadmap for determining whether compelled commercial speech should be deemed to violate the First Amendment, to advance its interests or at least not to be inconsistent with its directives or the interests it is designed to foster.

Under What Circumstances Does Compelled Commercial Speech Violate the First Amendment?

In determining whether or not compelled commercial speech is constitutionally prohibited, there are two approaches one can employ. On the one hand, one could begin with the default presumption that compelled commercial speech is constitutionally prohibited, and the burden would then be on those seeking to compel such speech to provide sufficient reasons to overcome that presumed constitutionally dictated prohibition. On the other hand, one could begin constitutional analysis with the opposite

---

[70] C. Edwin Baker, *Scope of the First Amendment Freedom of Speech*, 25 UCLA L. Rev. 964, 996 (1978).

presumption: compelled commercial speech is permitted, unless those opposing such compelled statements can overcome that presumption by affirmatively demonstrating ways in which the compelled expression undermines important First Amendment values. It might be possible, however, to blend the two perspectives, by imposing a standard that includes both "qualifiers" (i.e., prerequisites that compelled commercial speech needs to satisfy to be constitutional) and "disqualifiers" (i.e., fatal defects, automatically rendering compelled commercial speech unconstitutional). Such an approach would provide a significant level of protection for commercial speech while simultaneously recognizing the need for compelled expression in situations in which a showing of special need to protect and inform the public has been made.

To summarize the procedure envisioned by the model of compelled commercial speech advanced here: The initial burden would be placed on those seeking to justify compelled commercial speech. If they fail to satisfy that burden, compelled commercial speech is deemed unconstitutional. If, however, they do satisfy that burden, then those opposing compelled speech can assert, as an affirmative defense, factors that effectively disqualify compelled speech, despite the initial showing of qualification.

The concept of the qualifier requirement begins with the presumption of the baseline value of allowing any speaker to determine for itself what to communicate and what not to communicate to its listeners or readers. In two situations, however, government should be recognized to possess legitimate authority to compel a commercial speaker to convey information that it would not itself have chosen to communicate: (1) when the additional information is necessary to enable the listeners or readers to protect their health or keep them safe or (2) when the additional information is necessary to protect the readers or listeners from being economically defrauded by the commercial speaker. In other words, health, safety, and fraud prevention are categorically to be deemed sufficiently compelling interests, thereby justifying a departure from the presumption against compelled commercial speech. While at first glance these categorizations may appear to restrict government to only narrow situations in which it may compel commercial speech, as a practical matter, these categories cover basically all of the reasons that government should be deemed to possess a legitimate concern in compelling commercial speech in the first place. An example of the first qualifier would be the required inclusion of the risk of possibly harmful side effects in advertisements for prescription drugs. The second qualifier is simply an incorporation by reference of the *Zauderer* doctrine, which upholds governmental requirements of disclaimers in commercial speech when, absent the disclaimer, a serious risk of misleading and ultimately defrauding the consumer would exist.[71]

Under the blended approach to the constitutionality of compelled commercial speech which I propose, however, the mere fact that a particular governmental compulsion falls within one of the compelling categorical justifications (or "qualifiers," as I have called them) does not automatically lead to a finding of constitutionality. In addition, the compulsion of commercial speech would have to avoid contravening the "disqualifiers" that must be imposed in order to keep government from interfering communications between private speaker and private listener in a constitutionally pathological manner. Those disqualifiers include the following situations: (1) when the commercial speaker reasonably disputes the factual accuracy of some or all of the information the government wishes to require it to communicate or (2) when communication of the required information would, purely as a physical matter, have the indirect impact of effectively interfering with the commercial speaker's ability to convey its own information or opinion to the reader or listener.

The first disqualifier is grounded in the need to avoid the confusion and dilution pathologies. But invocation of this disqualifier cannot serve as a "get-out-of-jail-free" card, effectively permitting a speaker to avoid compelled expression simply by asserting the conclusory claim that it disputes the factual or scientific accuracy of the government's required statements. It is only when the private speaker's dispute is reasonably grounded in plausible scientific theory or fact that the pathologies of compelled speech are triggered. In other words, the court must be convinced that there exists a reasonable scientific dispute on the issue in question. Here, too, the devil will ultimately be in the details. One might therefore understandably criticize acceptance of this disqualifier on the ground that it will require the reviewing court to immerse itself in factual or (even worse) scientific disputes to determine the reasonableness of the private speaker's dispute with the government. But much like Churchill said about democracy, this approach is the worst one – except for all the others.[72] Neither of the conceivable alternatives to requiring the court to delve into the reasonableness of the speaker's dispute of the substance of the government's compelled expression is particularly palatable. On the one hand, one could posit that anything government wishes the private speaker to say is constitutionally acceptable, regardless of how legitimate the speaker's

---

[71] See discussion *supra* at 116–17.
[72] "No one pretends that democracy is perfect or all-wise. Indeed it has been said that democracy is the worst form of government except all those other forms that have been tried from time to time." (Winston Churchill, Speech to the House of Commons, November 11, 1947) (as quoted in The Oxford Dictionary of Quotations 150 (3rd ed. 1979)).

dispute with the substance of the government's compelled speech may be. Such an approach would risk triggering most or all of the pathologies brought about by compelled speech.[73] The only other alternative is to permit the speaker to exercise an unreviewable veto power over compelled speech – certainly an abuse of the First Amendment right against compelled speech. The only viable alternative, with all of its warts, is to require the court to proceed case by case, determining the reasonableness of the speaker's objection to the substance of the compelled speech.

In making a determination of the reasonableness of the speaker's scientific dispute with the government's dictated speech, a court need not find the speaker's version of the facts or science to be conclusively accurate and the government's version indisputably wrong. All that should be required to support a finding in favor of the speaker should be a showing of some plausible scientific or factual evidence supporting the speaker's version. To put the issue in technical procedural terms, the court should ask whether it would grant summary judgment against the speaker's position on the basis of the inadequacy of the evidence the speaker presents in support of its position. If it would deny such a hypothetical motion against the speaker, the court should find the governmentally dictated compelled speech to violate the First Amendment.

This does not mean that the government's version is necessarily inaccurate; it means only that the speaker's rejection of the government's version has some reasonable grounding, and therefore to require the speaker to parrot the government's version likely triggers all four of the pathologies to which compelled speech gives rise. Nor does it mean that government is powerless in its efforts to convince the populace of the correctness of its version of the facts. The government can conduct its own publicity campaign to disseminate its view in an effort to convince the populace of its correctness. What it cannot constitutionally do is use the private speaker as a conduit for that dissemination, lest it risk the very same kind of confusion, dilution, and psychological manipulation that the First Amendment's prohibition on compelled speech is designed to prevent.

The second disqualifier contemplates a situation in which the potential First Amendment problem is not the substance of the compelled speech, but rather its size in relation to the physical space available for the private speaker's message. In considering this disqualifier, it is important to keep in mind that commercial advertisers are generally not giving speeches or publishing articles. Commercial speech generally takes a variety of forms – billboards, pop-

---

[73] See discussion *supra* at 112–14.

up Internet ads, radio and TV ads, newspaper ads, and packaging information. It is conceivable that government could require the commercial speaker to include pictures or wording of such a nature as to effectively consume most or all of the physical space available for the commercial speaker to convey its message to the consuming public. Under this analysis, it does not matter whether or not the substance of the compelled speech is factually indisputable and important in protecting the public's health or safety. Such compulsion indirectly operates as suppression by severely limiting the commercial speaker's ability to convey its message, due simply to the physical realities of the expressive platform.

An example that should at least trigger First Amendment inquiry under the analysis of this disqualifier is the government's effort to require cigarette packages to include graphic pictures vividly underscoring the health dangers of smoking.[74] The First Amendment issue for present purposes is not whether the required pictures convey a factually or scientifically accurate message (though it is at least conceivable that such an issue could arise as well), but rather whether the required presence of the graphic messages as a practical matter leaves the commercial speaker with sufficient room on the pack to convey its message to the consumers in an effective manner. I make no judgment on how that issue should be resolved. The resolution would turn on the specifics of the individual case. Rather, I am merely suggesting that the case lends itself to such a First Amendment inquiry to determine whether the indirect suppressive disqualifier should be deemed applicable.

When the dust settles, the approach to compelled commercial speech proposed here requires that government avoid two disqualifiers and satisfy at least one of the two qualifiers before it can constitutionally compel a commercial speaker to include specific statements in its advertising. First, in order to qualify for constitutional validity, the compelled speech in question must either further the government's legitimate interest in protecting the health or safety of the public, or prevent imposition of a fraud on the public that could reasonably be expected to result in a financial loss.

Even if the compelled speech in question satisfies one or the other of the two qualifiers, in order to satisfy the First Amendment it must also avoid contravening either one of the two disqualifiers. It must not require the commercial speaker to utter statements whose accuracy it reasonably disputes, either on a factual or scientific level, and it must not consume so much of the available space as to significantly undermine the ability of the commercial speaker to express its message to the consuming public.

[74] See *R.J. Reynolds Tobacco Co. v. FDA*, 696 F.3d 1205 (D.C. Cir. 2012).

Admittedly, the standard proposed here will not always be easy or simple to apply to specific situations. This fact will no doubt upset those who yearn for reflexive, easy solutions to First Amendment problems. But when one realizes that either of the two options that potentially result from the use of a superficial, mechanical standard – i.e., either automatic protection or automatic exclusion from the First Amendment's protective scope – give rise to extremely dangerous consequences, one will recognize the need for the reviewing court to do the intellectual heavy lifting required by a more refined categorical analysis of the competing constitutional and policy interests involved.

COMPELLED COMMERCIAL SPEECH AND THE EQUIVALENCY PRINCIPLE: MAY NONCOMMERCIAL SPEECH EVER BE COMPELLED?

I have argued throughout this book that it is illogical and unprincipled to assert that, at least in the context of suppression, commercial speech is deserving of less First Amendment protection than noncommercial speech.[75] To be sure, this is not the view taken by a number of leading First Amendment scholars who have written on the subject.[76] But I have already explained throughout this book, in the simplest terms possible, why this is so,[77] and I have never seen a persuasive response to this reasoning. I have referred to this theory as the "equivalency principle."[78] This does not necessarily mean, however, that commercial speech will be protected as often as noncommercial speech will be. The explanation of this seeming paradox turns on the premise that First Amendment protection against governmental suppression is not absolute. Rather, it is widely accepted by both courts and scholars that even fully protected expression may be regulated in the presence of a compelling competing interest. Protection of the public's health and safety against immediate threats, I have argued, constitutes such a compelling interest, and commercial speech is, as a categorical matter, more likely to give rise to such a compelling danger than noncommercial speech is.[79] The same is true, I reasoned, of an immediate threat of intentional economic fraud, which also must be recognized as a compelling interest.[80] Thus, commercial speech can be recognized

---

[75] See, Chapter 1, *supra*.
[76] See, e.g. Frederick Schauer, *Commercial Speech and the Perils of Parity*, 25 Wm. & Mary Bill of Rts. J. 965 (2017).
[77] See Chapter 1, *supra*.
[78] See generally, Chapters 1, 2 & 3, *supra*.
[79] id.
[80] id.

as equivalent in value to noncommercial speech, yet at the same time be subject to a greater number of instances of constitutionally justified suppression.

In prior chapters, I did not consider the question of whether or not the equivalency principle similarly applies to governmental *compulsion* of speech, as well as to suppression. But years of experience immersed in the scholarly commercial speech wars make me anticipate the argument that unless I can demonstrate that my equivalency principle applies to *compelled* speech, my assertion that it applies to *suppressed* speech falls apart. Were such an argument to be made by those who oppose commercial speech parity in any form, I would categorically reject it. The contexts of suppression and compulsion are not necessarily fungible for this purpose. For example, one could argue that from the listener-centric perspective of free speech analysis,[81] suppression of the expression of information and opinion undermines the ability of the would-be recipients of that expression to govern their lives effectively and therefore undermines performance of the self-governing process. Yet compelled speech, in some cases,[82] may actually foster or facilitate performance of such inherently democratic functions.

It is true that, in the context of individual speakers, compelled speech may demoralize and psychologically manipulate the compelled speaker, and it is debatable whether those same harms exist in the context of a corporate speaker.[83] Thus, some may believe that there exists at least an arguable basis for rejecting the equivalency principle in the compelled speech context. But this possible difference is irrelevant in the suppression context; deprivation of potentially valuable information to the populace, standing alone, constitutes a sufficient constitutional pathology to justify a finding of unconstitutionality, regardless of the suppression's pathological impact on the speaker. Thus, even assuming – solely for purposes of argument – that one were to reach the conclusion that *suppression* of commercial speech causes more harm to interests and values protected by the First Amendment than *compulsion* of commercial speech, it surely does not logically follow that the equivalency principle is inapplicable in the regulatory suppression context. If the listener-centric model is deemed to be undermined by suppression of the speech of those *opposing* commercial sale of a product (as all anti-commercial speech

---

[81] See Chapter 1, *supra*.
[82] Note that in my proposed standard for determining the constitutionality of compelled commercial speech I have sought to separate situations in which such compelled speech would facilitate performance of the self-governing function or undermine it. See discussion *supra* at 120–23.
[83] See discussion *supra* at 119.

scholars presumably would conclude), then logically it is undermined by suppression of the speech of those *advocating* commercial sale (once again, at least absent the showing of a competing compelling interest justifying such suppression). This is so, even if we assume, for purposes of argument, that the same is not true in the context of compelled speech.

Thus, logically it matters not at all to the regulatory suppression context whether the equivalency principle applies as well to the regulatory compulsion context. But it is nevertheless appropriate to turn to that question. Should the standard proposed here for measuring the constitutionality of compelled commercial speech be deemed also the proper measure of the constitutionality of compelled noncommercial speech, thereby triggering the equivalency principle's applicability to the compulsion as well as to the suppression context? The answer, I believe, is most definitely yes.

The first point to note is that despite the Court's eloquent (if largely vacuous) defense of the First Amendment's prohibition of compelled noncommercial speech in cases like *Barnette* and *Wooley*,[84] in neither of those landmark decisions was there even an arguably compelling governmental interest justifying the compulsion. *Barnette*, it should be recalled, dealt with whether the state could require a Jehovah's Witness school girl to pledge allegiance to the flag. *Wooley* concerned the question whether a Jehovah's Witness couple could be required to display New Hampshire's slogan, "Live Free or Die," on their license plate. Both cases went to the heart of the regulatory-centric model of First Amendment analysis: governmental attempts to control the thought processes of its citizens. On the other hand, neither case involved even an arguably compelling governmental interest to justify such *prima facie* constitutional violations. Thus, as important as both decisions are in the history of First Amendment doctrine, neither tells us the slightest thing about the extent to which the prohibition on compelled noncommercial speech is absolute.

Even in the more traditional context of governmental suppression, First Amendment absolutism has never been accepted by the Court,[85] and only rarely advocated by First Amendment scholars. If absolutism is categorically rejected in the suppression context, there is no reason to assume it applies in the compulsion context. I am unaware of any Supreme Court decision invalidating compelled noncommercial speech in the face of even an arguably compelling governmental interest. Indeed, there are at least two instances

---

[84] See discussion *supra* at 109–11.
[85] See, e.g., *Brandenburg v. Ohio*, 395 U.S. 444 (1969) (per curiam); *New York Times Co. v. Sullivan*, 376 U.S. 254 (1964).

where the Court has been very willing to uphold governmentally compelled speech on the part of noncommercial speakers. One is in the context of contributions to political campaigns, where the Court has upheld forced disclosures of names of both the contributors and the candidates to whom they contributed.[86] Such required disclosures serve two important public interests: to deter corruption, and to inform the electorate of who is supporting which candidates.

The other situation concerns the Court's decision in Red Lion v. FCC,[87] upholding the FCC's Fairness Doctrine for broadcast licensees. The Court reasoned that licensees could be required to air positions with which they disagreed because such a requirement actually furthered the Meiklejohnian First Amendment listener-centric interest in keeping the voters informed.[88] To be sure, the Court's reasoning, grounded largely in assumptions of technological scarcity, will generally be inapplicable (indeed, it is now inapplicable in the context of Red Lion itself), as the Court has recognized.[89] But the decision nevertheless recognizes that in certain instances, because of the public's interest in receiving a wide variety of information and opinion, a speaker may be compelled to provide a platform for expression of views with which the speaker disagrees. In any event, anyone who takes the absolutist position that compelled noncommercial speech is always unconstitutional should take note of the judiciary's ability to compel witness testimony, without anyone ever suggesting the existence of a First Amendment problem with such compelled speech.

Thus, even in the noncommercial speech context, it is reasonable to assume that compelling interests exist that would justify compulsion. The only question is when, where and why. If one proceeds on the assumption that the showing of a compelling governmental interest is capable of justifying compelled noncommercial speech, one must of course determine what constitutes a sufficiently compelling interest in this context. In making this determination, it would seem reasonable to start with governmental efforts to protect against proximate threats to public health and safety. After all, it is difficult to imagine more compelling interests than these. Hence if, absent inclusion of some sort of required disclaimer, noncommercial speech presents a serious and proximate threat to health or safety, such a justification could reasonably be deemed compelling. This does not necessarily mean, however, that

---

[86] See Buckley v. Valeo, 421 U.S. 1 (1976).
[87] 395 U.S. 367 (1969).
[88] id. at 392.
[89] See, e.g., Miami Herald Pub. Co. v. Tornillo, 418 U.S. 241 (1974).

commercial and noncommercial compelled speech will receive identical treatment. As a general matter, it is likely that noncommercial speech that threatens health or safety will give rise to a less proximate danger, since it may not be as widely distributed as commercial speech nor contain as direct a promotion of sale as commercial speech generally does. This illustrates the potentially varying application of the equivalency principle. But this analysis would of course require a case-by-case inquiry, rather than a categorical *ex ante* classification, to make a final determination in individual cases.

Also seeming to satisfy this high bar to justify compelled noncommercial speech would be governmental efforts to prevent an intentional fraud that causes significant economic harm to members of the public. It is difficult to imagine a theory of the First Amendment, possibly short of one characterized by the most extreme form of unbending absolutism, that would deem commission of the crime of intentional economic fraud on the public to be constitutionally protected. Indeed, such expression could, consistent with the First Amendment, be suppressed by government. A *fortiori*, it could be allowed to be expressed only on the condition that it include some sort of disclaimer. Of course, as is the case in commercial speech, to satisfy First Amendment protections the compelled disclaimer would have to satisfy particular criteria – similar in many ways to my qualifiers and disqualifiers, used to determine the constitutionality of compelled commercial speech.[90]

Ultimately, this approach to compelled speech in the noncommercial speech context appears strikingly similar to the approach I have proposed for compelled commercial speech. And on some level, it would make little sense to reach any other conclusion. Consider the situation of the honey seller I described earlier.[91] If the honey seller takes out an advertisement stating that scientific proof exists showing that consuming honey either prevents or cures particular diseases, at the very least under *Zauderer*[92] he could be required to include a disclaimer stating that the FDA does not necessarily agree with his assertions. Such compelled speech could be deemed to protect against threats to public health and the potential threat of economic harm due to fraud. But what if, instead of including the assertion about the beneficial qualities of honey in an advertisement, the honey seller writes a book, or a newspaper op-ed column, making the exact same claim? Are we to conclude that all of a sudden, because the speech is no longer classified as commercial speech, the disclaimer requirement violates the First Amendment? Such

---

[90] See discussion *supra* at 120–24.
[91] See discussion *supra* at 118.
[92] *Zauderer* v. *Office of Disciplinary Council*, 471 U.S. 626 (1985).

a rigid dichotomy would place form over substance, ignoring the fact that possibly the exact same dangers arise when the claims are made in a more traditional form of noncommercial communication. Thus, assuming a finding has been made that the reach of the communication and the demographic of those exposed to the communication is virtually identical in both instances, drawing a distinction for First Amendment purposes between the two situations makes no sense.

One could reasonably impose on the health-safety exceptions to First Amendment protection against compelled speech the requirements that the threat be shown to be serious, clear, and proximate. But there exists no legitimate reason why those very same qualifiers should not apply with equal force to application of the health-safety exception to the constitutional ban on compelled commercial speech. Similarly, in allowing government to require inclusion of some form of disclaimer, we need to keep in mind that the nature of advocacy allows some selectivity in choice of facts and arguments. An advocate need not make the opposition's case for it.[93] Thus, required inclusion of all counterarguments could have a devastating impact on the exercise of First Amendment rights. Therefore, it should only be where the danger has been shown to be both serious and proximate that government should be permitted to depart from this foundational precept of free expression. This is surely true in the case of political speech, and there is every reason for commercial speech to be treated in the same manner.

It should once again be emphasized that, as in the case of First Amendment protection of false factual claims,[94] this does not necessarily mean that governmentally compelled commercial speech will be invalidated as often as compelled noncommercial speech will be. This is so, even if one starts with the premise, as I would, that compelled commercial speech risks giving rise to many of the same fatal constitutional pathologies deemed to dictate the unconstitutionality of compelled noncommercial speech.[95] For example, situations will often arise where the commercial speech, because of its wide distribution, the directness and intensity of its promotion of sale, and the demographic qualities of the audience reached, may give rise to a more serious threat to public health or safety than would, say, the same claims made in a less widely distributed scholarly article, seen only by a much smaller and more intellectually discerning audience. But recognition of this possibility does not

---

[93] This concern is consistent with my theory of the adversary First Amendment. See Martin H. Redish, *The Adversary First Amendment: Free Expression and the Foundations of American Democracy* 1–15.
[94] See Chapter 2, *supra*.
[95] See discussion *supra*.

in any way alter the basic fact that, much like my proposal for the treatment of compelled commercial speech, the long-standing First Amendment prohibition on compelled noncommercial speech is subject to an exception for compelling interests. Thus, I think it is fair to conclude that under the approach I propose for First Amendment treatment of compelled commercial speech, the equivalency principle between commercial and noncommercial speech for First Amendment purposes properly applies.

CONCLUSION

The First Amendment law concerning compelled speech is not as clear-cut as many may think it is. Many likely assume that compelled speech is automatically unconstitutional in the context of noncommercial speech and automatically constitutional in the commercial speech context. But if so, they would be wrong. While the classic cases concerning compelled noncommercial speech, such as *Barnette* and *Wooley*, were easily resolvable in favor of a finding of unconstitutionality, neither involved even an arguably compelling governmental interest to justify the compulsion. To the contrary, both represented paradigmatic invasions of the regulatory-centric model's categorical prohibition of governmental efforts to engage in citizen thought control.[96] On the other hand, the Supreme Court has correctly recognized that compelled commercial speech may trigger many of the classic – and fatal – First Amendment pathologies to which compelled speech gives rise, even if it does not necessarily trigger all of them.

In this chapter, I propose a concededly complex standard to determine the constitutionality of compelled commercial speech, including an inquiry into both qualifiers and disqualifiers central to making the determination of constitutionality.[97] Under this standard, it is only when government seeks to protect against a clearly defined, serious, and proximate threat to public health or safety or the imposition of an intentional economic fraud on the public that it may overcome the standing presumption against governmental interference in communications between private speaker and private listener. Moreover, in order to qualify for a finding of constitutionality, the compelled speech must not include facts or scientific statements with which the compelled speaker reasonably disagrees. Nor may the compelled speech, regardless of its content, effectively consume the expressive platform in question, thereby disrupting the

---

[96] See discussion *supra* at 106–07.
[97] See discussion *supra* at 120–25.

commercial speaker's ability to communicate its message to its potential customers.

Whether such a standard, even assuming it were to be accepted in the context of commercial speech, should be deemed equally applicable to test the constitutionality of compelled noncommercial speech remains doctrinally unresolved at this point in time. Even if one were to reject fungibility between compelled commercial and noncommercial speech, that would have no logical impact on the extent to which commercial and noncommercial speech should be deemed equivalent for purposes of judging the constitutionality of direct suppression. But it is my belief that, as a matter of both logic and policy, the standard I have developed to judge the constitutionality of compelled commercial speech applies with equal justification in the context of compelled noncommercial speech. As in other areas of First Amendment law, though many scholars of free expression seem to be unable to understand or accept the inescapable logic of this position, the equivalency principle between commercial and noncommercial speech is applicable to instances of compelled, as well as suppressed, expression.

5

Scientific Expression and Commercial Speech: The Problem of Product Health Claims

INTRODUCTION

Issues of commercial speech protection become especially complex when they arise in the context of scientific expression. In this chapter, I focus on broad issues concerning application of the First Amendment to scientific claims made in the context of commercial advertisements. This analysis leads to the conclusion that scientific claims made in the context of commercial promotion deserve a level of First Amendment protection equivalent to that given to comparable scientific claims made to a similar audience. As counterintuitive as this may seem at first, it flows logically from the dictates of the equivalency principle. As a general matter, commercially motivated scientific claims serve much the same expressive values as similar claims made in other contexts. To the extent the two are to be distinguished, it is only because the differences between the two contexts make one more dangerous than the other. To the extent such situations arise, as will be seen, use of appropriate disclaimers can in most cases circumvent the problems caused by the context of commercial expression.

PRODUCT HEALTH CLAIMS AND THE FIRST AMENDMENT: RECOGNIZING THE SCIENTIFIC-COMMERCIAL SPEECH CONUNDRUM

Imagine for a moment that Congress enacts the False and Misleading Medical and Scientific Reporting Act of 2021. The law is premised on a fear that scientific quackery may cause significant societal harm by confusing the public and inducing its members to seek out costly, worthless, and possibly harmful medical cures or supposed scientific advances. The Act establishes a special commission of scientific and medical experts to rule on the accuracy of any proposed scientific or medical theory that conceivably could cause public harm or confusion. Such scientific or medical assertions must be substantiated to the commission's satisfaction, or the speaker risks issuance of a cease and desist order, imposition of criminal penalties or both.

Only the narrowest of free speech theorists[1] would find this statute to satisfy the First Amendment. Indeed, most observers[2] would recoil at the creation of such a governmentally imposed 'Big Brother' of scientific inquiry. In part, this is because imposition of a governmental pall of intellectual orthodoxy is inconsistent with the assumptions traditionally deemed to underlie a free society. The ability to engage in uninhibited intellectual inquiry and communication is essential to the mental and personal development of the individual.[3] This development is indispensable if individuals are to participate actively in the governing of their lives, an activity inherent in a democratic system.[4]

The instinctive repugnance felt toward this hypothetical statute derives from another premise of a fundamentally democratic society: what might be labeled the "principle of epistemological humility." This principle posits that whatever the currently prevailing beliefs may be, history teaches us that scientific or moral advances may at some future point make those beliefs appear either silly or monstrous.[5] Accordingly, the Supreme Court has said "there is no such thing as a false idea" under the First Amendment.[6] "However pernicious an opinion may seem, we depend for its correction not on the

---

[1] One such exception, at least prior to his confirmation hearings, would have been Judge Robert Bork, who wrote that "[t]here is no basis for judicial intervention to protect any ... form of expression [other than political speech], be it scientific, literary or that variety of expression we call obscene or pornographic." Bork, *Neutral Principles and Some First Amendment Problems*, 47 Ind. L. J. 1, 20 (1971). Robert Nagel is another scholar who would provide only very limited protection to speech of any kind. See Robert Nagel, *Constitutional Cultures: The Mentality and Consequences of Judicial Review* (Berkeley, CA: University of California Press, 1989), pp. 27–59. He appears to make no special mention of scientific expression, however.

[2] See, e.g., Alexander Meiklejohn, *The First Amendment Is an Absolute*, 1961 Sup. Ct. Rev. 245, 263 (urging protection of scientific speech); see also Thomas Emerson, *The System of Freedom of Expression* (New York: Random House, 1970), pp. 6–7 stating: "[F]reedom of expression is an essential process for advancing knowledge and discovering truth. An individual who seeks knowledge and truth must hear all sides of the question, consider all alternatives, test his judgment by exposing it to opposition, and make full use of different minds. Discussion must be kept open no matter how certainly true an accepted opinion may seem to be; many of the most widely acknowledged truths have turned out to be erroneous."

[3] See Thomas Emerson, *supra* note 2, at 6. My own analysis of this free speech value appears in Martin H. Redish, *Freedom of Expression: A Critical Analysis* (Miche Co. 1984), pp. 19–29.

[4] See Walker, *A Critique of the Elitist Theory of Democracy*, 60 Am. Pol. Sci. Rev. 285 (1966). John Stuart Mill is often associated with the developmental value of democracy. See generally John Stuart Mill, *On Liberty* (1978).

[5] See discussion *infra* at 161.

[6] *Gertz v. Robert Welch, Inc.*, 418 U.S. 323, 339 (1974).

conscience of judges and juries but on the competition of other ideas."[7] While the Court was quick to distinguish assertions of basic fact,[8] assertions of *scientific* fact traditionally are viewed as similar to the expression of ideas,[9] because both fall within the zone of the epistemological humility principle. Hence, any attempt by the government to impose a national scientific orthodoxy could undermine or inhibit the advance of scientific knowledge, thus undermining a key value fostered by the First Amendment.[10]

Despite the protection given by traditional First Amendment theory to scientific assertions, when the very same assertions are made as part of a commercial promotion of a product, attitudes change dramatically. Governmental regulation of product health claims demonstrates the clearest application of this dichotomy today. Because of both the public's strong desire for information about how the use or consumption of a product may affect one's health and the often uncertain, controversial, and the constantly changing nature of medical science, the government on numerous occasions has regulated health claims made on behalf of various commercial products. Both the Federal Trade Commission (FTC)[11] and the Food and Drug Administration (FDA)[12] exercise regulatory authority

---

[7] id. at 339–40.
[8] id. at 340.
[9] See sources cited in *supra* note 2.
[10] See Burt Neuborne, *Free Speech – Free Markets – Free Choice: An Essay on Commercial Speech* (1987), p. 2 (footnote omitted): "The laws that govern the physical and social universe can never be revealed except through a vigorous exchange of hypotheses and information that permits the identification of error and the recognition of scientific progress. We rightly sense that interference with free speech threatens to freeze conventional perceptions of reality into permanent intellectual prisons."
[11] The FTC's authority derives from § 12 of the Federal Trade Commission Act (Act), 15 U.S.C. § 52 (1988), which provides:

> It shall be unlawful for any person, partnership, or corporation to disseminate, or cause to be disseminated, any false advertisement . . . [b]y any means, for the purpose of inducing, or which is likely to induce, directly or indirectly, the purchase in or having an effect upon commerce of food, drugs, devices, or cosmetics. In addition, § 5 of the Act, 15 U.S.C. § 45 (1988), which applies to advertising for more than merely foods, provides that "unfair or deceptive acts or practices in or affecting commerce, are declared unlawful." According to one group of authorities, "A central principle in FTC law is that if advertising claims are not adequately substantiated they will be regarded as deceptive or unfair."

> J. Calfee & J. Pappalardo, *How Should Health Claims for Foods be Regulated? An Economic Perspective* (1989), p. 7.

[12] J. Calfee & J. Pappalardo, *supra* note 11, at 5 (footnote omitted): "FDA authority over disease prevention claims in food marketing arises from the Food Drug and Cosmetic Act . . . which prohibits the sale of misbranded foods or drugs in interstate commerce." Section 403(a) of the Food Drug and Cosmetic Act provides that "[a] food shall be deemed to be misbranded [if] its labeling is false or misleading in any particular." 21 U.S.C. § 343 (1988). See generally Hutt, *Government Regulation of Health Claims in Food Labeling and Advertising*, 41 Food Drug Cosm. L. J. 3 (1986).

over health claims made for various products. Regulation also has been sought at the state level, primarily through attempted judicial enforcement against allegedly deceptive product health claims.[13]

As shown in prior chapters,[14] in most situations modern commercial speech doctrine has evolved since the early days of its creation to provide a level of constitutional protection to commercial speech roughly equivalent to that extended to noncommercial speech, even as to regulations imposed in the name of health.[15] Yet a number of free speech scholars no doubt find little constitutional difficulty with governmental regulation of scientific claims made in the context of commercial advertising. Many commentators believe that commercial speech is either automatically rendered beneath First Amendment concerns,[16] or at least deserving of significantly reduced protection.[17] Moreover, it remains at the very least uncertain how the Supreme Court would rule in a First Amendment challenge to government regulation of commercial scientific claims, and it is certainly true that up to now, government's power to impose such regulations appears to be well accepted, if only tacitly. Surely, federal regulatory agencies assume such authority every day.

I have argued throughout this book that this disparate treatment of commercial speech is not justified by any legitimate understanding of First Amendment theory,[18] and I believe the same to be true of government regulation of scientific claims made in the context of commercial advertising. Under the equivalency principle advocated throughout this book, such speech appropriately is viewed not merely as commercial, but rather as scientific expression, made for purposes of commercial sale. To hold otherwise would

---

[13] An example was the proceeding brought in Texas state court by the State of Texas against the Quaker Oats Company. The State alleged that "Quaker has embarked upon a campaign of deception, designed to entice Texans who are concerned about their cholesterol levels and the risk of heart attack to buy and consume Quaker's oatmeal and oat bran products ... as a substitute for traditional medical treatment" and that Quaker is "motivated solely by the base purpose of selling as much of Quaker's products as possible." Plaintiff's Original Petition at 3, *Texas v. Quaker Oats Co.* (Dist. Ct., Dallas County, Texas, Sept. 7, 1989) (No. 89-10762-M).

[14] See Chapter 1, *supra*; Chapter 2, *supra*; Chapter 3, *supra*.

[15] See, e.g. *Lorillard Tobacco Co. v. Reilly*, 533 U.S. 525 (2001); *Thompson v. Western States Medical Center*, 535 U.S. 357 (2002).

[16] See, e.g., C. Edwin Baker, *Commercial Speech: A Problem in the Theory of Freedom*, 62 Iowa L. Rev. 1 (1976); Thomas Jackson & John Jeffries, *Commercial Speech: Economic Due Process and the First Amendment*, 65 Va. L. Rev. 1 (1979).

[17] See, e.g., Chapter 1, *supra*; Chapter 2, *supra* (discussing theories of Robert Post).

[18] See Redish, *supra* note 3, at 60–68. See generally Martin H. Redish, *The First Amendment in the Marketplace: Commercial Speech and the Values of Free Expression*, 39 Geo. Wash. L. Rev. 429 (1971).

be to penalize traditionally protected expression for no reason other than the communicator's personal motivation for making that expression. Motivation never has influenced the level of protection given to speech in other contexts[19] and its use cannot be rationalized under First Amendment theory.[20] This conclusion is dictated by the logic of the equivalency principle, shaped in prior chapters.[21]

This does not mean, of course, that assertions of scientific theory contained in commercial advertisements deserve absolute protection. The Court never has provided such an extreme degree of protection to even the most traditional subjects of expression.[22] Therefore, full protection to scientific-commercial speech would not require an absolute constitutional shelter. In the presence of either a truly compelling governmental interest[23] or a finding of conscious or reckless falsity, all speech may be regulated.[24] The same should be true of scientific-commercial speech. Under the equivalency principle, scientific-commercial speech should receive the same level of constitutional protection given to pure scientific expression with only one limited exception required by certain historical differences. Under the approach advocated here, before a court upholds governmental regulation of assertions of scientific theory contained in commercial advertisements, it first must inquire whether the regulation of the same assertion, made to the same audience by an individual lacking a direct profit motive, would be upheld. Certain guidelines may be provided to help answer this question in specific instances.[25] Regardless of how the reviewing court chooses to resolve this issue, the answer generally should not vary on the basis of the presence or absence of the profit motive.

As is true of other categories of expressive regulation explored in these pages, however,[26] application of the equivalency principle as I have defined it will not necessarily mean that the First Amendment outcomes will always be

---

[19] See discussion *infra* at 143–46.
[20] See discussion *infra* at 144–46.
[21] See Chapters 1–4, *supra*.
[22] See, e.g., *Heffron v. International Soc'y for Krishna Consciousness, Inc.*, 452 U.S. 640, 650 (1981) (stating that as "a general matter, it is clear that a State's interest in protecting the 'safety and convenience' of persons using a public forum is a valid governmental objective"); *New York Times v. Sullivan*, 376 U.S. 254, 279–80 (1964) (defamation of public official not protected if said with knowledge of falsity or reckless disregard of truth or falsity); *Dennis v. United States*, 341 U.S. 494 (1951) (political advocacy of unlawful conduct is not protected); *Feiner v. New York*, 340 U.S. 315 (1951) (speech prohibited to prevent reaction by a hostile audience).
[23] See cases cited *supra* note 22.
[24] See *Gertz v. Robert Welch, Inc.*, 418 U.S. 323 (1974); *New York Times*, 376 U.S. at 254.
[25] See discussion *infra* at 155–56.
[26] See, e.g., Chapter 2, *supra*; Chapter 3, *supra*.

identical in cases of commercial and noncommercial speech regulation. It means, simply, that they both are to be judged by the same standards in determining whether a sufficiently compelling competing interest exists to justify regulation. It is conceivable that, because of differing levels of distribution and differences in the expertise and intellectual sophistication of the audience reached, harmful commercial speech may cause far greater damage than parallel noncommercial speech. For example, commercial advertisements given general societal distribution may reach a much larger and different audience than scientific journal articles, thereby possibly causing far more harm than the scholarly articles. In such a situation, it is possible that the First Amendment would allow the commercial advertisements to be regulated while not finding a sufficiently compelling interest to justify suppression in the case of the scientific scholarly works. But both will nevertheless have been judged under identical standards, and both will be assumed to possess identical scientific value.

Governmental regulation of product health claims can have one of three general goals, depending on the nature of the government's asserted interest for the regulation. Initially, the government conceivably might wish to prohibit all health claims concerning a particular group of products, despite their scientific accuracy, because of a fear that the public could misconstrue or unduly exaggerate the extent of such claims. Second, the government might wish to prohibit claims for products that are legally sold, because the government wishes to deter the sale or use of those products. Finally, government might seek to suppress as false or deceptive those claims found either to be inconsistent with scientific consensus or to fail a type of cost-benefit analysis that weighs the potential benefit of the advertising against its potential harms. The first type of regulation has been employed in the past by the FDA in the labeling of foods.[27] The second regulatory category includes attempts to suppress tobacco advertising.[28] The third category traditionally has been used by the FTC in the regulation of product advertising,[29] and a similar approach is likely to be employed in the future by the FDA.

---

[27] See Calfee & Pappalardo, *supra* note 11, at iv (noting that more "health information had not appeared in food labeling earlier because the Food and Drug Administration ... officially prohibited this use of health findings for many years").

[28] See generally, Martin H. Redish, *Tobacco Advertising and the First Amendment*, 81 Iowa L. Rev. 589 (1996).

[29] See id. Calfee & Pappalardo, *supra* note 11 at viii. While the FTC employed the "consensus" method in negotiating a ban on tar and nicotine advertising in 1960, its current "substantiation" doctrine is an application of what Calfee and Pappalardo refer to as the "expected value" rule, which states: Under this doctrine the decision to allow or prohibit an advertising claim is based upon a comparison of the likely costs and benefits of each action. A rigid

These regulatory options give rise to distinct First Amendment problems, and the remainder of this chapter is devoted to their examination. The next section considers the constitutionality of a total ban on health claims by certain products, and concludes that such a ban is unconstitutional even under the reduced level of protection given by the Supreme Court's commercial speech precedents.[30] The section that follows examines the government's authority to regulate scientific assertions concerning products' health effects when those assertions are deemed to be inconsistent with current consensus.

BANNING ALL PRODUCT HEALTH CLAIMS: CONSTITUTIONALITY UNDER THE COMMERCIAL SPEECH DOCTRINE

No federal regulatory agency presently adheres to the policy that all health claims by certain product categories are impermissible.[31] Indeed, today numerous prescription drugs are regularly advertised on television. However, an examination of the constitutionality of such a practice can serve as a valuable working measure as to how far regulators may go in inhibiting scientific-commercial expression.

A total ban on product health claims violates the First Amendment, regardless of whether or not my argument that product health claims be deemed fully protected scientific expression is accepted. Even under the standard protection that the Supreme Court accords to commercial speech, a total ban would almost certainly be held unconstitutional.

In *Central Hudson* the Supreme Court adopted a four-part standard for commercial speech protection under the First Amendment: (1) it must concern lawful activity and not be misleading; (2) the government's interest must be "substantial"; (3) the regulation must directly advance the governmental interest asserted; and (4) it must not be more extensive than necessary to serve that interest.[32] While in its early years this test was construed to provide a very limited level of constitutional protection, more recently it has served as a strong protection of commercial speech.[33]

---

consensus is not uniformly required to support accurate claims. Put simply, the FTC's policy allows manufacturers to use information surrounded by scientific debate as long as the scientific finding is accurately represented, the degree of evidence is not misrepresented, and the claim passes a rough cost-benefit test. id. at viii–ix.

[30] See discussion *infra* at 139–42.
[31] See Calfee & Pappalardo, *supra* note 11, at iv–v.
[32] id. at 566.
[33] See Chapter 2, *supra*.

In the case of a total ban on product health claims, the state's asserted interest in preventing the public from exaggerating the implications of concededly truthful claims is not "substantial" and is inconsistent with the precepts underlying the First Amendment,[34] because it is premised on the fear that the public cannot be trusted to make valid judgments about truthful expression. For example, in *Virginia State Board of Pharmacy v. Virginia Citizens Consumer Council, Inc.*[35] the Court invalidated a prohibition on the advertising of prices of prescription drugs, rejecting the argument that consumers might give such information undue weight. The Court, in referring to this approach as "highly paternalistic," reasoned that price information should not be assumed harmful in itself, because people will discern their best interests when they are well informed through free and open, rather than closed, channels of communication. In any event, said the Court, the First Amendment has made the choice "between the dangers of suppressing information, and the dangers of its misuse if it is freely available."[36]

The same logic would seem to apply directly to the government's asserted interest in banning truthful health claims. Allowing the government to require the withholding of truthful information relevant to lawful activity because of a fear that the public will misunderstand that information abandons the essential premise of democratic government, namely that the individual can assess competing information and make lawful, life-affecting choices on the basis of that assessment.

Justice Stevens's plurality opinion for the Court in *44 Liquormart v. Rhode Island*[37] underscores this conclusion. In that case, the state of Rhode Island imposed a statutory bar on price advertising of liquor other than at point of sale. In finding this law to be a violation of the First Amendment's protection of commercial speech, Justice Stevens reasoned that "[p]recisely because bans against truthful, nonmisleading commercial speech rarely seek to protect

---

[34] See Justice Brandeis's famed concurring opinion in *Whitney v. California*, 274 U.S. 357, 375–77 (1927) (Brandeis, J., joined by Holmes, J., concurring):

> "Those who won our independence believed that the final end of the State was to make men free to develop their faculties. They believed that freedom to think as you will and to speak as you think are means indispensable to the discovery and spread of political truth and that the fitting remedy for evil counsels is good ones. Believing in the power of reason as applied through public discussion, they eschewed silence coerced by law .... If there be time to expose through discussion the falsehood and fallacies, to avert the evil by the processes of education, the remedy to be applied is more speech, not enforced silence."

[35] 425 U.S. 748 (1976) (the decision initially recognizing substantial protection for commercial speech).
[36] id. at 770.
[37] 517 U.S. 484 (1996).

consumers from either deception or overreaching, they usually rest solely on the offensive assumption that the public will respond 'irrationally' to the truth. The First Amendment directs us to be especially skeptical of regulations that seek to keep people in the dark for what the government perceives to be their own good. That teaching applies equally to state attempts to deprive consumers of accurate information about their chosen products."[38]

In this statement, Justice Stevens effectively applied the equivalency principle at least in the context of governmental regulation of truthful commercial speech. He recognizes the danger of what I have called "reverse dilution": that the paternalism inherent in government's selective suppression of truthful speech in order to manipulate citizens' lawful behavior is fundamentally pathological to the precepts of the liberal democratic social contract.[39] While this is unquestioningly true of governmental efforts to suppress truthful political, social, or scientific advocacy, it is now understood that the very same dangers to liberal democracy arise, even when the suppressed speech is made by the seller of a lawful product.[40]

Regulatory agencies' inability to impose a general ban on health claims for particular products, however, does not necessarily mean that they lack authority to prohibit or penalize health claims found to be false or misleading. If such claims were characterized as commercial speech, the courts would no doubt deny them constitutional protection because they clearly fail *Central Hudson's* first prerequisite: that the speech not be false or misleading.[41] Nevertheless, it should now be clear at least that truthful product health claims, even though they are unambiguously characterized as commercial speech, are to receive the same level of First Amendment protection afforded truthful speech of any kind.

In earlier chapters, I explained why the equivalency principle logically applies in the context of false commercial speech, as well as truthful commercial speech.[42] This is so, even though constitutional doctrine has never been modified to reach that conclusion. In the section that follows, however, I plan to make a type of fallback argument: Even if one were to reject the categorical rejection of *Central Hudson's* first requirement that protected speech be

---

[38] id.
[39] See Chapter 1, *supra*.
[40] This reasoning flows from the precepts of the "regulatory-centric" perspective, explained in Chapter 1, *supra*.
[41] *Central Hudson Gas & Elec. Corp. v. Public Serv. Comm'n*, 447 U.S. 557, 566 (1980). But see Chapter 2, *supra*, arguing against the categorical exclusion of false or misleading commercial speech from First Amendment protection.
[42] See Chapter 2, *supra*.

truthful and nonmisleading, one should nevertheless accept that the categorical falsity prohibition should be rejected selectively, at least in the context of what can be called "scientific" commercial speech. This is because the concept of "falsity" takes on an entirely different, more nebulous quality in the category of scientific speech. In many situations, an assertion of fact is, as a practical matter, usually either true or false – for example, it is raining outside; Tom shot Bill. In the context of scientific speech, however, the concept of truth, and therefore also falsity, is somewhat more nebulous. That distinction has enormous implications for the scope of First Amendment protection. The point, in short, is that even were one to reject the categorical application of the equivalency principle to false commercial speech – if only for purposes of argument – one should nevertheless apply it in the much narrower context of scientific speech.

REGULATING "FALSE" PRODUCT HEALTH CLAIMS: ESTABLISHING THE INTERSECTION OF COMMERCIAL AND SCIENTIFIC EXPRESSION

Scientific Expression and the Principle of Epistemological Humility

Virtually no free speech observer would find constitutionally tolerable a widespread system of governmental suppression of scientific opinion,[43] even when that opinion differed dramatically from the prevailing scientific consensus. The validity of the principle of epistemological humility in the scientific context is shown by recalling only a few of the many times throughout history when widespread scientific consensus subsequently proved to be pitifully inaccurate. From the suppression of Galileo's adoption of Copernicus's theory that the earth rotates around the sun[44] to the medical profession's early rejection of Pasteur's germ theory[45] to the pre-relativity theory assertion by a leading physicist that only minor advances remained for physics[46] to the FTC's contention, as recently as 1950, that cigarette

---

[43] See discussion *supra* at 133–34.
[44] See *Moore v. Gaston County Bd. of Educ.*, 357 F. Supp. 1037, 1042 (W.D.N.C. 1973) (recounting Galileo's story). See generally G. De Santillana, *The Crime of Galileo* (1955).
[45] See R. Dubos, *Louis Pasteur: Free Lance of Science* (1950), p. 248.
[46] In 1899, famed physicist A.A. Michelson stated: "The more important fundamental laws and facts of physical science have all been discovered, and these are so firmly established that the possibility of their ever being supplanted in consequence of new discoveries is exceedingly remote our future discoveries must be looked for in the sixth place of decimals." F. Richtmyer, E. Kennard & J. Cooper, *Introduction to Modern Physics* (6th ed. 1969), p. 43.

smoking was not harmful to healthy adults,[47] by now we should have learned our lesson. Indeed, in recent times some have begun to challenge the consensus concerning the connections between certain foods and cholesterol, on the one hand, and between high cholesterol and heart disease, on the other hand.[48] Thus, viewed from the broad perspective of history, any attempt by the government to lock in a prevailing scientific consensus is likely to be either futile, dangerous, or a combination of both. In addition, such attempts undermine both the search for knowledge and the development of a free and open exchange of information and opinion, traditionally deemed central values served by the right of free expression.

The belief that the very same scientific claims automatically lose their full level of constitutional protection when made by a product manufacturer in a commercial advertisement requires some logical basis, in terms of free speech theory, for the drawing of such a strict dichotomy. It is doubtful, however, that such a basis may be found.

Economic Motivation and Free Expression: The Difficulty of Defining Commercial Speech

Those who conclude that commercial speech deserves either only limited First Amendment protection[49] or none at all[50] naturally bear the burden of defining that concept. Presumably, any principled definition should turn on the reason for separating commercial speech from other forms of expression. For example, if the basis for this dichotomy is the assumption that the First Amendment is designed solely to facilitate the processes of self-government,[51] and that commercial speech is irrelevant to attainment of that value,[52] then the definition of commercial speech will depend on the subject matter of the expression. The logic behind this assumption would have to be that the subject of the comparative merits of commercial products is irrelevant to political decision making.

The adoption of that definition, however, would also logically exclude from First Amendment protection speech such as information from consumer

---

[47] "The record shows ... that the smoking of cigarettes ... in moderation by individuals who are accustomed to smoking and who are in normal good health ... is not appreciably harmful." R. J. Reynolds Tobacco Co., 42 F.T.C. 706, 724 (1950); see Calfee, *The Ghost of Cigarette Advertising Past*, REG. Nov.–Dec. 1986, at 35, 37.
[48] Moore, *The Cholesterol Myth*, Atlantic Monthly, September. 1989, at 37.
[49] See discussion *supra* at 135–36.
[50] See, e.g., Bork, *supra* note 1.
[51] See, e.g., Meiklejohn, *supra* note 3. Bork, *supra* note 1.
[52] See, e.g., Baker, *supra* note 16.

advocates about certain products or the findings contained in *Consumer Reports* magazine, because those necessarily concern the identical subject matter discussed in commercial advertisements. Yet the Supreme Court clearly has not provided a reduced level of First Amendment protection to *Consumer Reports*,[53] and that treatment is fully consistent with the Court's general definition of commercial speech. In *Virginia State Board of Pharmacy v. Virginia Citizens Consumer Council, Inc.*[54] and subsequent decisions, the Court has characterized commercial speech as "speech which does 'no more than propose a commercial transaction.'"[55] Very few advertisements actually do nothing more "than propose a commercial transaction," including many of the advertisements characterized by the Court as commercial speech.[56] Thus, the Court seems to mean that the proposal of a commercial transaction is a necessary, though perhaps not sufficient,[57] condition for inclusion within the definition of commercial speech. This approach excludes from the definition of commercial speech both *Consumer Reports* and expression by consumer advocates because in neither case is the speaker proposing a commercial transaction.

Under this definitional structure, one could understand how scientific claims asserted in commercial advertisements might – though need not[58] – be distinguished, for First Amendment purposes, from the same claims when made by those lacking a direct financial interest. Commercial advertisements "propose a commercial transaction," but the scientific claims made by so-called objective experts do not. The logic of the Court's definitional approach

---

[53] See *Bose Corp. v. Consumers Union of United States, Inc.*, 466 U.S. 485 (1984) (recognizing the applicability of the *New York Times v. Sullivan* conscious-or-reckless-falsity test to a magazine article about a commercial product).

[54] 425 U.S. 748, 762 (1976).

[55] See, e.g., *Bolger v. Youngs Drug Prods. Corp.*, 463 U.S. 60, 66 (1983) (quoting *Virginia State Board*, 425 U.S. at 762, and *Pittsburgh Press Co. v. Pittsburgh Comm'n on Human Relations*, 413 U.S. 376, 385 (1973)). In *Central Hudson*, 447 U.S. 557 (1980), the Court defined "commercial speech" as "expression related solely to the economic interests of the speaker and its audience." id. at 561. After *Bolger*, however, the Court "again seems to equate commercial speech and commercial advertising," and "seemed to equate the two even in *Central Hudson*." Shiffrin, *The First Amendment and Economic Regulation: Away From a General Theory of the First Amendment*, 78 Nw. U. L. Rev. 1212, 1222 n.70 (1983).

[56] *Bolger* is an illustration. See discussion *infra* at 150–51.

[57] A persuasive argument could be fashioned that when the predominant element of the communication necessarily concerns a traditionally protected subject, the inclusion of a proposal for a transaction should not be enough to render a statement commercial speech. See discussion *infra* at 145. Purely as a predictive doctrinal matter, however, the Court probably would deem any statement including such a direct proposal to be "commercial." See discussion *infra* at 150.

[58] See Chapter 1, *supra*.

reasonably may be questioned, however, because it is unclear why an otherwise fully protected statement loses full protection when a proposal for a commercial transaction is appended.

The presence of a proposal for a commercial transaction cannot, consistent with the dictates of both the rationalist-centric and regulatory-centric perspectives explained earlier in this book,[59] serve as the sole element to determine whether speech is commercial speech if one rationalizes reduced protection on the grounds that commercial speech is unrelated to effective self-government.[60] The same is of course true of any comment on commercial products that contains no such proposal. Arguably, inclusion of a proposal for a commercial transaction takes the speech out of the realm of the pure exposition of ideas and brings it closer to the concept of conduct, or "action."[61] The First Amendment, however, never has been thought to be the exclusive preserve of abstract ideas.[62] Advocacy of action has long been considered to fall within classic concepts of protected expression.[63] Indeed, there would be no small degree of irony in rationalizing reduced protection for commercial speech on the grounds that the proposal of a commercial transaction constitutes "action," while a consumer advocate's urging of the public *not* to buy a product simultaneously is viewed as fully protected "expression."

As we have already seen in other contexts throughout this book, the only other conceivable rationale for the Court's reliance on the presence of a commercial proposal in its definition of commercial speech is the simple fact of the profit motivation for the speech. The Court must be understood as saying that otherwise fully protected speech loses some or all of its constitutional protection when the speaker stands to profit financially from the

---

[59] See Chapter 1, *supra*.
[60] See, discussion *supra* at 134–35.
[61] Professor Emerson has argued that "a fundamental distinction must be drawn between conduct which consists of 'expression' and conduct which consists of 'action.' 'Expression' must be freely allowed and encouraged. 'Action' can be controlled, subject to other constitutional requirements, but not by controlling expression." T. Emerson, *supra* note 2, at 17. Thus, "when the communication is so close, direct, effective, and instantaneous in its impact that it is part of the action," he believes it should not be protected by the First Amendment. id. at 404. That Professor Emerson would define a communication merely including a proposal for a transaction as "action," rather than "expression," however, is highly doubtful under these definitions.
[62] As Justice Holmes wrote, "Every idea is an incitement. It offers itself for belief and if believed it is acted on unless some other belief outweighs it or some failure of energy stifles the movement at its birth." *Gitlow v. New York*, 268 U.S. 652, 673 (1925) (Holmes, J., joined by Brandeis, J., dissenting).
[63] See, e.g., *Brandenburg v. Ohio*, 395 U.S. 444 (1969). See generally Martin H. Redish, *Advocacy of Unlawful Conduct and the First Amendment: In Defense of Clear and Present Danger*, 70 Calif. L. Rev. 1159 (1982).

listener's acceptance of the argument being made.[64] But this logic is seriously flawed from the perspective of First Amendment theory. A speaker's motivation, standing alone, never has reduced the level of constitutional protection given particular types of expression. For example, one who defames a public figure may speak out of the most evil motives of spite, religious or racial hatred, or vengeance, yet those statements remain protected often unless uttered with knowledge of their falsity or reckless disregard of their truth or falsity.[65] Similarly, a newspaper usually includes expression for the sole purpose of financial gain, yet that expression is fully protected under the First Amendment.[66] Scholars have defended the Court's penalization of commercial speech because of its profit motivation by arguing that "whatever else it may mean, the concept of a First Amendment right of personal autonomy in matters of belief and expression stops short of a seller hawking his wares."[67] This mode of reasoning, however, which might be labeled "proof by hyperbolic pejorative," does little either to advance the analysis or to explicate the Court's logic.

Professor Edwin Baker presented a somewhat more tempered – though no less fallacious – rationale in the exposition of his "liberty model" of free speech.[68] Professor Baker believed that a fundamental rationale for free speech protection is the desire to foster communication that defines or develops "the self."[69] Because "the values supported or functions performed by protected speech result from that speech being a manifestation of individual freedom and choice,"[70] Baker concluded that speech which "does not represent an attempt to create or affect the world in a way which can be expected to represent anyone's private or personal wishes" is undeserving of First Amendment protection.[71] Baker reasoned that although the speech may cause change or advance knowledge, if it "is not a manifestation of the speaker's values," it does not serve this liberty value and is not protected.[72]

[64] For a response to the specious argument that commercial speech constitutes conduct and therefore extending First Amendment protection to such activity would constitute the indirect resurrection of the widely discredited economic substantive due process doctrine of *Lochner v. New York*, see Chapter 1, *supra*.
[65] *New York Times Co. v. Sullivan*, 376 U.S. 254 (1964); see also *Hustler Magazine v. Falwell*, 485 U.S. 46, 53 (1988) (holding that constitutional protection of public discourse does not depend upon the motivation for the expression).
[66] *New York Times*, 376 U.S. at 266.
[67] Jackson & Jeffries, *supra* note 16, at 14.
[68] C. Edwin Baker, *Scope of the First Amendment Freedom of Speech*, 25 UCLA L. Rev. 964 (1978).
[69] id. at 992.
[70] Baker, *supra* note 16, at 3.
[71] id.
[72] Baker, *supra* note 68, at 991 n.86.

Market forces, rather than individual choice, dictate what and how much a commercial enterprise will advertise, he argued,[73] and, therefore, commercial advertising should not receive First Amendment protection.

Excluding scientific assertions made by commercial advertisers from the scope of fully protected expression while fully protecting identical assertions when made by a seemingly neutral scientist or when reported in a newspaper makes perfect sense, if Professor Baker's theory were to be accepted. Professor Baker's fallacies, however, are both numerous and fatal.[74] Initially, if the First Amendment right consists at least in part of the listener's right to receive information,[75] then the speaker's motive logically should be irrelevant to the analysis.[76]

An equally important point, largely ignored by Professor Baker,[77] is that many people make a living by means of self-expressive work.[78] Many speakers stand to achieve direct personal gain in one way or another from the listener's acceptance of their speech – from the political candidate seeking election to the picketing welfare recipient seeking an increase in benefits. If the constitutional protection of speech were reduced or eliminated solely on the basis of a speaker's motivation for personal gain, considerably more than commercial advertising would be affected. Indeed, one could argue persuasively that even objective scientists have strong personal interests in the acceptance of the truth of their assertions, because disbelief of those assertions will do little to help their careers. Similarly, a newspaper obviously possesses a strong commercial interest in the public's acceptance of its claims about the health impact of certain products. For example, when a sensationalist tabloid proclaims that onions prevent heart attacks,[79] many purchase the newspaper because they wish to learn a new method of improving their health; they presumably would not buy the newspaper unless they thought the claim had at least some basis in fact.

---

[73] See generally Baker, *supra* note 16.
[74] I previously explored the fallacies of Professor Baker's analysis in detail in Martin H. Redish, *Freedom of Expression: A Critical Analysis* (Michie Co., 1984), pp. 30–36, 49–52.
[75] Both respected commentators and the Supreme Court have stated this view in the context of noncommercial speech. See Chapter 1, *supra*. See also *First Nat'l Bank v. Bellotti*, 435 U.S. 765, 783 (1978) (stating that "the Court's decisions involving corporations in the business of communication or entertainment are based not only on the role of the First Amendment in fostering individual self-expression but also on its role in affording the public access to discussion, debate, and the dissemination of information and ideas."); *Red Lion Broadcasting Co. v. FCC*, 395 U.S. 367, 390 (1969) (stating that it "is the right of the viewers and listeners, not the right of the broadcasters, which is paramount"); Meiklejohn, *supra* note 2.
[76] See Chapter 1, *supra*.
[77] See Redish, *supra* note 74, at 50–52.
[78] id. at 50.
[79] See *The Globe*, February 20, 1990, at 7, col. 1.

Perhaps support for Professor Baker's analysis can be found in the theories of the liberal civic republican scholars, who have decried the existence of interest groups and their influence over a political process that should be defined by the common good.[80] Because commercial advertisers presumably are motivated solely by the desire to increase profits, the modern republican theorists might wish to exclude commercial speech from the scope of First Amendment protection. The civic republicans, however, are misguided in their efforts to define a coherent, objective concept of common good, because they effectively are attempting to superimpose their externally derived political values on the populace in total derogation of the fundamental notion of self-determination. The essential premise of self-determination is that individuals may choose to govern their lives in the manner they believe best, even if that includes acting in their own self-interest. The civic republicans' belief in imposition of a distinct common good directly conflicts with this value.[81] In any event, even modern republican scholars acknowledge that private interests may constitute relevant inputs into politics.[82] Thus, their acceptance of Professor Baker's "liberty model" as the exclusive measure of free speech protection is not clear.

The Court has never adopted Professor Baker's "liberty model." For example, the Court has provided full constitutional protection to corporations' contributions to debate about public issues, despite the obvious profit motivation for those communications.[83] Professor Baker acknowledges that these decisions are wholly inconsistent with his theoretical framework,[84] and the decisions themselves make clear that the Court has not adopted Professor Baker's "liberty model." In these decisions the Court has noted that a company has the full panoply of protections available to its direct comments on public issues.[85]

This concession by the Court makes all but unintelligible its prerequisite to the categorization of expression as commercial speech that the speech

---

[80] See, e.g., Cass Sunstein, *Beyond the Republican Revival*, 97 Yale L. J. 1539, 1540, 1550 (1988) [hereinafter *Beyond the Republican Revival*]; see also Cass Sunstein, *Interest Groups in American Public Law*, 38 Stan. L. Rev. 29 (1985).

[81] See Martin H. Redish, *Federal Common Law, Political Legitimacy, and the Interpretive Process: An "Institutionalist" Perspective*, 83 Nw. U. L. Rev. 761, 761–64, 775–83 (1989).

[82] See, e.g., *Beyond the Republican Revival*, supra note 80, at 1541.

[83] See, e.g., *Citizens United; Pacific Gas & Elec. Co. v. Public Utils. Comm'n*, 475 U.S. 1 (1986) (newsletter mailed with utility bill); *Consolidated Edison Co. v. Public Serv. Comm'n*, 447 U.S. 530 (1980) (same); *First Nat'l Bank v. Bellotti*, 435 U.S. 765 (1978) (advertisement giving bank's views on proposed tax).

[84] *Bolger v. Youngs Drug Prods. Corp.*, 463 U.S. 60, 68 (1983) (citing *Consolidated Edison*, 447 U.S. at 530).

[85] See discussion *supra* at 147.

propose a commercial transaction, because combining these two principles results in the following enigma: Speech solely concerning commercial products or services is not necessarily commercial speech, because, under the Court's definition, if the discussion of products or services does not propose a commercial transaction it is considered fully protected speech.[86] Yet the mere presence of a profit motive for expression does not automatically render speech "commercial," because by the Court's own acknowledgment a corporation's direct contributions to public debate are fully protected. Thus, under the Court's precedents, neither a commercial subject matter nor the presence of a profit motive is a sufficient condition for a finding that particular expression constitutes commercial speech. The Court, then, seems to require the presence of both a commercially oriented subject matter and a speaker motivated by profit to support a finding of commercial speech. Yet the Court's willingness to find speech fully protected when either one of the two is absent renders dubious its willingness to reduce protection when both are present. Think of it in the following manner: If discussion of commercial products is not included automatically within the commercial speech category, and if the existence of a profit motive fails to achieve the same result, the Court effectively has acknowledged that neither factor renders speech "commercial." Why, then, does the combination of the two justify a reduced level of First Amendment protection? After all, as the Court has acknowledged, neither factor disqualifies speech from protection.

Those who oppose protection of commercial speech could conceivably respond that the answer is simply to deny full protection to the profit motivated speaker in all contexts, despite the reference to public issues and the absence of a direct request for purchase. That analysis, however, would effectively undermine the well-established principle that a speaker's motivation is irrelevant to the level of First Amendment protection given particular speech.[87] More importantly, such an analysis would effectively punish a speaker solely because of his profit motivation and would, therefore, constitute an irrational insertion of an anti-capitalistic philosophy into a supposedly politically neutral free speech theory.[88]

---

[86] See discussion *supra* at 143–45.
[87] See *Police Dep't v. Mosley*, 408 U.S. 92, 95 (1972) (stating that "above all else, the First Amendment means that government has no power to restrict expression because of its message, its ideas, its subject matter, or its content"); *Kingsley Int'l Pictures Corp. v. Regents of N.Y.U.*, 360 U.S. 684, 688 (1959). See generally Geoffrey Stone, *Content Regulation and the First Amendment*, 25 Wm. & Mary L. Rev. 189 (1983).
[88] *Bolger*, 463 U.S. at 68.

A synthesis of the Court's "propose-a-commercial-transaction" prerequisite for a finding that speech is commercial and its simultaneous acknowledgment that a corporation enjoys "the full panoply of [First Amendment] protections available for its direct comments on public issues,"[89] reasonably might conclude that a commercial enterprise would have a fully protected right to discuss the scientific merits of its product, as long as it did not urge purchase directly. While probably accurate, this conclusion is by no means certain. In *Central Hudson Gas & Electric Corp. v. Public Service Corp.* the Court recognized a distinction between fully protected "institutional and informational" messages, on the one hand, and those "clearly intended to promote sales," on the other.[90] Because any statement by a commercial enterprise about the scientific properties of its product could be deemed "intended to promote sales," it is conceivable that the Court would characterize any such statement as proposing a commercial transaction. The problem, however, is that the Court erroneously has viewed statements that are "informational" and those which are "intended to promote sales" as mutually exclusive. This need not be the case. The confusion results primarily because the Court has evolved this commercial versus informational distinction in cases in which the informational statement and the promotional element actually are severable; in product health claims, on the other hand, the two issues are intertwined inextricably.

A synthesis of the Court's approach to the dichotomy may be derived by contrasting three decisions: *Bolger v. Youngs Drug Products Corp.*,[91] *Consolidated Edison Co. v. Public Service Commission*,[92] and *First National Bank v. Bellotti* (the predecessor of the controversial decision in *Citizens United*).[93] In *Consolidated Edison* the Court invalidated the state public service commission's suppression of bill inserts by the company that discussed controversial public issues.[94] The Court relied on its earlier decision in *Bellotti*[95] to reject the assertion that a state may restrict corporate speech to specified issues.[96] In *Bellotti* the Court had framed the question for decision as "whether the corporate identity of the speaker deprives ... proposed speech of what otherwise would be its clear entitlement to protection." Justice Powell,

---

[89] 447 U.S. 557, 562 n.5 (1980).
[90] 463 U.S. 60 (1983).
[91] 447 U.S. 530 (1980).
[92] 435 U.S. 765 (1978); see also *Pacific Gas & Elec.*, 475 U.S. at 1.
[93] *Citizens United v. Federal Election Comm'n*, 558 U.S. 310 (2010).
[94] 447 U.S. at 544.
[95] 435 U.S. at 765.
[96] *Consolidated Edison*, 447 U.S. at 533.

answering the question in the negative, noted that "the Court has not identified a separate source for the right of free speech when it has been asserted by corporations."[97] He reasoned that "the Court's free speech decisions involving corporations in the business of communication or entertainment are based not only on the role of the First Amendment in fostering individual self-expression but also on its role in affording the public access to discussion, debate, and the dissemination of information and ideas."[98] He therefore could "find no support ... for the proposition that speech that otherwise would be within the protection of the First Amendment loses that protection simply because its source is a corporation."[99] While the Court was unwilling to define the outer reaches of this corporate right,[100] it did note that "especially where ... the legislature's suppression of speech suggests an attempt to give one side of a debatable public question an advantage in expressing its views to the people, the First Amendment is plainly offended."[101] Doctrinally, under both *Consolidated Edison* and *Bellotti*, once it is acknowledged that a product's scientific properties or impact on health represent "public issues," a corporation must have a First Amendment right to contribute to debate on those issues. This right is subject to the strong protections of a compelling interest analysis, which is above and beyond its more limited commercial speech right.

In *Bolger*, however, the Court attempted to explain the factors that determine whether the exercise of corporate speech falls within the comment-on-public-issues category or under the less protected commercial speech heading. *Bolger* concerned a First Amendment challenge to a federal statute[102] that prohibited the mailing of unsolicited advertisements for contraceptives. Youngs, a contraceptive manufacturer, proposed a mailing of advertisements that would include informational material discussing "public" issues such as venereal disease and family planning.[103] While the Supreme Court ultimately found the postal service's prohibition of Youngs's mailing to be unconstitutional,[104] it initially ejected Youngs's argument that the pamphlets should not be deemed less protected commercial speech because they

---

[97] *Bellotti*, 435 U.S. at 780.
[98] id. at 783.
[99] id. at 784.
[100] id. at 777.
[101] id. at 785–86 (footnote omitted).
[102] 39 U.S.C. § 3001(e)(2) (1988).
[103] *Bolger*, 463 U.S. at 62 & n.4.
[104] Youngs, said the Court, was proposing commercial speech presenting "truthful information relevant to important social issues" and, therefore, was protected by the First Amendment under the commercial speech doctrine. id. at 69.

included discussion of social issues. The mere fact that these pamphlets constitute advertisements does not require the conclusion that they are commercial speech, and "the reference to a specific product does not by itself render the pamphlets commercial speech," Justice Marshall's opinion reasoned.[105] Additionally, Youngs's economic motivation alone clearly would be insufficient to turn the materials into commercial speech.[106] Somewhat curiously, however, Justice Marshall concluded that "the combination of all these characteristics ... provides strong support for the District Court's conclusion that the informational pamphlets are properly characterized as commercial speech."[107] Under the *Bolger* analysis, then, the combined presence of the advertisement context, the reference to a specific product, and an economic motivation for the expression appear to dictate a finding of commercial speech.

One might assume, under *Bolger*'s three-factor test, that an advertisement by a manufacturer discussing a product's scientific properties would be classified as commercial speech and thus receive the somewhat reduced protection provided by the *Central Hudson* test,[108] although that same information, if conveyed by a neutral party, undoubtedly would be characterized as fully protected speech. That conclusion, however, does not necessarily follow, as can be seen by examining the specific factual context in which the *Bolger* Court developed its test. In *Bolger* the information about public issues and the commercial promotion were linked gratuitously. As the Court expressly recognized,[109] Youngs quite easily could have distributed pamphlets discussing the general problems of venereal disease and family planning without simultaneously promoting its specific products. In developing its test, the Court made its concern clear: "Advertisers should not be permitted to immunize false or misleading product information from government regulation simply by including references to public issues."[110]

When, however, a public issue directly concerns a product – for example, the effect of oat bran on cholesterol – to characterize everything a manufacturer says about the scientific properties of its product as

---

[105] id. at 66.
[106] id. at 67.
[107] id.
[108] See discussion *supra* at 139–40.
[109] *Bolger*, 463 U.S. at 66–67.
[110] id. at 68. Of course, to the extent the discussion of venereal disease or family planning concerned the role of prophylactics, as a genetic matter, in the treatment of the former or the implementation of the latter, the situation in Bolger would be quite similar to the case of product health claims. In such an event, the Court's conclusion that the advertisement and the public discussion were not inextricably intertwined would have been incorrect.

commercial speech effectively revokes a corporation's "full panoply of protections available to its direct comment on [that] public issue[],"[111] a right conceded by the *Bolger* Court itself. Thus, when a particular product and a public issue are intertwined inextricably, if *Bolger*'s definition of commercial speech is not to consume the fully protected corporate right to comment on public issues,[112] certain ground rules would have to be recognized. If a real scientific debate about the health impact of a product exists, the manufacturer would retain a fully protected right to comment on that debate, as long as it did not promote simultaneously and directly the sale of the product. This comment would receive full First Amendment protection, even though the likely and intended impact of the comment on the listener would be the creation of a desire to purchase that product.

One reasonably could criticize this doctrinal resolution because it may be thought to draw irrational distinctions. On the one hand, if we begin with the premise that a manufacturer's promotion of its product deserves only the reduced First Amendment protection which many scholars believe is due commercial speech, it should make no difference whether the promotion is direct or indirect. On the other hand, if a corporation is recognized as having a fully protected First Amendment right to comment on public issues, even if the corporation has a concrete financial interest in that issue, and if it is conceded generally that the health impact of a corporation's product is a public issue, why is that corporate right any less valuable once the corporation adds a direct promotion?[113]

One response to these criticisms is that, purely on the narrow doctrinal level,[114] this resolution is the only conceivable means of reconciling the two coexisting lines of Supreme Court precedent on the matter. If one were ultimately to conclude, however, that this suggested doctrinal resolution is fatally illogical, then it should be clear, in terms of fundamental free speech

---

[111] Id.

[112] See discussion *supra* at 150–51 (discussing *Bolger*).

[113] Of course, if one were to reject a corporation's First Amendment right to comment on even purely political issues, as a number of leading free speech scholars do, then the logic of my argument breaks down. The issue of corporate speech in the context of purely political speech is beyond the scope of this book. However, for my views explaining why corporate political speech deserves full First Amendment protection, see Martin H. Redish, *Money Talks: Speech, Economic Power and the Values of Democracy* (New York: New York University Press, 2001), pp. 63–114. In any event, it is clear at least as a matter of First Amendment doctrine that corporations continue to possess full First Amendment protection for comments on public issues. See *Citizens United v. Federal Election Comm'n*, 558 U.S. 310 (2010).

[114] See Jefferson Powell, *Reaching the Limits of Traditional Constitutional Scholarship* (Book Review), 80 Nw. U. L. Rev. 1128, 1136–37 (1986).

theory, which of the two doctrinal lines should prevail. When a product's health impact is characterized as a public issue, a corporation must possess a fully protected right to state its side of the argument, because those on the other side of the public debate will retain the "full panoply of protections"[115] for their commentary. Otherwise, the public would be deprived of information and opinion on one side of the argument, in direct contravention of fundamental precepts of free speech theory.[116] Exclusion of corporate commentary on regulatory issues, for example, effectively amounts to a governmental preference for speech advocating regulation and governmental disdain for belief in a free market economy, because the speech of those advocating regulation will receive full protection, but those with the strongest incentive to oppose regulation – the corporations subject to that regulation – will receive only the reduced protection given commercial speech. Just as "the Fourteenth Amendment does not enact Mr. Herbert Spencer's Social Statics,"[117] neither does the First Amendment embody their rejection.[118] To the contrary, the First Amendment was largely designed to prevent just such governmental viewpoint preference.[119]

Similarly, to rationalize an exclusion of corporate commentary from full protection because corporations have a direct financial interest in the outcome of the debate would alter dramatically traditional First Amendment values. If such grounds exclude corporations from full First Amendment protection, then comments by Michigan automobile workers urging an increase in automobile import tariffs or urgings by senior citizens for an increase in social security benefits logically would have to receive reduced protection as well, because the speakers clearly possess a direct financial interest in the outcome of the public debate to which they directed their commentary. These examples, in which no one seriously could doubt that full First Amendment protection would be provided, should make clear that the First Amendment never has been interpreted to reduce protection because of a speaker's private economic motivation. The public may appropriately discount a speaker's commentary on the basis of an economic motivation, but this does not mean that such commentary is inherently false or lacking in persuasive value. Indeed, this is especially likely to be true for product health claims when those possessing both the

---

[115] See discussion *supra* at 150–51.
[116] See Chapter 1, *supra*.
[117] Lochner v. New York, 198 U.S. 45, 75 (1905) (Holmes, J., dissenting).
[118] See *Citizens United, supra*.
[119] See Chapter 1, *supra*.

most substantial resources to fund research and the strongest incentive to do so are the commercial manufacturers.

Establishing the Contours of Constitutionally Valid Regulation

It should be clear at this point that a corporation's truthful health claims for its products must receive full First Amendment protection. But the Supreme Court, of course, never has equated full First Amendment protection with absolute protection. A compelling governmental interest may justify regulations of content.[120] It is necessary, then, to set out the contours of constitutionally valid governmental regulatory authority over product health claims.

Initially, the Court has never extended First Amendment protection to either conscious falsehoods or to statements made with reckless disregard of truth or falsity when those statements cause significant harm.[121] Thus, if one making a health claim for a product – either the manufacturer or an objective scientific observer – is found knowingly to have communicated a falsehood or to have been reckless about the issue of falsity, the First Amendment would have no applicability.[122] Because knowledge is a wholly subjective factor, it is naturally difficult to prove. This difficulty, however, has not prevented the Court from employing the knowing-or-reckless-falsehood standard in the defamation area,[123] quite probably because of the unattractiveness of the alternatives – either allowing even conscious falsehoods to go unregulated or regulating even factual assertions made without knowledge of their falsity.

In the context of scientific speech, however, the problem of proving knowledge of falsity may not prove to be as difficult as it is in other contexts. Reasonable inferences drawn from objective data often may prove state of

---

[120] See *Young v. American Mini Theaters*, 427 U.S. 50, 66 (1976) (stating that the "question whether speech is, or is not, protected by the First Amendment often depends on the content of the speech"). The Court has recognized that even fully protected expression may be regulated on the showing of a compelling governmental interest. See *Consolidated Edison Co. v. Public Serv. Comm'n*, 447 U.S. 530, 533–34 (1980).

[121] See *New York Times Co. v. Sullivan*, 376 U.S. 254, 279–80 (1964); see also Chapter 2, *supra*.

[122] The Court has considered various aspects of the fact-finding process on the knowledge-of-falsity issue in several decisions. See, e.g., *Anderson v. Liberty Lobby, Inc.*, 477 U.S. 242 (1986) (concerning appropriate summary judgment standard); *Herbert v. Lando*, 441 U.S. 153 (1979) (concerning scope of discovery on knowledge-of-falsity issue); *St. Amant v. Thompson*, 390 U.S. 727 (1968) (significantly curbing the jury's fact-finding authority in determining whether a defendant in a defamation action brought by a public figure acted with reckless disregard of the truth or falsity of his or her statements). On this issue, see the detailed discussion in Chapter 2, *supra*.

[123] See Chapter 2, *supra*.

mind. Thus, in the area of product health claims, a complete absence of even arguably probative scientific data to support the claim reasonably could be found to constitute recklessness, if not actual knowledge of falsity, which renders regulation or suppression of those scientific claims constitutional. However, the mere fact that a health claim departs from governing scientific consensus should not, standing alone, constitute a sufficient basis to justify a finding of either knowledge of falsity or recklessness, because the principle of epistemological humility plays such an important role in both free speech theory in general and free scientific inquiry in particular.[124] Thus, reliance by federal regulatory agencies on departure from scientific consensus as a basis for the prohibition of health claims should be deemed to violate the First Amendment, at least to the extent commercial advertisements containing scientific claims are deemed to be fully protected expression. The knowledge-or-reckless-disregard standard probably could be applied, however, when the advertiser or communicator misrepresents the current state of the scientific consensus, even though reasonable difference of opinion may exist over the scientific reality. Nevertheless, because the need for open scientific debate is so ingrained in our constitutional tradition, governmental regulation should be allowed only when the danger to the public is great, and the advertiser's claim is patently inaccurate. Arguably, under certain circumstances a compelling interest may be found to justify regulation, even in the absence of a finding of conscious or reckless falsity. If the government can demonstrate that serious physical harm may result from the listener's belief of what is universally deemed a scientifically inaccurate health claim made about a product, the governmental interest in regulation conceivably could be deemed compelling. Because in such a case the government always has available the option of prohibiting the actual sale,[125] however, and because, by hypothesis, at least an arguable scientific basis for the health claim is assumed to exist,[126] First Amendment interests would be served better by prohibiting regulation of the claim. In any event, to the extent the First Amendment interest is deemed outbalanced by the compelling governmental interest in safety, the result logically should be similar for claims made by neutral scientists, as well as commercial advertisers.

---

[124] See discussion *supra* at 142–43.
[125] Such economic activity is classifiable as conduct rather than protected speech.
[126] As previously noted, if there existed absolutely no evidentiary basis to support the scientific claim, it is likely that the claim reasonably could be found to have been made with either knowledge of falsity or reckless disregard of truth or falsity.

EQUATING COMMERCIAL AND SCIENTIFIC EXPRESSION: THE DILUTION DANGER

Pursuant to the equivalency principle advocated here, the standards adopted for the regulation of a manufacturer's health claims[127] must be nearly identical to those employed to test the constitutionality of the hypothetical regulation of the same comments made by neutral scientists to roughly the same audience. Full protection for one must translate to full protection for the other. If distinctions in the amount of protection are to be drawn, it must be because the difference in the source of the communication somehow gives rise to a difference in the amount or nature of harm caused by the expression, justifying the finding of a compelling interest in one situation but not the other.[128] Some may reasonably raise the fear that extending equivalent protection to commercially based scientific claims would lead to a dilution in or reduction of protection given to more traditionally expressed scientific assertions, simply to allow regulation of the commercial claims. In earlier portions of this book, I have acknowledged and sought to respond to this so-called dilution danger.[129] Here, I do so in the special context of scientific claims, where the danger could arguably be considered significantly greater. In most other contexts, one can probably distinguish discussions of commercial products and services from traditionally protected categories, at least if one believed such a distinction justified.[130] In the context of scientific speech, however, drawing such a distinction would effectively be impossible; the substance of the assertions would be identical in both contexts.[131] Thus, if governmental regulators were required by the First Amendment to treat commercial scientific claims in the exact same manner in which they treat noncommercial scientific claims, it is conceivable that they would choose to regulate both, rather than neither, thereby seriously diluting First Amendment protection for scientific speech.

The problem should not arise, however. As shown throughout these pages, the equivalency principle demands only that commercial speech be treated as having the same constitutional value as traditionally protected categories of expression. It does not demand identical treatment, when it can be established that the commercially grounded scientific claim gives rise to a significantly

---

[127] See discussion *supra* at 154–56.
[128] See Chapter 1, *supra*.
[129] See Chapter 1, *supra*; Chapter 2, *supra*.
[130] But see id.
[131] A similar concern arises in the context of the equivalency principle's attack on the right of publicity. See generally Chapter 3, *supra*.

greater amount of harm. In such a situation, it is conceivable that the commercial scientific claim could be deemed to satisfy a compelling interest standard, when comparable noncommercial scientific claims do not.

In one sense, a health claim made by a product's manufacturer, rather than by a supposedly neutral scientist, is actually likely to *reduce* the danger of harm to the public caused by the communication because common sense tells us that a consumer is much more inclined to be skeptical of claims made by an interested manufacturer than by an objective observer.[132] In another sense, however, a claim made by the manufacturer, at least when it is included in a product advertisement or label, may be given greater credence by consumers, because of the reasonable assumption on the part of those consumers that the governmental regulatory agencies would not permit a manufacturer to make such claims if those agencies had deemed them to be false or deceptive. This is not an assumption that a consumer reasonably could or would likely make about the claims of an objective scientific observer, because there would be no reason to assume that a federal agency reviewed every assertion or theory proposed by a scientist in a scholarly journal. Moreover, it would be reasonable to assume that the audience for claims made in scientific scholarly journals will be far smaller and far more expert than the audience for commercial claims. Nor would such an audience be anywhere near as likely to act upon those scholarly scientific claims as would potential consumers. That distinction, however, would not justify a ban on health claims found to be inconsistent with governing scientific consensus because a compelling interest standard demands that governmental regulation be structured narrowly to be no more intrusive than necessary.[133] Requiring inclusion of a disclaimer of governmental approval could easily satisfy the legitimate governmental interest in avoiding consumer confusion in this matter. Thus, the FTC reasonably might require an advertiser to state that the Commission takes no position on the validity of the health claim being made. In this manner, the legitimate regulatory interest may be satisfied without significantly interfering with the advertiser's right to contribute to the public debate concerning the product's health impact.

Other than this one exception, no legitimate basis in First Amendment theory exists to justify differentiating the scope of constitutionally valid regulatory authority between the scientific claims made by a commercial

---

[132] See Redish, *supra* note 18, at 461 n.163 (stating that it "should be questioned ... whether the consuming public would be more likely to believe Dr. Linus Pauling or the orange juice companies when they say that vitamin C cures colds").

[133] See the discussion of this issue in Chapter 4, *supra*.

manufacturer and those made by an objective scientific observer. Thus, there exists no basis for assuming dilution were the two types of claims to be afforded equal protection.

In any event, the dilution concern fallaciously places the conceptual cart before the horse. Unless one can justify rationally, at the outset, a distinction in treatment for First Amendment purposes between the different types of expression in terms of free speech theory, the dilution criticism is illogical. If one assumes that the two forms of speech serve the same values and give rise to the same danger of harm, then those concerned about the danger of dilution logically should focus their criticism on the Court for irrationally failing to raise the level of constitutional protection it gives to commercial speech. If, on the other hand, one finds that a compelling interest justifies the Court's upholding of commercial speech regulation, and if one still cannot find a theoretically sound basis for providing greater protection to the traditional form of expression, then logically one should not fear the effect caused by the equation of the two types of speech.

One who believes that free speech theory logically justifies reduced protection for commercial speech[134] need not rely on the dilution fear to justify the distinction. Those who rely on nothing more than the concern over dilution to reject commercial speech protection, then, simply are evoking the intuitive, irrational assumption that speech by a commercial advertiser is somehow beneath traditional First Amendment concerns, for the circular reason that it is commercial.[135] My goal here has been to demonstrate that speech by a commercial enterprise concerning the scientific properties of its product deserves as full First Amendment protection as similar statements made by an objective scientific observer. Unless one accurately can point out the fallacies in my logic, the fear that the level of constitutional protection given pure scientific expression may be reduced as a result should carry no weight.

EPISTEMOLOGICAL HUMILITY, CONSTITUTIONAL FACT, AND JUDICIAL REVIEW OF ADMINISTRATIVE FINDINGS OF FACT

Assume, as is the likely case under existing doctrine, that scientific claims, when included as part of a direct commercial promotion, are deemed to constitute commercial speech and receive the reduced level of First

---

[134] See sources cited *supra* notes 2, 3.
[135] See generally Baker, *supra* notes 16.

Amendment protection provided by the *Central Hudson* test.[136] Under the first prong of this standard, a finding of the claim's falsity automatically removes the speech from the scope of the First Amendment, but a finding that the claim is truthful will lead to a substantial degree of constitutional protection against governmental regulation.[137] The truth or falsity of the advertiser's claim, then, often will be outcome determinative of the constitutionality of the challenged regulation.

In light of this analysis, it is amazing that the post-*Bolger* lower court decisions so uniformly have ceded enormous discretion to the administrative regulator to determine the truth or falsity of the advertiser's claim.[138] Both statutory[139] and judicial[140] traditions have granted broad judicial deference to administrative fact-finding within the scope of the agency's expertise. An equally venerable tradition,[141] however, requires that issues of "constitutional fact" must be examined de novo by the reviewing court.[142] A "constitutional fact" is a factual determination that, if resolved one way, will render governmental action constitutional and, if resolved another way, will render it unconstitutional. When the issue of constitutionality implicates liberty interests,[143] the Supreme Court consistently has held that our system of separation of powers demands independent judicial determination of such

---

[136] See discussion *supra* at 139–41.
[137] See discussion *supra* at 139.
[138] A leading example is the decision in *Federal Trade Comm'n v. Brown & Williamson Tobacco Corp.*, 778 F.2d 35 (D.C. Cir. 1985). The FTC had sought to enjoin the advertising of cigarette tar content alleged to be deceptive. The company disputed the application of the FTC's method employed to test the ratings. The D.C. Circuit, in affirming the grant of the injunction, noted that a court can overrule an agency's decision only when that decision is arbitrary or capricious. id. at 44; see also *Bristol-Myers Co. v. Federal Trade Comm'n*, 738 F.2d 554 (2d Cir. 1984), cert. denied, 469 U.S. 1189 (1985); *Federal Trade Comm'n v. Pharmtech Research, Inc.*, 576 F.Supp. 294 (D.D.C. 1983).
[139] See 5 U.S.C. § 706(2)(A) (1988) (arbitrary or capricious standard of review).
[140] See *Citizens to Preserve Overton Park, Inc. v. Volpe*, 401 U.S. 402, 416 (1971).
[141] This tradition is associated primarily with the famed decision in *Crowell v. Benson*, 285 U.S. 22 (1932).
[142] In *St. Joseph Stock Yards v. United States*, 298 U.S. 38 (1936), the Supreme Court modified *Crowell*'s requirement that the reviewing court hold a de novo hearing on the issue of constitutional fact, but reiterated the requirement of de novo review.
[143] While the *Crowell* doctrine generally fell into disrepute in property rights cases as the level of constitutional protection for those rights diminished, see Schwartz, *Does the Ghost of Crowell v. Benson Still Walk?*, 98 U. Pa. L. Rev. 163 (1949), in personal liberty suits it has retained vitality. See, e.g., *Cross v. United States*, 512 F.2d 1212, 1217 (4th Cir. 1975) (reviewing grocery store's qualification for food stamp program); *Jenkins v. Georgia*, 418 U.S. 153 (1974) (finding film Carnal Knowledge not obscene); *Jacobellis v. Ohio*, 378 U.S. 184, 190 n.6 (1964) (finding of obscenity).

factual issues. The reasons for the rule are clear. As I have argued previously in another context:

> Nonjudicial administrative regulators of expression exist for the sole purpose of regulating; this is their raison d'etre. They simultaneously perform the functions of prosecutor and adjudicator and, if only subconsciously, will likely feel the obligation to justify their existence by finding some expression constitutionally subject to regulation. Such a systematic danger does not plague the functioning of a judicial forum. In addition, the tradition of independence from external political pressure provides grounds for preferring judicial to administrative adjudication.[144]

Accordingly, the Supreme Court has held that, because obscene expression falls outside the scope of First Amendment protection,[145] findings of obscenity are constitutional facts subject to de novo judicial review.[146] No basis exists for distinguishing findings of falsity for commercial speech. Moreover, the framework established by the principle of epistemological humility should give us pause before we allow a formal governmental finding that a certain scientific assertion is false. Thus, even if one were to acknowledge that in extreme cases the government may make such findings, and even if we concede that such scientific assertions are to receive only the reduced protection associated with commercial speech, at the very least we should demand that such findings be made by the single independent governmental organ ultimately entrusted with the task of protecting free and open communication: the judiciary.

IMPLICATIONS OF THE SCIENTIFIC-COMMERCIAL SPEECH OVERLAP

Recognizing the Overlap between Commercial Speech and Traditional Categories of Protected Expression

A number of respected scholars have either categorically rejected extension of First Amendment protection to commercial speech[147] or proposed significant

---

[144] Redish, *supra* note 3, at 148–49 (footnotes omitted). See also Martin H. Redish & Kristin McCall, *Due Process, Free Expression, and the Administrative State*, 94 Notre Dame L. Rev. 297 (2018).
[145] *Miller v. California*, 413 U.S. 15, 23 (1973).
[146] *Jacobellis*, 378 U.S. at 190 n.6. See generally Martin H. Redish & William D. Gohl, *The Wandering Doctrine of Constitutional Fact*, 59 Ariz. L. Rev. 289 (2017).
[147] C. Edwin Baker, *Commercial Speech: A Problem in the Theory of Freedom*, 62 Iowa L. Rev. 1 (1976).

restrictions on its protection,[148] reasoning that the profit motivation of the speaker distinguishes it from more traditionally protected categories of expression. But as the preceding analysis has demonstrated, in the case of scientific expression, there exists no rational basis on which to distinguish so-called pure scientific expression from commercially motivated scientific expression for purposes of First Amendment theory.

Recognition of this theoretical inseparability underscores a broader point about the intersection of traditionally protected expression and commercial speech for purposes of American political theory. In this section, I explore that theoretical intersection, as well as its broader implications for the scope of constitutional protection appropriately extended to commercial speech in general.

The Underlying Postulates of the Theory of Free Expression

There are many different, and often conflicting, theories of free expression. There are, however, certain core postulates of political theory without which any system of free expression would be incoherent. At some level, dispute may well exist as to the exact number and content of these postulates. But there are at least four such postulates that are clearly contravened by the governmental suppression of scientific commercial speech. This is so, even though most, or all, of the expression suppressed by the government's prohibition is properly described as commercial speech.[149]

The four core postulates of free speech theory are the following:

1. Government may not attempt to manipulate lawful citizen behavior by means of the selective suppression of truthful expression advocating lawful activity.
2. The self-motivated nature of expression does not automatically render it false or misleading, thereby removing it from the scope of constitutional protection.
3. Government has greater power to regulate conduct than it has to regulate expression.
4. Government may not hold fully protected expression hostage as a means of extortion.

---

[148] Robert Post, *The Constitutional Status of Commercial Speech*, 48 UCLA L. Rev. 1 (2000).
[149] Though at the margins the definition of "commercial speech" is subject to some confusion, [see discussion *supra* at 149–54; see also, *Kasky v. Nike, Inc.*, 2 P.3d 1065 (Cal. 2000)], it is generally accepted that expression in the form of an advertisement by a profit-making seller that promotes sale of a commercial product or service falls within that definition. See, e.g., *Bolger v. Youngs Drug Prods. Corp.*, 463 U.S. 60 (1983).

When viewed in the context of noncommercial speech, presumably no educated observer could dispute the accuracy of these postulates, or their centrality to any coherent system of free expression. Indeed, if there existed a book entitled "Free Expression for Dummies," these postulates would almost undoubtedly appear within the first few pages. Violation of any of these four postulates would correctly be deemed to undermine core notions of free speech theory. The social contract implicit in the relationship of citizen to government in a liberal democratic society would be undermined if government could disrespect the intellectual dignity of its citizens. Yet the exact same pathologies may occur when government violates these core postulates in the context of commercial speech, just as much as it does when other types of expression are suppressed; the same lines between government and citizen have been improperly crossed in both contexts. To demonstrate this point, I will consider each of the postulates separately.

Postulate One: Government May Not Attempt to Manipulate Lawful Citizen Behavior by Means of the Selective Suppression of Truthful Expression Advocating Lawful Activity

In a democratic society, basic choices of policy are, ultimately, made by the populace, if only indirectly, through their elected representatives. To be sure, in certain instances the Constitution imposes limitations on majority choices, but even in those cases a super-majority of the populace may alter constitutional commands where it deems them to be no longer acceptable.[150] Government may, of course, prohibit certain behavior, but the inherent logic of democracy prevents it from prohibiting the populace from debating the merits of those prohibitions. Where government has left behavioral choices to the individual, the premises of liberal democracy prevent the government from attempting to influence those choices through selective suppression of one side of a debate.

The point can be made clearer by viewing it through the lens of traditional political debate. If the First Amendment means anything, it prohibits government from suppressing one side of a political debate because it fears that the public might be convinced to make "the wrong" choice. For example, had the government sought to suppress opposition to the Iraq war because it feared that the public might be convinced to end that war, the suppression would undoubtedly have been found to infringe the First Amendment. In

---

[150] U.S. Const. art. V (authorizing amendment of the Constitution through a super-majoritarian process).

a democratic society, government may seek to influence the choices of the populace, not by means of selective suppression, but rather by making its own contributions to that debate. Indeed, it is impossible to point to a single respected First Amendment scholar who would deem such a selective ban to be constitutional. The reason is that vesting such power in government would necessarily prove too much, for it would undermine the fundamental premise underlying the commitment to self-government in the first place – namely, the citizen's ability to make lawful choices on the basis of free and open debate.

Given that no one could seriously challenge the constitutional pathology of paternalistically driven selective suppression in political debate, it is puzzling that so many have no difficulty authorizing such paternalism when the subject of the speech is commercial, rather than political. There is no way one may legitimately compartmentalize respect for citizens' ability to make lawful choices on the basis of free and open debate. Either a democratic society trusts citizens to make such choices, or it does not – in which event it automatically transforms from a democratic society to an authoritarian one. The fact that a dictatorship is benevolent does not make it a democracy. Yet if citizens are deemed incapable of making lawful choices on the basis of free debate in the commercial realm, why all of a sudden do we deem them capable of making such choices in the political realm? When viewed through the lens of the relationship between government and citizen, the fact that in the commercial realm the speaker is seeking to make a profit is wholly irrelevant; the pathology in terms of democratic theory is not so much the suppression of the speaker's right as it is the lack of respect for the citizen's ability to make lawful choices – a lack of respect that inheres in the government's selective suppression, regardless of the speaker's purposes.[151]

Recognition of this fundamental element of the liberal democratic social contract between government and individual, then, leads to a rejection of the core distinction drawn between commercial and political speech.

Postulate Two: The Self-Interested Nature of Expression Does Not Automatically Reduce the Level of Constitutional Protection

As noted throughout this chapter, those who oppose full First Amendment protection for commercial speech would readily extend full protection to the

---

[151] It is worth noting that in many contexts, the commercial speech would be directed at trained members of the medical profession, rather than laymen. Under the logic of this premise of democratic theory, however, it is doubtful that that element should be deemed outcome determinative.

exact same speech when uttered by someone who lacked a commercial motivation. The assumption implicit in that dichotomy is that the self-interested nature of the promotion somehow renders the expression both less worthy and more dangerous. As previously noted,[152] the logic of such a dichotomy, to the extent it were to justify categorical suppression, is inherently inconsistent with the Supreme Court's commitment to the protection of commercial speech in the first place. Under the Court's definition, all commercial speech is manufacturer speech; yet under the Court's doctrine it is extended a significant level of constitutional protection. Thus, the categorical suppression of speech for no reason other than the fact that it is made by an economically self-interested party is inconsistent with accepted Supreme Court jurisprudence.

Beyond its doctrinal difficulties, it is interesting to explore the consistency of such discriminatory treatment from the broader perspectives of constitutional and political theory. In a democracy, it is generally understood that individuals will often act out of their own self-interest, and will employ expression as a means of convincing others to take actions to advance that self-interest. The long history and current power of political interest groups is conclusive proof of that political reality. In the world of noncommercial speech, no one would seriously suggest that the self-interested nature of expression somehow reduces the level of First Amendment protection it receives. Yet those who draw such a distinction appear to have made the wholly unsupported, *ex ante* assumption that commercially motivated speech will be inherently distorted, and therefore easily suppressed, for no reason other than the self-interested economic nature of the speaker's expression.[153] Once again, when viewed through the lens of accepted political practice and modern democratic theory, the categorical discrimination against sellers for no reason other than the fact of the self-interested nature of their expression is rendered wholly incoherent.

Postulate Three. The Government Has Greater Power to Regulate Conduct Than It Has to Regulate Speech

In the traditional world of free expression, no one would ever question that expression has considerably greater constitutional protection than most forms of conduct. For example, under certain circumstances, at least, one has the

---

[152] See Chapter 1, *supra*.
[153] It should be emphasized that, even were one to assume the correctness of the FDA's concern, under controlling commercial speech doctrine the problem could be solved by the far less invasive use of required disclaimers, rather than direct suppression. See discussion *supra* at 158.

right to advocate unlawful conduct;[154] yet one surely has no constitutional right to engage in that unlawful conduct. While some scholars have challenged the conclusion that speech is truly "special,"[155] it is not all that difficult to grasp the key differences. Expression deals more directly with the unique ability to think and reason on multidimensional levels – qualities that are essential in a democratic society.[156] Moreover, while of course expression can cause harm, as an *ex ante* matter it is reasonable to presume that the harm caused by expression will generally be less immediate and concrete than harm caused by physical conduct. For purposes of a constitutional protection in which broad judgments must be made, it is therefore reasonable to draw a categorical distinction between expression and conduct. By providing special protection to expression, this is exactly what the First Amendment does.

In the area of commercial speech, the distinction has not always been so clearly understood. After its decision in *Posadas de P.R. Associates v. Tourism Co. of P.R.*, the Court proceeded on the wholly misguided assumption that government's greater power to regulate conduct subsumed the "lesser" power to regulate expression advocating that conduct, even where the conduct is not prohibited.[157] This "logic," of course, completely ignores the fact that because the First Amendment extends greater protection to expression than to conduct, it is, in reality, the regulation of the expression that is the "greater" power. Indeed, acceptance of this logic outside of the commercial speech context (and there is no logical basis for confining it in such a manner) would overturn over eighty years of Supreme Court jurisprudence in the constitutional protection of unlawful advocacy.[158] In his opinion announcing the judgment of the Court in the 1996 decision in *44 Liquormart v. Rhode Island*,[159] Justice Stevens categorically and vigorously rejected the specious logic of prior Supreme Court jurisprudence.[160] The Court's vigorous protection of commercial speech since that decision[161] confirms that the Court as a whole has concurred in Justice Stevens's rejection of the "greater includes the lesser" logic.

---

[154] See, e.g., *Brandenburg v. Ohio*, 395 U.S. 444 (1969) (per curiam).
[155] Frederick Schauer, *Must Speech Be Special?*, 78 Nw. U. L. Rev. 1284 (1984).
[156] See Martin H. Redish, *The Value of Free Speech*, 130 U. Pa. L. Rev. 591 (1982).
[157] See *Posadas de P.R. Assocs. v. Tourism Co. of P.R.*, 478 U.S. 328 (1986).
[158] For a description of that jurisprudence, see Redish, *supra* note 74, pp. 173–212.
[159] 517 U.S. 484 (1996).
[160] id. at 509 ("[O]n reflection, we are now persuaded that *Posadas* erroneously performed the First Amendment analysis ... [T]he advertising ban [in that case] served to shield the State's ... policy from the public scrutiny that more direct, nonspeech regulations would draw.").
[161] See Chapter 1, *supra*.

The Court's decision in *Posadas* had turned the First Amendment on its head, creating an Alice-in-Wonderland world in which speech receives less constitutional protection than the conduct it advocates. Such an inversion of constitutional values would surely not be permitted when traditionally protected noncommercial speech is involved; there is no basis in logic or experience to justify its use in the context of commercial speech.[162]

Postulate Four: Government May Not Hold Fully Protected Expression Hostage as a Means of Extortion

At various points in time, governmental agencies have sought to justify their suppression of speech not on the grounds that the speech in question is inherently false, harmful or dangerous, but rather on the grounds that suppression of that speech will induce the speaker to take certain actions.[163]

This is particularly true in the context of so-called "off-label" advertising. Certain prescription drugs, approved by the FDA only for a particular purpose, have been found to provide additional benefits, above and beyond the purpose for which they were FDA-approved. Such uses are perfectly legal. Indeed, many of these off-label uses constitute foundational treatment for a variety of serious diseases. Thus, doctors often prescribe prescription drugs for such off-label purposes, to the substantial benefit of patients. Yet drug manufacturers are, for the most part, prohibited from advertising the drug for these off-label purposes. To enable the manufacturer to advertise the drug for such purposes without restriction, it must obtain FDA approval. In order to advertise these off-label uses in their own words, manufacturers must obtain FDA approval for such uses. This process requires manufacturers to prepare expensive and detailed scientific studies supporting the efficacy and safety of the off-label use, something they understandably are often not inclined to do. By substantially prohibiting their ability to promote off-label use despite the often widely accepted beneficial impact of such uses, the FDA is able to pressure them into undertaking the necessary steps to make the uses on-label. In effect, the government is asserting that it is constitutionally authorized to suppress speech

---

[162] As explained earlier, it appears that the rationale for suppressing promotion while simultaneously failing to regulate the activity being promoted originally was grounded largely in political, rather than regulatory, considerations. See discussion *supra* at 166.

[163] The Food and Drug Administration, for example, took the position that it could suppress even truthful manufacturer promotion of off-label uses of prescription drugs – wholly legal conduct – on the grounds that to do so pressures the manufacturer to seek to satisfy the requirements for making that off-label use on-label. See Coleen Klasmeier & Martin H. Redish, *Off-Label Prescription Advertising, The FDA and the First Amendment: A Study in the Values of Commercial Speech Protection*, 37 Am. J. Law & Med. 315, 342 (2011).

that it readily concedes, if only for purposes of argument, is on its four corners fully deserving of protection, in order to extort certain actions out of private entities that have absolutely no legal obligation to undertake such action.

It is hard to imagine government even attempting such outrageous actions when the speech in question is noncommercial, but if it did so, there can be little doubt that its actions would be held unconstitutional. By much the same reasoning, government could presumably prohibit individuals from attending religious services unless individuals engaged in specified behavior, despite the existence of the First Amendment's Free Exercise Clause. One shudders to think what might result if government sought to achieve the same result by suspending citizens' Eighth Amendment right against cruel and unusual punishment.

Where citizen behavior on its face falls within the scope of a constitutional protection, it would be absurd to permit government to suppress that behavior in order to induce citizens to engage in behavior in which they have no legal obligation to engage. The surreal aspect of such extortive behavior is underscored by the fact that the federal government generally possesses full constitutional authority to directly require the behavior in question without in any way suppressing expression as an indirect means of achieving its goal.[164] Whether it would be simpler – or simply more expedient – for the government to achieve its goal indirectly by suppressing protected speech is irrelevant to the constitutional inquiry. The suppression of fully protected, potentially valuable expression is far too high a price to pay for governmental convenience.

CONCLUSION

The public today is sensitive to the impact of the foods it consumes and the products it uses to improve its health. As a result, manufacturers also have become more sensitive to the implications that their products have for public health. In the true tradition of American capitalism, commercial enterprises have determined that health sells, and to a large extent they have devoted their research, marketing, and advertising resources toward both improving the health impact of their products and informing the public of those improvements.[165] Thus, allowing manufacturers to emphasize the health implications of their products likely will increase public awareness of these

---

[164] U.S. Const. art. I, § 8, cl. 3 (Commerce Clause); U.S. Const. art. I, § 8, cl. 18 (Necessary and Proper Clause).

[165] One illustration is the cereal market, in which there exists "clear evidence that ... producer advertising and labeling added significant amounts of information to the market and reached groups that were not reached well by government and general information sources." P. Ippolito & A. Mathios, *Health Claims in Advertising and Labeling: A Study of the Cereal*

health concerns. Expression by those with the greatest incentive to speak will increase the level of public awareness about issues that directly will affect their lives and over which they have control. This represents the classic role that free expression can and should play in our society. The level of public interest in communication and information concerning the health implications of everyday products is no less when that information comes from the manufacturer of those products than when the same information comes from an objective scientific or medical expert.

When speech is allowed to be "uninhibited, robust, and wide open,"[166] there exist risks of misinformation, confusion, and even deception. Recognition that such communications deserve full First Amendment protection, however, does not imply that society is defenseless against intentional economic fraud. The First Amendment, even in its most classic applications, is not an absolute. Because of the historical lessons taught us by the principle of epistemological humility, however, we should hesitate to stifle scientific assertions simply because they are inconsistent with current scientific consensus. One of the fundamental premises of the First Amendment is that, except in the most extreme cases, the proper response to speech we deem inaccurate is not repression but rather counter speech.[167] The Court adheres to this principle for political speech, regardless of the speaker's motivation. There is no reason, in either logic or history, to treat good faith, scientific expression any differently.

Market (1989), p. ix. The same authors assert that "producer advertising was a significant source of information on the potential benefits of fiber." id. at xi.

[166] *New York Times Co. v. Sullivan*, 376 U.S. 254, 270 (1964).

[167] *Whitney v. California*, 274 U.S. 357, 377 (1927) (Brandeis, J., joined by Holmes, J., concurring); see also *Gertz v. Robert Welch, Inc.*, 418 U.S. 323, 339–40 (1974) (stating that "[h]owever pernicious an opinion may seem, we depend for its correction not on the conscience of judges and juries but on the competition of other ideas").

Conclusion

Making the Case for First Amendment Protection

This book has sought to achieve two goals. First, it is designed to rationalize full First Amendment protection for commercial speech by means of a new "four perspective" approach – a speaker-centric perspective, a listener-speaker perspective, a regulatory perspective, and a rationalist perspective.[1] In order to rationalize First Amendment protection, each of these perspectives must be viewed as sufficient, but not necessary. Qualification under any one of these perspectives justifies full First Amendment protection.

Application of these conceptual approaches establishes that commercial speech achieves the exact same First Amendment goals attained by more traditional categories of protected expression. Commercial speech fosters the interest in enabling speakers – individuals or entities – to self-realize by employing persuasive expression as a means of attaining the goals they have set for themselves. While some scholars debate whether corporate speakers can actually self-realize, it is important to keep in mind that human beings are employing the corporate device as a means of achieving their goals. Those individuals self-realize by the use of expression as a means of achieving their goals.

Commercial speech also fosters the interests of listeners by providing them with information or opinion that can help them make choices to facilitate the process of individual self-government. First Amendment protection of commercial speech also prevents government from violating the liberal democratic social contract by paternalistically manipulating lawful citizen choices by means of selective suppression of competing expression. Finally, under the rationalist perspective, protection of commercial speech prevents government from drawing indefensible, irrational, and discriminatory distinctions in the regulation of expression.

While over the years the Supreme Court has extended constitutional protection to commercial speech in a manner approaching the level of

---

[1] See generally Chapter 1, *supra*.

protection extended to more traditionally protected categories,[2] it has done so largely without any recognition that it is establishing this equivalence and without any coherent, carefully reasoned underlying theory. In these pages, I have sought to provide that underlying theory to support what I have referred to as "the equivalency principle" – that is, the dictate that, as a matter of valid free speech theory, commercial speech deserves a level of First Amendment protection that is equivalent to the level of protection traditionally afforded fully protected categories of noncommercial expression.

Second, the book has focused on four important subcategories of commercial speech in which the Supreme Court has either improperly failed to extend First Amendment equivalency or has left the issue of equivalency unresolved. These four areas are false commercial speech,[3] First Amendment limits on the common law or statutory right of publicity,[4] compelled speech,[5] and scientific speech.[6] In each area I have demonstrated, by application of the four-perspective framework described earlier, that each of these areas deserves constitutional treatment under the equivalency principle.

It is important to understand, however, exactly what the implications of the equivalency principle are, and are not. The equivalency principle does not mean that commercial speech will receive absolute protection, any more than the First Amendment dictates absolute protection for noncommercial speech. Indeed, the equivalency principle is agnostic to the actual level of First Amendment protection to be extended. All it means is that commercial speech is to receive the First Amendment version of a most favored nation clause: Commercial speech is to be judged by the exact same standard of constitutional protection by which noncommercial speech is judged.

It is also important to understand that application of the equivalency principle will not necessarily dictate an identical First Amendment outcome for governmental regulations of commercial and noncommercial speech in all cases. All it means is that regulations of both forms of expression are judged by identical standards. Instances may arise in which, due to the nature and size of the audience reached, commercial speech may cause more harm than comparable noncommercial speech, thereby justifying regulations that would be deemed unconstitutional when applied to noncommercial speech. For example, under the equivalency principle when an assertion of scientific

---

[2] See Chapter 1, *supra*; Chapter 2, *supra*.
[3] See Chapter 2, *supra*.
[4] See Chapter 3, *supra*.
[5] See Chapter 4, *supra*.
[6] See Chapter 5, *supra*.

fact is made in a commercial advertisement, for reasons explained earlier in this book it is to be measured by the exact same standard of First Amendment protection as is a comparable assertion of scientific fact made by a scientist in a scholarly journal.[7] However, if the scientific claim, though neither reckless nor knowingly false, is controversial, the First Amendment may well tolerate a requirement that the commercial advertisement contain a disclaimer, indicating that the claim has not been approved by the Food and Drug Administration. This would be acceptable under the equivalency principle, even though imposition of a comparable disclaimer requirement on the exact same claim made in a scholarly journal would be unconstitutional. This is because, absent the disclaimer, the public might well assume that regulatory agencies would not allow questionable scientific claims to be made by commercial advertisers, so the disclaimer would be required to disabuse them of this notion. In contrast, in the case of a scientific claim made in a scholarly journal it would be reasonable to assume either that members of the general lay public would never see the claim in the first place or if they did, they would have no reasonable expectation that governmental regulatory agencies would have previewed the claim.[8] Thus, in a narrow category of instances, application of the equivalency principle to commercial speech regulation will demand the precision of a scalpel, rather than the blunt strokes of a hatchet.

In many areas of commercial speech regulation, the Supreme Court has already approached, if not adopted, the equivalency principle.[9] The problem is, however, that the Court itself appears not to have recognized that it has done so. Rather, for the most part it has purported to apply standards developed first in the 1970s and early 1980s, when commercial speech was treated as the First Amendment's second class citizen.[10] While more recently the Court appears to have recognized that *legislative* discrimination against commercial speech must be subject to strict scrutiny,[11] it has mysteriously failed to recognize that, at least on its face if not in most applications, the Court's existing test for commercial speech protection itself discriminates against commercial speech.[12]

In one sense, this concern is more academic than real, since in most cases of commercial speech regulation the Court, while purporting to apply its largely under-protective standards of days gone by, has extended to commercial

---

[7] See Chapter 4, *supra*.
[8] See id.
[9] See Chapter 1, *supra*; Chapter 2, *supra* at; Chapter 3, *supra*.
[10] See Chapter 1, supra. See also Martin H. Redish, *The Adversary First Amendment: Free Expression and the Foundations of American Democracy* (Stanford, CA: Stanford University Press, 2013).
[11] See Chapter 1, *supra*.
[12] See Chapter 1, *supra*.

speech a level of First Amendment protection virtually fungible with that given to more traditionally protected categories.[13] However, the Court's total failure to grasp the theoretical underpinnings of the need to extend First Amendment equivalence has led to two dangerous constitutional pathologies. First, its theoretical vacuum has allowed poorly reasoned scholarly rejections of commercial speech protection to fill that vacuum. Second, it has caused both the Court and the judiciary as a whole to apply the equivalency principle in an aberrational and irrational manner. For reasons explained in detail in the prior chapters, the Court's selectively negative treatment of several important categories of commercial speech regulation is unjustified by either logic or First Amendment policy. Thus, Chapter 2 explains why the Court has improperly failed to apply the equivalency principle to false commercial speech. Chapter 3 explains why the judiciary's failure to recognize that prima facie commercial speech violations of the right of publicity deserve First Amendment protection equivalent to that received by profit-making media. Chapter 4 provides a theoretical basis for treating compelled commercial speech in a manner equivalent to the First Amendment treatment afforded compelled noncommercial speech. In Chapter 5, I critique the general failure of the courts to afford scientific claims made in commercial advertisements a level of First Amendment protection equivalent to that given to scholarly assertions of scientific theory or fact. These are important and troubling judicial failures to extend the proper level of First Amendment protection to commercial speech, on both theoretical and practical levels.

Of course, in response to my theoretical critique one could always point to the intuitive difficulty in giving *any* commercial speech a level of First Amendment protection equivalent to that extended to such traditionally protected expressive categories as political speech, art, or literature. But for reasons explained throughout this book, reliance on unsupported intuition to discriminate against commercial speech is easily shown to be irrational when that intuitive conclusion is subjected to analysis under the regulatory-centric and rationalist-centric perspectives, described earlier.[14] Allowing government to suppress commercial speech undermines classic values fostered by the constitutional guarantee of free expression. It threatens to harm both speaker and listener interests, and often undermines the liberal-democratic social contract by enabling government to paternalistically manipulate citizens' lawful choices.[15]

---

[13] See id.
[14] See Chapter 1, *supra*.
[15] See id.

In recent years, the Court has gone part of the way toward recognizing the need for First Amendment equivalence. This book will hopefully provide both theoretical and doctrinal bases to enable the Court to take the further steps necessary to provide commercial speech the level of First Amendment protection it truly deserves.

Index

Actual Malice Test, 43–45; 49; 154–56
Autonomy Rationale for Right of Publicity, 70–71

Baker, C. Edwin, 12; 146–48
Blair, Jayson, 54
Brandeis, Louis, 64
Brennan, William J., 94; 95
Breyer, Stephen, 32; 34

Churchill, Winston, 122
Campaign Contributions, 104–05
Central Hudson Test, 5; 22; 30–31; 33; 42; 50; 83; 87–88; 99–100; 114
Chilling Effect, 18
Commercial Speech Passim
Compelled Commercial Speech, 103–32; 171; 173
Congressional Medal of Honor, 45–46
Constitutional Fact Doctrine, 160–61
Consumer Reports Magazine, 144
Corporations, 12; 118–20; 155; 170
Cruise, Tom, 94; 97

Democracy, 7; 10; 12; 40–41; 173
Dilution, 18–20; 39–41; 141; 157–59

Eighth Amendment, 168
Emerson, Thomas, 145
Epistemological Humility, 134–35
Equivalency Principle Passim

Fairness Doctrine, 128
False Speech, 17–20; 21–58; 104; 130; 134; 137; 142–43; 160–61; 171; 173
Federal Trade Commission, 135; 138; 142; 158

Feinerman, Gary, 91
First Amendment Passim
Flag Burning, 12
Flag Salute, 109
Food and Drug Administration, 129; 135; 138; 167; 172
Frank, Jerome, 66
Fraud, 54–55 (see also "False Speech")
Free Exercise Clause, 168
Freedom of the Press Clause, 97–98

General Motors, 6; 38
Glass, Stephen, 54

"Incidental Use" Exception, 76

Jackson, Robert, 109
Jacksonian Democracy, 12
Jehovah's Witnesses, 109; 110; 127
Jordan, Michael, 91

Kennedy, Anthony, 45–46
King, Martin Luther Jr., 113
Kozinski, Alex, 83

Listener-Centric Model of Free Speech, 2; 9; 14–15; 104; 106; 112
Locke, John, 68

Madow, Michael, 67
Marquess of Queensbury Rules, 7
Marshall, Thurgood, 152
Meiklejohn, Alexander, 11; 14; 37; 90; 103; 104; 108
Misleading Speech, 57–58 (see also "False Speech"; "Fraud")

Nader, Ralph, 6; 35; 38
New Deal, 4
New Republic, 54
Newsworthy exception to right of publicity, 72–73; 76; 97
Nike, 35; 38
Nimmer, Melville, 68
North American Free Trade Agreement, 13

Off-Label Advertising, 167
Optimistic Skepticism, 9

Pasteur, Louis, 142
Perspective Framework, 8; 9–17
Phillip Morris Company, 21
Post, Robert, 12; 13; 37; 49; 90; 91; 162
Predominant Use Test, 80–81
Privacy Right, 64–65
Private Self-Government, 35
Product Health Claims, 133–69
Property Rights, 4
Prosser, William, 65
Publicity Right, 60–102; 171; 173
Public Choice Theory, 15–16

Rationalist-Centric Model, 2; 9; 10; 16–17; 106; 107; 112; 145; 173
Regulatory-Centric Model, 2; 9; 10; 15–16; 17; 106; 107; 112; 173
Restatement (First) of Torts, 65
Rhode Island, 140

Scalia, Antonin, 6
Scientific Expression, 133–69; 171; 173
Self-Realization, 35; 170
Social Contract, 9; 173
Spencer, Herbert, 154
Speaker-Centric Model, 2; 9; 104; 106; 112
Stevens, John Paul, 16; 140–41; 166
Stewart, Potter, 48
Supreme Court Passim

Transformative Use Test, 78–80

Viewpoint Discrimination, 6; 38–39
Virginia Slims Cigarettes, 21

Warren, Samuel, 64
Westlaw, 82
White, Vanna, 83

For EU product safety concerns, contact us at Calle de José Abascal, 56–1°,
28003 Madrid, Spain or eugpsr@cambridge.org.

www.ingramcontent.com/pod-product-compliance
Ingram Content Group UK Ltd.
Pitfield, Milton Keynes, MK11 3LW, UK
UKHW020209060825
461487UK00018B/1648